THE OTHER SIDE OF SILENCE

[THE LIVES OF WOMEN IN THE
KARAKORAM MOUNTAINS]

FARIDA AZHAR-HEWITT

iUniverse, Inc.
Bloomington

The views expressed in this work are solely those of the author and do not necessarily reflect the views of the publisher, and the publisher hereby disclaims any responsibility for them.

iUniverse books may be ordered through booksellers or by contacting:

iUniverse
1663 Liberty Drive
Bloomington, IN 47403
www.iuniverse.com
1-800-Authors (1-800-288-4677)

Because of the dynamic nature of the Internet, any Web addresses or links contained in this book may have changed since publication and may no longer be valid. The views expressed in this work are solely those of the author and do not necessarily reflect the views of the publisher, and the publisher hereby disclaims any responsibility for them.

Any people depicted in stock imagery provided by Thinkstock are models, and such images are being used for illustrative purposes only.

Certain stock imagery © Thinkstock.

ISBN: 978-1-4502-8767-8 (sc)
ISBN: 978-1-4502-8768-5 (hc)
ISBN: 978-1-4502-8769-2 (ebook)

Printed in the United States of America

iUniverse rev. date: 02/17/2011

Dedication

This book is dedicated to my four daughters, Sonia, Nina, Sian, and Tara; and to the memory of my son, Berwick.

Contents

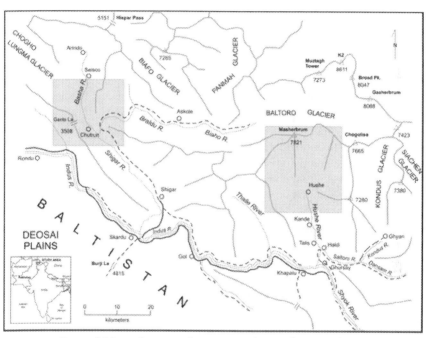

General Map, showing the River Indus with two tributary valleys of River Shigar-Basha and River Hushe.

Preface

This is a book about women who live in remote villages in the Karakoram-Himalaya mountains that span the borders between Pakistan, India, and China. In the eyes of the modern Westernized world, they are poor, traditional, Muslim, and secluded by custom. As far as the rest of the world is concerned, a wall of silence surrounds them which, at best, their menfolk can cross. Even though some visitors have observed them from afar and written about them, it is without a knowledge of their own language. It has been my privilege to have lived on the other side of their silence.[1]

This is not to say that the women are silent. Indeed, they are always talking—in the fields, in the bathhouse, on the pathways, around the hearth in their own or a neighbour's home. Even when they are alone, their lips are moving! The silence exists in relation to "strangers" or to the world so often seen as "outside."

The people of the region have experienced two kinds of transformations in the last few decades. One is the change instituted by nongovernmental agencies (NGOs), international agencies, and government and other officials who have entered their villages and valleys for the purposes of so-called development. The other is that some community members have been able to embrace these changes while others have been left out, or left behind. The difference between "modernized" people and those left behind is noticeably a gender difference. That is partly why women are silent: their voices are not heard outside their world, or even by most of those outsiders who move in and out of their world. However, their separation is not absolute. Part of the current generation of young women, having had some schooling and learned Urdu (the official language of Pakistan), have opportunities to be different and *their* daughters in turn may be even more articulate in public space.

---

1 See George Eliot, *Middlemarch*, chap 2.

The history of past silence haunts and frustrates them too. I experienced this silence in my early days of living in the village. As I sat by the fire watching my hostess cook, we suddenly looked at each other and laughed. "*Zuban met!* I don't know the language!" I said ruefully.[2] She nodded and spread out her hands. We had so much to talk about, so many questions to ask each other, but we could not talk.

This book is based on my travels and residence in the high mountain villages of the Karakoram-Himalaya in the past two and a half decades. It foregrounds and is built around narratives of the daily life, customs, significant events, and recent changes in the lives of those people. Most of the material was observed first hand as a direct participant. Some was recounted to me by the villagers in whose homes I stayed. This is a first-person account of sojourns with a little-known group of people, whose level of technology seems more like the Middle Ages in Europe than today's world—and yet they are living in today's world.

My initial approach to this work was perhaps extreme—to carry as little baggage as possible, both figuratively and literally. On our first visit my six-year-old daughter and I went with the bare essentials in the way of clothing, food, and supplies—but the intention was also to carry as few preconceptions about the place and people as possible: no "tools" except my eyes and notebooks (although I did take a small camera which turned out to be an asset). I particularly wanted not to prejudge what was important to the women so I had no prepared questions—just a readiness to learn from what they wanted to show me.[3] I still regard this approach to be appropriate community research. Nevertheless, after each stage, upon returning to Canada I searched in (at that time) mostly feminist literature for those with parallel experiences to mine to help me articulate and make comparisons with my findings.

In deciding to write this book in the form of stories, I was influenced by the approach of life historians. Life stories take the form of conversations with the addition of biographical detail drawn from other sources. The information need not cover the entire lifespan of a person, but needs to focus on relevant details.[4] In this way my narratives are set around an event or an issue concerning an individual, family, or group of friends. It is particularly useful in oral cultures such as this where, in the absence of written documentation, the practice of collecting life stories and handing

2   Literally, "I have no tongue!"
3   Abu-Lughod, *Veiled Sentiments: Honor and Poetry in a Bedouin Society*, 23-24.
4   Bertaux, ed. "Introduction," in *Biography and Society*, 7.

them down is part of people's heritage.[5] More will be said about this approach once I give some sense of the world in which it is applied.

The stories portray the lives and conditions of traditional peasant women living on the margins of the modern world. Their lives are organized around a well-defined annual cycle of activities and related spaces in the villages and surrounding lands. Everyday life is absorbed mainly in cultivation, herding, refining the products of field and pasture, and practices concerning childbearing, caring for their families, and participating in religious and cultural events. I pay special attention to women's work and its place in the material life of their societies. The stories, set in the villages where I lived, act as a framework to interpret how women's lives are organized around gender, labour, economic, religious, and cultural matters. In most cases I refrain from identifying actual individuals to protect their privacy and avoid the possibility of embarrassment. In particular, I use aliases for the women who so kindly took me into their homes to reveal rare glimpses of their lives.

I first went to the Karakoram in 1961. With a friend, I spent the summer camping and walking in the valleys of Naltar, Gupis, and Punial beyond Gilgit, meeting local people, eating apricots from the trees, and admiring the landscape of mountains, glaciers, and rivers, which have drawn most outsiders to these valleys. It was later that I went on formal treks over glaciers and high passes to see the "other" world of the high pastures, mainly a men's world, but in some special cases, women's as well. But I have spent most of my time living in the villages in homes with families, attempting to learn about their culture, to study the life-worlds of women in traditional societies, and to make sense of the changes brought about by modernizing influences.

I formally embarked on this study in 1986 when I went to the Hopar villages in Nagir Province for a summer. My six-year-old daughter Tara went with me, partly because I had been impressed by Dervla Murphy's account of her travels in Baltistan with her young daughter. Much like Murphy, I received especially warm welcomes and developed friendships because of the way the local women took to a child and mother together.[6] Meanwhile, I marvelled at how well my daughter adapted to this new life. We returned to the mountains in Baltistan in 1989, spending about eight months in one village and then again in 1993 for three months. Since then, I have visited several times for shorter periods, going to other valleys and

5   Kohli, "Biography: Account Text, Method," in Bertaux ed., 4).
6   Murphy, *Where the Indus Is Young.*

other villages with or without with my daughter, sometimes crossing one glacier or another.

How I Did My Research

I am a human geographer, although much of what I do is akin to anthropology and sociology. My emphasis is on who does what and how, in relation to place. Relationships are central to the choice and content of the stories—relations of women and men to land, to resources, to work, and to each other. In that sense my book is about the geography of experience.

The women with whom I have lived, while secluded in accordance with conservative Islamic principles, are nonetheless a vital and productive part of their village and larger economy. I began to understand this when comparing my experiences with Lila Abu-Lughod's accounts of her life with Bedouin women.[7] Abu-Lughod, an anthropologist of Arab-American descent, lived in a Bedouin camp for extended periods of time. Her research concerns the lives of women—their place in society, and their relationships with men, in particular through poetry and song. I was inspired by her methods and have used her works as a model for mine. Like Abu-Lughod, I have chosen to locate myself in the women's world—to gain their trust and learn from and about them, and like her, to let the occasion guide my research.

This qualitative approach was refined through feminist participant observation and biographical interviews. This implies that it was not done for its own sake, or only to collect material for a book, but to make a positive difference in the study area by listening to those best able to articulate their concerns and hopes.[8]

Where local medical clinics (which are called dispensaries and funded by the government) are ill-equipped at best, my knowledge of first aid enabled me to help people who seldom see a doctor.[9] Also, since language is an important tool in gathering information, I learned Balti, the local Tibetan-derived dialect. I already knew the national language, Urdu, but Balti was essential with women who did not generally speak Urdu. I could talk directly with the villagers, with little need for the intervention of male

---

7   Abu-Lughod, *Veiled Sentiments*.

8   "From the alternative viewpoint, the purpose of research is not merely to describe or uncover interpretations of social dynamics, but to do something about social contradictions and inequities" (Maguire, *Doing Participatory Research: A Feminist Approach*, 19).

9   The dispensary is staffed by (generally) a male nurse, who is trained in first aid.

interpreters who so often distance themselves from the speaker and/or change the meaning of what is being said.[10]

The "Outsider" Theme

In dealing with this approach I borrow the concept of the "outsider" from Alfred Schutz.[11] The stranger comes from outside, but aims for an "insider" view of the community. Initially, s/he is confused by the signals and codes of a linguistically and culturally different society, but in time s/he begins to understand how the community functions. I use this as an analogy for my own experience since I also entered the village society as a stranger. My history was not their history. Yet as I learned their language, ate their food, and adopted their ways, I began to accept the new routines as my own and to live with them, like them.

Initially this created a dilemma. I tried to fit in and "belong" but I was uninvolved in the choices, decisions, and actions taken in daily living—I did not own land, livestock, trees, or home. This meant that, in the beginning, my behaviour was viewed by the in-group with caution and even skepticism because, in Schutz's words, it was "void of the underlying spirit."

After living in the village for seven months, literally on the eve of my departure, I learned that I had at first been suspected of being a *jasoos*, a spy. Some villagers, who had congregated in a house to bid me farewell, said, "When you first came here we thought you were a spy. Now we don't want you to leave." The family I rented the roof from for our tent refused to accept money for the daily loaf of bread they made me. "You are family now." I was even urged to buy a plot of land in the village and build a small house, so deeply ensconced were my daughter and I in village society.[12]

It took time and perseverance to be admitted into the community, but eventually, I could gossip with the women. News I had to give was eagerly listened to and news was given to me.[13] If I left, people waited eagerly for my return. From this stance, I was able to identify with the villagers and particularly the women. In other words, I experienced their taken-for-

---

10 Rogers, *The Domestication of Women: Discrimination in Developing Societies.*
11 Schutz, "The Stranger: An Essay in Social Psychology," 499-550.
12 I will say more about our levels of acceptance later.
13 In *Return to Laughter: An Athropological Novel*, Bowen discusses how one belongs by learning and sharing knowledge (105).

granted world, *while being aware that I was doing so.*[14] The experience of the stranger as geographer is part of the methodology used in this book—as Schutz states, because the stranger is from outside, s/he is able to mediate between the host group and the outside world.

I've been asked whether I was being dishonest and concealing my true identity from the villagers, and I have to say no—people knew my home was in Canada. My daughter and I talked about our life and family in answer to their questions and showed them photographs of our home. When a letter came for us, it was no secret, since the postmaster or his wife would bring it to our tent, accompanied by curious children. Passersby would stop to ask me if all was well at home, and was there any special news. They would sit down around me while I recounted tidbits from the letter. When they heard that one of my other children was ill, they beat their breasts in sympathy.

All in all, having more of an insider's perspective than a casual visitor gave me a better view of Balti women's world than an outsider could have, although there are still limitations with this approach. Sometimes the challenges I faced were those of both an insider and outsider. The following excerpt from my diary gives an example:

> Trying to maintain a detached view as well as being a participant observer is so difficult. Perhaps it is a tribute to my immersion here that I come up against jarring incidents and feel annoyed that the people are presuming too much about me. On the other hand, Tara's reactions are more straightforward. She throws herself wholeheartedly into experiences such as bathing in the common bathhouse, having a nap with other children, carrying bare-bottomed babies around, going wherever they lead, while I hold back. Of course, I also want more privacy than she does.

While the book records original material that should be of interest to teachers and scholars, I hope it will have appeal for those interested in other cultures. It has elements of a travel book—I delighted in travelling to and through these high valleys—but primarily the stories are used to interpret some basic principles of organization and the ethics of village life in a changing and sometimes dangerous context.

---

14   Bowen refers to the difficulty of both belonging to the in-group and as an anthropologist, being an observer aiming for objectivity (122-23).

The village landscape in Baltistan is almost entirely human-made, consisting of levelled, terraced, arable land, shade and fruit trees, water channels—as well as fields, houses, and gardens. Although its greenness appears to have always been there, the reality is that it does not occur naturally in the midst of what is, mostly at these elevations (2,500 to 4,000 metres), stark, barren rocks and steep, arid slopes overlooked by some of the most rugged mountains in the world. The "oases" have been created by the painstaking effort and meticulous labour of generations of farmers, the work of women as much as men.

Over the centuries they have made fertile soil where there was none and led streams in the desert to water seeds and saplings.[15] The settlements are placed at confluences with main rivers where tributary glacial-melt streams enter them and where level ground, water, and sediment are available. Years of cultivation, tending, and building give the scenery a permanent, timeless appearance. Even what appears wild and "natural" to an outsider is usually someone's fallow field, woodlot, orchard, or pasture.

There is plenty of evidence to show that modern, urban people look at a strange landscape without understanding what commonplace objects right in front of their eyes can teach them.[16] Their preconceptions get in the way. Henri Lefebvre, among others, urges us to pay attention to the material evidence found in everyday life. He says we need to observe the landscape carefully, much as a detective would, in order to unravel the history that lies behind the visible features. In this case, the history is largely of a human-made landscape and not a "natural" one.

In looking at the lives of people very different from us, too often we try to find explanations in encyclopedias, epistemologies, and methodologies which may be *about* the everyday, but which generally take us away *from* it. My view is that understanding should begin with what we observe in detail first hand. Interpretations should flow from this and from conversations about it with those whose lives are the main concern. The stories here describe the life and culture of villagers in intimate, yet ordinary situations that are not normally available to outsiders or casual visitors. I interpret this world through the stories by taking the reader directly into the everyday to "hear" and "see" the Baltis. For the most part, I refrain from philosophical discussions based in Western literature concerned mainly with Western

---

15   One inhabitant of a village in Nagir estimated that it was nine hundred years old.

16   Lefebvre, *Everyday Life in the Modern World*.

ideas and theories about other places. Instead, I include explanations of the main issues in each chapter as well as in footnotes.[17]

---

17 I use British nouns and verbs for certain words that local people would use if they spoke in English. For example, torch, not flashlight, dispensary, not pharmacy, plait not braid. This is because Pakistan was part of a British colony for over one hundred years and retains British linguistic and cultural features.

Chapter 1   BEGINNINGS

Rabia's Story: A Farmer's Life

Every evening, Rabia unlocks the gate of woven saplings and goes into her garden. She has been working hard since she got up, like any busy farmer's wife with a large family, but when she enters her garden, she relaxes. Her satisfaction in being there is evident. She stoops down, skillfully transplanting tiny onion and tomato seedlings, pruning the tomato plants, deftly picking greens and coriander leaves for their evening meal. She plucks a red poppy for the baby and tucks it behind her ear. She may spend as much as two hours in her garden. All the while she answers her children's questions as they come and go, delegates reponsibilities, and nurses the new baby when she cries.[1]

"If I could, I would spend the whole day here," she says, as her eyes travel over the garden with pride: neat beds of onions, tomato bushes trailing over the fence, tiny green spinach leaves poking out of the dark earth, ridges for potatoes and mounds for squash plants, hot peppers in flower. This work—while producing their daily sustenance—is not performed solely out of duty. It is a pleasurable, even therapeutic activity. In the serenity of the garden, she looks back on her long day.

Her days typically begin at 5:00 am—anticipating the dawn, bathing in the hot spring where she also washes last night's dishes. Then she heads home again to cook, feed her family, sweep the floor, clear the debris. She has spent most of the daylight hours weeding, watering, and tending their fields, accompanied everywhere by her baby and other small children. After leaving the garden she still has to milk the goat, gather in young

---

1   There was a new addition to the family every two or three years. In the span of fifteen years, Rabia's family increased from four to nine children.

chicks from the garden for the night, and prepare and serve the evening meal.

At one point, Rabia leaves the garden and climbs down the ladder into her *katza*, her underground cellar, with a small metal tray and shovel in hand. She goes to a dark corner where their winter woodpile has been stored and digs out the soft, dark, mouldering earth. "This is very good for the *drumba*, kitchen garden," she explains. She also takes the ashes out of the now-cold winter fireplace. "I put this *tsillsirr* around the tomato plants." Apart from vegetables in the small garden, flowers grow here and there to add colour and beauty—*allo*, *gulchin*, *lamgan*, hollyhocks, marigolds, poppies. In a corner, there are baby *chuli* and *starga*, apricot and walnut trees. Rabia has planted and is nurturing them, until they are big enough for her husband to plant outside the *drumba*. The care of this garden is woman's work—sowing, transplanting, weeding, watering, harvesting—when all her other work is done.

Surrounding her garden are fields of wheat and barley, crisscrossed by paths and water channels. Dotted here and there among them are mud and stone houses along with fruit and nut trees. They are set in a valley amidst towering snow-capped peaks, some of them over 7,000 metres high. From her garden, she can see the Kosar Range in the Braldu valley in the southwest. Far up a mountainside across the river from her, a waterfall is visible, silenced by the distance. Below it, hidden from view, is the wide, brown Basha River, which can be heard winding its way south to join the Shigar and then on to the Indus—another 2,400 kilometres to the Indian Ocean.

I was living in Rabia's home on one of my periodic visits to the mountains. She allowed me to join her in her daily routines as a farmer's wife, so that I could understand something of the complex and intricate rituals of traditional living. She knew that I was writing a book about her homeland.[2] My friendship with Rabia developed gradually. She was one of the many friendly women who greeted me on the pathways and came to visit me on my roof when we first arrived. Her daughters were among Tara's friends. But Rabia stood out above the others with her natural good manners, grace, and intelligence and, when I visited her home, by the pleasant and quiet atmosphere there. After my first visit to Chutrun, I always stayed there.

---

2   In return for her help, I promised not to compromise her privacy or that of her neighbours.

Rabia's life is at once unique and typical of women in this and other valleys who pursue a life of herding and cultivation that has been largely unchanged for several centuries, although inroads of modernity are becoming increasingly evident. It is a life bound above all by the round of seasonal activities and changes.

Outsider on the Inside: My Story

Skardu at last! We were going north to Baltistan, a region with some of the largest glaciers and highest mountains in the world. Intersected by five major rivers, its sharp peaks, deep gorges, and fast-flowing, flood-prone rivers have kept casual holiday-makers away, except from the main town and airport. But it is a much-desired destination for serious mountaineers, trekkers, and research scientists from all over the world. "Outsider" women and children rarely visit, much less stay, in the *nallahs,* as the interior valleys and settlements are known.[3]

Tara and I were up at 4:00 AM to go to the Islamabad airport for our flight to Skardu. It was still dark outside, made darker by heavy rain, thunder, and lightning. While it was a hot, humid dawn in Islamabad, when we arrived in the mountains we would need warm clothing. With this in mind, I had packed sweaters and light jackets in our carry-on bags. My mother came in with mugs of tea, worried about our adventure, giving advice and warnings for our safety.

I, on the other hand had other worries. The Boeing does not fly by radar alone, since it must negotiate its way among and sometimes below the height of some of the world's highest peaks, many over 7,000 metres high. Fog, low clouds, heavy rain, or strong winds are reasons to cancel the flight. The inclemency of the weather might mean that we would not fly today.

When we arrived at the airport, a crowd of mostly men was milling about, anxiously scanning the sky. Much of the conversation was about the weather. I have grown used to such uncertainty now, having made the trip many times since. I have gone to the airport only to be turned back and once even flown up to and over the Skardu basin before returning to Islamabad without landing. The clouds had been too dense above the landing strip that day. As it turned out, this time we were delayed at the airport for only an hour while the pilot made up his mind about the flight.

---

3 This is a local term for settlements in the interior valleys.

As we sat in the waiting room after being cleared for boarding, I looked around at the other passengers. They were mostly men, dressed in traditional *salwar kamiz*, baggy pants and shirt, in shades of grey and beige.[4] Most of them wore round woollen caps with rolled edges, typical of the northern regions. There were only three women, accompanied by their men, who sat to one side in an area reserved for ladies. Their heads were covered with *chaddars*.[5] Two small children, dressed in miniature like their mothers in *salwar kamiz*, played around the women. I was glad that Tara and I were appropriately dressed, although our heads were not covered. I still had not decided what to do about that issue, although I had been warned that local women in the conservative north covered their heads.[6]

Much to our relief, the pilot's final decision to fly was announced and we filed on board the small Boeing. After leaving the city behind, we flew north over the flat Indus plains, which merged gradually into the foothills of the Himalayas. The view changed when we reached the high mountains. The blue-grey ribbon of the river was enclosed in a deep gorge, edged by green. Occasionally, in narrow valleys, we glimpsed villages like fly specks on green patches. Bare brown slopes stretched up to snow and clouds on high mountains.

"On the right we are passing Nanga Parbat," the pilot intoned over the sound system. Through ragged grey clouds we saw the famous mountain outlined against the sky. At over 8,000 metres, it is the third-highest mountain in the region. I recognized its sharp cone-shaped peak with the twist at the end from postcards. It seemed as though the wing of our plane might almost brush against it.

An hour later we landed in Skardu on an airfield ringed by bare, brown mountains. The airport was a small bungalow, the garden full of zinnias, roses, geraniums, and hollyhocks. It was a beautiful sunny morning. After collecting our baggage from a trolley wheeled in by porters, we stepped outside while I scanned the waiting crowd for a familiar face. Sure enough, there she was, standing beside a jeep—the cousin of a "friend of a friend"

---

4   This is the traditional dress of Pakistan for men and women.

5   Urdu. They are veils or shawls in various materials and colours. They can be or-nately patterned, embroidered, or plain. *Dakhun* in Balti.

6   After being in Chutrun for a few days, a young boy politely asked me to cover my head, in order to maintain my *izzat*, my self-respect. My daughter, who loved dress-ing up and play acting, was already observing this practice.

whom I had met in Islamabad as a contact.[7] Saleema was Balti, an educated woman involved in local politics. She was plump and fair, smartly dressed in a pastel-coloured suit of *salwar kamiz*. She took us to the Yurt and Yak Hotel where we were installed in a spacious and carpeted yurt-like tent. The foam mattresses folded up as couches for daytime. There were two tables, two chairs, a table lamp, and a water cooler. A bare light bulb hung down from the centre pole of the tent.

There was a rustle of the curtain as a young Balti boy brought in a tray of tea and biscuits. Our new friend left after arranging for us to have a jeep and, after our tea, we also left on our errands. First, we went to see an Aga Khan Rural Support Program officer about choosing a village for my research.[8] The white jeeps of this organization are a familiar sight in the streets. Again, this was a contact we had established in Islamabad through the social network.

I had originally intended going to Arindu, at the snout of the Chogholungma Glacier. The name had appealed to me in the travel books

---

7   Social networks are common in the absence of official programs; they are usually more helpful and certainly more pleasant.

8   The Aga Khan Rural Support Program in Pakistan (AKRSP) is a non-governmental organization, aided by the Netherlands, Canada, and Britain, that helps small farmers with credit, appropriate technology, and skill-training in the Northern Areas. It is an Ismaili organization headed by the Aga Khan, but its work is non-denominational. While it focuses mainly on men's work, women are also recipients of aid. The programs for women have been more successful in the progressive Ismaili villages of Hunza and some adjoining parts of Nagir, than in the orthodox Shia communities of most of Nagir and Baltistan. Since I had no knowledge of this region, I was grateful for the initial advice, transport, and contacts I received from the officers of this organization.

I had read. It means *big stream* in Balti.[9] I had also heard that, in Arindu, women instead of men go up to the high mountain pastures with the herds. The village is at an altitude of approximately 3,000 metres. A smaller glacier nearby had surged and engulfed fields and houses the year before and I wanted to learn how they had coped with the flood.

But instead Mr. Darjat (the manager) said that I should reconsider my plan since I had a young child with me. "The village is isolated," he said. "It is at the end of the Basha valley and difficult to reach because you will have to walk the last ten to twelve kilometres on a rough dirt track that is often under water. What will you do if the child is sick?" He suggested Chutrun on the Basha River, about eighteen kilometres south of Arindu. The name Chutrun means hot spring, from *chhu*, water and *trunmo*, hot.

"How big is it?" I asked.

"I think the village has thirty-five *chulas,* so it is not very big."[10] It is their custom to count houses by the number of fireplaces, since each home has one. "The advantage is that it is on a jeep road," he replied. "AKRSP had a flood reclamation scheme there, but the people showed no interest, so we abandoned it." I was delighted with this piece of news, because I wanted to go to a village as unaffected by "modernization" as possible to be able to see traditional Balti culture. "Another advantage is that it has a natural hot spring. Your daughter will like that," he continued.

"Can we bathe in it?" I asked. This was news indeed! The hot spring would be a boon in the winter months we planned to be there.

---

9   Balti is derived from an archaic Tibetan language that comes from Zanskar. After the seventh century, following conversion to Buddhism from earlier religions like Pon or Bon, Balti was written in Tibetan script. That changed to Persian script after the fourteenth century when Islam was introduced, but when Baltistan became part of Pakistan in 1948, the script changed again to Urdu. With the addition of Farsi and Urdu words, Balti has been evolving from its origins. Currently, in Skardu, there is an initiative to revive Balti language and Tibetan script. Syed Abbas Kazmi explains in "The Balti Language" that since there are no Balti words for new and invented things, Urdu and English words are commonly used, for example, *bijli* Urdu for electricity, *bittery* (battery) English for torch. It is a difficult language to learn and to speak. Some words begin with three or more consonants, for example *lzgot* (moon) each of which is sounded. I had bought A.H. Read's *Balti Grammar and Vocabulary* in Islamabad. The book was written by a Moravian missionary who had travelled in these parts in the 1930s. However, I mainly learned from my female companions.

10   The hearth is synonymous for home. According to Mircea Eliade in *The Sacred and the Profane*, this shows the centrality of fire to premodern people.

"Oh, yes," he answered with a smile. "The locals seem to do nothing else. It's always busy." He added, "I don't know how they get any work done." His tone was patronizing. So it was decided. Mr. Darjat kindly agreed to send us the next day in an AKRSP jeep that was going that way.

After visiting the AKRSP office, I asked the jeep driver to take me to the bazaar so that we could equip ourselves for the trip. The rough road was shared with pedestrians (men and boys), small donkeys pulling loaded carts, bicycles, and other jeeps. I went to small shops, some no bigger than large, wooden upturned crates, piled high with trinkets, plastic toys, kitchen utensils, medicines, and cosmetics. There were also vegetables and spices along with canned, dried, and baked goods, cloth, shawls, shoes, postcards, and stationery. Altogether, I bought 1,500 rupees worth of groceries, essential items for our use, and gifts for new friends.[11]

I had left Tara with Saleema's cousin's wife. When I went to pick her up, she was playing happily in the garden with Mrs. K, who has no children. Her house of brick and stone was set on top of a hill. The garden was full of flowers, fruit trees, and neat vegetable beds in a corner. We were served tea in the garden on a tray with china cups and we feasted on biscuits, strawberries, dark red cherries, and mulberries, all from the garden, of course. Then Mr. K drove us back to the Yurt and Yak Hotel with a basket of mulberries and cherries. Increasingly, I realized that the reason everyone was so kind is that I had a child with me.

Arrival in the Village

Nothing could have prepared us for the journey to Chutrun the next day. We arrived at night after a tiring five-hour drive, going north-northwest along the Shigar River. The paved road out of Skardu soon petered out into an expanse of sand and rock. The driver seemed to discern a track in what seemed to me a desert as we slithered and slid in the jeep towards a point where the mountains narrowed and then the track followed the river northward, keeping the river to the left of us. The sand changed to a rocky untarred track along and above the Shigar River, at times wide enough for only one vehicle to pass at a time.

Where tributaries from the east joined the Shigar, the fair-weather track dipped and widened as villages appeared—a collection of low mud-and-stone dwellings surrounded by neat fields. Then the road would rise

---

11   In 1989 this was equivalent to $125.00 Canadian.

again, often with a steep drop down to the river on the left. When we saw a jeep coming towards us, I would hold my breath as the driver expertly manoeuvred his vehicle to one side (we were on the outside) in the smallest of spaces to let the other pass. At one point, in the rearview mirror I saw our rear wheel perched on the edge. "Sit still," I whispered. Even a change in the distribution of our weight might end in a catastrophe—it was too far down to see the river, but not to hear it. A phrase from Dervla Murphy's book came to mind— she quotes a local man, who said "Always, jeeps are falling down into the Indus."[12]

Our jeep shook and rattled along the road, hugging the mountain on one side. The slopes were covered sparsely with stunted, grey-green artemesia bushes through which red earth and rocks were visible. Clumps of white or cream flowers sprouted up among them, the flowers of the *isman* bush. Once a *chakor* ran across the road. "We hunt the partridges," the driver said. "A *shikari* is sure to come along with a rifle." I felt he would have liked to be that hunter.

Most of the time we held tightly on to a strap to avoid hitting our heads on the roof or to avoid whiplash injury on the bumpy track. Where the road levelled through villages, groups of children came out to cheer and wave and women looked up from the fields. At Shigar, the largest settlement, really a town, we stopped for *chai* where the driver took us to see the seventeenth-century mosque, with pagodas and intricate carvings made of wood. It is an unusual mosque, because the architecture is Buddhist rather than Islamic.[13] Churrkha, Hashuppe, Alchori, Sildi, Kashumal, and Yuno slid by. At Hashuppe, the small tributary that flooded yearly had deposited its loads of sand through which the driver had to accelerate the jeep, skidding but managing to keep it upright, as if going through snow. We bypassed a small wooden bridge that sat unused and broken over the now-shrunken stream.

The River Shigar meets the River Braldu from the east and Basha to the north, where we were headed. At the confluence, we stopped in Hyderabad at a small *hotul* (local pronunciation for hotel) for lunch, before turning west towards Tissar and north to Chutrun. The cook, in a sleeveless vest and pyjamas, a towel over his shoulder, peered at us through

---

12   Murphy, *Where the Indus Is Young*, 37. He was referring to the Indus, but a gorge is a gorge.

13   This mosque is patterned after one in Kashmir, which also reflects Buddhist influence in the architecture. There are others built in the Buddhist style with pagodas insead of domes and minarets, at Thagas, Khapalu, and Keris.

the tiny serving window from the kitchen.[14] "Bring three *dal* plates, *roti*, and a coke for the child. We will have tea," the driver said. Some talk between the cook and the driver followed. Since that visit, whenever we stop at that hotel, I am welcomed as the *"api* of Chutrun."[15]

The last stretch of the journey, when we crossed the Basha over a solid-looking bridge ("No photos," the driver said, putting out a warning hand) and passed through Tissar, was one of the most difficult. Streams tumbling down from the west to reach the river had dislodged rocks and carved deep gullies in the soft surface of the road. The driver had to get out to move rocks, or drive fast, wheels churning through deep pools of water.

It was growing dark by the time we reached Chutrun. The resthouse keeper met us as we rolled to a stop in a clearing at the southern edge of the village.[16] We discovered later that the jeep is visible as it approaches the village from the south, a black, moving dot that slowly gets bigger. Its arrival is a lively diversion from routine so there is always a welcome party of men and boys, and sometimes, bolder girls, when it arrives in daylight.

Since we had arrived in the evening, most of the villagers were in their homes, but someone had obviously notified the *chowkidar*. Rapid talk followed between the driver and the resthouse keeper about our unexpected arrival. I peered out of the jeep into the gathering dusk. There were some cement buildings nearby, later identified as the resthouse and bathhouses.

Beyond the resthouse, looking north, I could dimly see fields and then what appeared to be houses, half-hidden by trees. *"Salaam ji,"* the *chowkidar* came around to our door. *"Aa jao, aa jao,"* he welcomed us, inviting us to alight. He was a small, neat-looking man with Tibetan features. He looked alert and ready for anything. We got out and stretched after our cramped position in the jeep. The driver and *chowkidar* conferred about where to erect our tent and chose the space behind the resthouse in an apple orchard. We put boxes of food in the resthouse kitchen for the

---

14 Traditionally, men wear pyjamas as well as the baggier *salwar*. Pyjamas are narrow, and more tapered than western nightwear, and usually of white cotton.

15 Men and women who appear to be older than forty years are called *apo* or *api* which means grandfather and grandmother, respectively.

16 Resthouses were instituted by the British in colonial times in far-flung places and were meant for visiting officers. They are still called by that name. Now, reservations have to be made in town from whichever agency operates them (e.g., Tourist, Water and Power, etc.)

night, keeping only our personal belongings with us in the tent. As he helped us unload, the *chowkidar* suggested we move into the village proper the next day. "It is not safe for women and children to be here alone, *ji*," he said tactfully. But we were too tired and overwhelmed by all the new experiences to make plans then.

We quickly unrolled our sleeping bags and went to sit on the steps of the resthouse veranda (we were not allowed to enter the building itself because we had not booked rooms from Skardu, but then it had never been our intention to live there like visitors). When our eyes became accustomed to the dusk, we looked at the view in front of us across the Basha River to high, jagged peaks covered with snow and a waterfall that seemed tiny in the distance, glistening as the moon rose. In the clear air, distances can be deceptive. The mountains seemed close and looming. I felt insignificant.

Behind us, in the kitchen in a separate small building, Ahmad *chowkidar* quickly prepared a meal of *dal* and *chapatis* from our supplies. The hissing of the kerosene stove and the louder murmuring of the river were the only sounds. Shortly, he came out of the kitchen. "*Lo ji*, here madam," he said respectfully, carrying a tray with bowls, a steaming dish of lentils, and hot *chapatis* wrapped in a cloth. A metal jug of water was placed before us with two metal mugs. Because we had been warned to drink only boiled water, we asked him please to make us tea instead. At that late hour, very obligingly, he did.[17]

We ate on the veranda by the light of a kerosene lantern. The food was comforting and helped to make me feel that things were going to work out. When we had finished, we rinsed our hands and faces with water from the jug and went back to the tent carrying our lantern, grateful to crawl into our sleeping bags. It started to drizzle. We fell asleep to the gentle sound of rain falling on canvas. As I snuggled into my sleeping bag, my last thought was that the tent appeared to be waterproof.

It rained all night on that first night in the village, a gentle, soothing patter on the canvas. Whenever I awoke and realized with some trepidation where I was, alone with a child, I was lulled back to sleep by the sound. It was still raining at dawn when the driver, Ghulam Abbas, came to say

---

17 Ahmad soon became a good friend and ally and a fund of stories and historical anecdotes. His brisk gait was easily recognizable to me from a distance; his trademark waistcoat, with many pockets for keys, cigarettes, and cash—and his woollen cap with rolled edges—added to his dapper appearance. He came from a learned family: his maternal grandfather, a Dogra, had been a teacher in the present agha's grandfather's household.

that he was returning to Skardu, and to remind me that I had promised to sell him my tent when I left.[18] I went back to sleep.

Voices outside woke me. Tara was fast asleep, worn out by the journey. Perhaps she was also feeling scared. I unzipped the flap and peeked out to see a ring of curious women and children, laughing and talking around us. They became very excited when they saw me and the level of noise rose. Here was something strange: overnight, a tent with a foreign woman and child had appeared literally in their midst![19]

It is not as if they are unused to outsiders, but those who come to the hot spring to bathe or stay in the resthouse are usually men, sometimes with their families. Unlike the curious crowd around our tent, Ahmad had taken our unannounced arrival in his stride. As our friendship developed, I came to appreciate his ability to remain unfazed. But even he had been puzzled by the news that two foreigners were going to live in the village and not as visitors in the resthouse.[20]

Later I realized that where we had camped was considered public space. It was not seemly for females to live there alone, hence Ahmad's suggestion that we move. Since some men who come to bathe are strangers—that is, they are not local—it would not do for women to be seen by, or to speak to them. Later I also learned that the orchard where we had camped was private property owned by Rabia's family (although she told me so only much later when we had become friends).

Ahmad shooed the women away. "*Sung, sung*, go, go. *Tamiz met?* Where are your manners?" but children remained, sitting in a wider circle, some perched on the wall and some in the trees, to see what we would get up to next. At his invitation, Tara and I went into the smoke-blackened kitchen and sat down on an old string *charpai* for breakfast: *chapatis* soaked in sweet tea (again, prepared from our supplies, handed gratefully to Ahmad; he was already becoming a familiar face in a bewildering world).

After breakfast, Ahmad first took us to a house to look at a stuffy, windowless room, which we did not like. Then as we were leaving, we saw another, bigger house along the alley with an unfinished second storey. On top of the roof, a turf roof and supporting pillars had been constructed. It

---

18   I had seen such tents put to many uses in the villages, for example to cover stacks of grain in the rain.

19   Logically, we had to be foreign, because we were in a tent.

20   It took a few weeks to convince the villagers that I was a Pakistani by birth. Because Tara and I often spoke English, they believed we were *angreze*. But all foreigners are called English.

was situated beside a large field and seemed airy and inviting. "You could put your tent up there," Ahmad suggested. "Can we go and look at it?" I asked.

A slim young woman came out of the open door when she saw us standing there. "*Chi'bya?* What's the matter?" she asked. Ahmad explained who we were and what we wanted. She was carrying a tiny baby wearing an embroidered wool cap decorated with pompoms, beads, and buttons, her big eyes ringed with *kohl*. Two other children clung to her knees, looking up in wonder at these strangers who had come into their house.

Her husband Husain joined her, a dark man with a brooding expression. He later proved himself to be a devoted father, patient with the children (unlike his hot-tempered young wife). "Ali! They are going to live here? Why?" They were plainly astonished. After more talk they agreed to let us set up our tent on the roof. We negotiated the monthly payment with the homeowners and Ahmad and Husain brought our bags from the resthouse.

All in all, in the morning everything appeared more hopeful and less confusing. We were happy with the place that was going to be our home for the next six months. Husain nailed *dhurries* onto the surrounding posts to afford privacy and to shelter us from the wind.[21] Our tent was pegged securely into the turf-and-sod roof. We had a roof above us to keep us dry in the rain (should the tent leak). We were right in the middle of the village, which turned out to be an excellent vantage point from which to view life and most importantly, we could use their *desi*, the outdoor toilet.

At the resthouse, we had used the bushes in the dark, which involved scrambling up a stony slope. The toilet was set a little apart from the rest of the house and encircled with *shuck*—a wall of woven willow. Inside were two rectangular openings. I pushed the burlap curtain aside and looked at it. Razia watched me. "How...?" I began in Urdu, leaving the question unfinished. With a little smile she used her hands expressively in answer. "*Duk, dena thalba tanse,*" making a squatting action and pointing to a shovel and a sand pile at the side. On the level underneath, as I discovered later, there was a bed of straw and sand that collected the human waste which, with the addition of livestock manure, becomes *lut* or compost.[22]

---

21 The homeowner was going to build another two rooms in that space. When we returned four years later, he invited us to come and stay in one, which we did.

22 Such toilets are also built by their owners in fields, for the convenience of those working there. A low circular wall surrounds them. When going past such a structure, one averts one's eyes if it is occupied, although I noticed children would look boldly, laughing and pointing.

Living with a family had another advantage. We were now part of their household so it was their duty to see that we were safe.[23] We were welcomed into other homes as Husain's "family."[24] Our family offered us hospitality, in the form of invitations to sit by their fire and partake of tea or food. There was an unspoken agreement that I, too, would reciprocate with favours.

When I gave Tara a biscuit, or candy, or crayons and paper, I gave the same to their two little children. When I needed a sharp knife, I had only to ask. My onions, spices, and salt were occasionally "borrowed." This immediately gave me the opportunity to observe and participate from the "inside." Of course, as time went by, other homes opened to us and the experience was extended from this beginning. Living in a home also helped me to learn the language. As she was feeding her baby, Razia asked me with gestures, *"Canada la ango chuchu min?"* and I was able to nod that yes, mothers breast-feed their babies in Canada.

One morning I heard her singing to her baby. The baby sat on her outstretched legs while she held her little hands, and rocked back and forth, in time to the tune (much like "Row, row, row your boat"). What are you singing?" I asked. "Oh, just a silly song." "What does it mean?" "It has no meaning," she replied with a laugh. Much later, when my Balti had improved, I asked her to sing and translate it. Here it is:

Suringe (cow's name), *onga* (milk), *grunntse* (sound made when churning),

Awalme (cow's name), *onga* (milk), *brunnste* (sound made when churning),

Blangmo, onga, grunnste,

Marstene, onga, brunnste,

Shogholme, onga, grunnste.

Singing nonsense songs to babies was something we had in common, then!

Despite our warm welcome, we did have an early setback. We tried to light the Coleman stove, which I proudly took out of its box, watched by

---

23   A woman and child alone are considered to be at risk. There is also the issue of respectability—to be unescorted violates the code of honour.

24   See Abu-Lughod, *Veiled Sentiments*. In traditional societies where kinship is an important organizing principle, relationships, even an honorary one like this one, enabled us to be more readily accepted by the villagers than if we had tried to live alone. Now, our hosts could vouch for our behaviour. I became *amma*, mother, or *baji*, elder sister. Tara was regarded as one of their children.

admiring eyes—and found I could not! It was missing the start-up fuel, which I had neglected to buy in Canada. The homeowner and *chowkidar* were very helpful but it refused to light up. So we had to pack that away and send for a simple contraption from the Skardu bazaar, which cost me 45 rupees.[25] The Coleman had cost ninety-four dollars.

In the meantime we were given permission to light a little fire in the middle of the rooftop, away from the tent in a makeshift *thap* or fireplace made with three large stones as andirons. We were also allowed to burn the wood chips and shavings left over from construction of the posts that supported our roof.

It may not seem like much, but it gave me much satisfaction in unfamiliar surroundings to be able to light a fire, balance a pot on three stones, and prepare a meal of instant soup, crackers, and tea. When we had finished, I extinguished the embers by throwing the dregs of our tea on it, while Tara proudly carried our tin bowls and mugs, spoons, and saucepan down to the channel to rinse them, copying what she had seen other girls do.

She was followed by various small children who appeared out of nowhere. Once she'd washed the dishes and they were put away in the box, we went for a walk around the village. Whatever we did and wherever we went thereafter, we were watched and followed by groups of children, usually small boys, or older girls carrying babies. I realized I would have to get used to a lack of privacy when we were outside our tent, and resisted the urge to keep ducking into it.[26]

Walking around the village soon became our way of spending the morning (that is, until Tara made friends. Then I went alone). After rinsing the breakfast dishes we would set out, observing, photographing (never, as I explain later, photographing people without their permission), often

---

25 This was nearly $4.00 in 1989.

26 The following morning, irked by the press of humanity that was crowding around the tent on our roof, speaking a language barely understood, I did a desperate thing. Looking back, I am amazed at my arrogance and their tolerance. "Back, back," I said firmly in Urdu, gesturing them to move. Then, kneeling down, I drew a line between us in the dirt. "This is *my* side," I said. "Do not come past it without permission." They were astonished. Had I bought the house? Did I own the land? Later, I began to understand their loose concept of ownership and private property. If a woman was working in a field adjacent to a neighbour's house, she would take a blanket from their roof to lay her sleeping baby down. No permission was asked and none was needed. But I had still to learn the unspoken rules by which their society worked. They laughed good-naturedly and quite rightly ignored what I had said.

being stopped on the pathways by inquisitive but mostly friendly villagers. "*Gar gwe*? Where are you going?" they would ask, gesturing with their hands. Some of the first Balti words I learned were "*Drulba khurba*, for a stroll," at which they would nod and smile, "*Liachmo*, good, nice." If I was alone they invariably asked "*Bongo*? (the *n* is nasal). Daughter?" twirling their fist.

On our first walk we met a pretty girl about Tara's age carrying her baby sister on her hip, accompanied by innumerable younger children. She immediately attached herself to us and with meaningful looks, smiles, and gestures we managed to understand each other quite well. "*Yeri mintakpo ch'iin*? What is your name?" I asked, using the phrase the jeep driver had taught us. "Jehan," she replied with a captivating grin. Every so often on that first walk, she would tug at my sleeve and beckon us to her house, "*Ango onn' dzerrat*. Mother says to come." She became our self-appointed guide thereafter. Whenever she saw us on a walk, she would run and join us, always accompanied by small girl cousins and sisters. I was grateful for her company. She seemed to be respected by other children who then were also friendly towards us.

As we walked that first day, we met a young fellow who hailed us politely in English. "Hello, please. I am student at Skardu Degree College. My name is Syed Jamal. Vhat is your good name?" He told us he was home for the holidays. He said *okay* when he meant *yes*, so we were not sure of exactly how much he understood, but he insisted on speaking in English in response to my Urdu. He told us proudly that he was from the "fust family," which I took to mean the leading or most prestigious family. In fact, he was the nephew of the agha or religious leader of the village and the entire Shigar-Basha valley. It was Syed Jamal who explained that aghas are the direct descendants of the Prophet Muhammad. Later, and throughout our subsequent visits to his village over the years, he remained a trusted ally and friend.

He took us to his and Jehan's home (he was her cousin, which would explain her popularity in the village). This was the large, sprawling mud-and-stone house dominating the village that we had noticed as we rounded the curve in the road just the evening before. So much had happened since then—it felt as if we'd been here much longer. The house was one of the few in the village with window panes, and blue painted woodwork.

His aunt came out of the kitchen onto the balcony, slowly wiping her hands on her *dakhun*. She took my hand in both of hers, pulling her long sleeves down so that our hands did not actually touch, and welcomed us warmly.[27] This was Jehan's mother. As soon as she had seated us, murmuring something to her nephew, she disappeared into the inner room and shortly came out bearing a tray. We were served very sweet tea in small china cups without handles and twists of sweet, fried bread called *azzuq*.

We sat on the carpeted balcony with bolster cushions behind us, overlooking a secluded garden that had a grape arbour and a stream trickling through it. A mother duck with her family of five sat in and beside the water. That was one of the things I came to love about this and other villages: wherever we went, there was the sound of running water.

Ascho Fauzia had six children.[28] She could speak Urdu because she came from a bigger village where there is a primary school for girls.[29] However, she was too shy to speak to me in Urdu (as I realized much later). As we reclined on the cushions and sipped tea, she answered my questions in Balti (always covering her mouth with her *dakhun*, a charming gesture used by many women to convey modesty), which her nephew translated. I caught the words "*tshelba onget*, I feel shame."

"*Sehrla gwerra?* Shall we go for a walk? I will show you our village," *Ascho* Fauzia suggested after tea. So we went on a little tour along secluded pathways. As a Sayyid woman, it would not have been proper for her to have been seen wandering around the village in the company of strangers—even female ones. We went to see the women's bathhouse—a small cement room. When we opened the door into the gloom (the only light came from a square opening in the roof) I could see a lot of mainly old women sitting

---

27   This gesture shows respect. It is also done when a woman shakes hands with a man so there is no skin contact. Traditional women's shirts, called *gunmo*, are voluminous garments with many pockets both inside and on the outside. The sleeve is long and has two openings. One is the conventional opening at the end; the other is higher up on the side. This is used when women perform ablutions before praying. Men's shirts do not have such openings. This may be because women are considered "unclean" when they are menstruating. More and more, however, younger women are beginning to wear the style worn in lowland Pakistan, which does not have special sleeves or many pockets. Then they pull their *dakhuns* down to cover their palms when shaking hands with a man.

28   *Ascho* is honorific for elder sister, because she belonged to a Sayyid family of aghas.

29   Chutrun did not have one in 1989. In 1993 a girl's room was added to the boy's school by the teacher who was also the agha 's cousin. (Actually, the boys' classroom became the girls' and the boys studied outside, as they had before. When the weather became cooler, they moved on to the verandah. School closes for the winter months). His first pupils were his daughter and nieces. Encouraged by this and because he was a familiar and respected figure, other parents began sending their daughters to school.

happily unclad around the edges of the pool of steaming water, chatting and scrubbing clothes or themselves. Some of them waved and called out to us cheerily as we stood in the doorway. "This is where we bathe," *Ascho* said, from behind her *dakhun*. This was my first introduction to village life in Baltistan.

In the years following, I made many friends in this and other villages. I gradually learned the language and began to feel more comfortable with social negotiations in the society. Alone or with my daughter and/ or husband, I stayed with my new friends in their home rather than in a tent. My daughter was an important reason for my being accepted into Balti society She readily adapted to their ways and picked up colloquial expressions while I struggled with Balti grammar and vocabulary.[30]

Without entering into a formal agreement, I made sure that I repaid our hosts with cash as well as gifts of food and clothing for their trouble.[31] But there was always one stipulation: that I have a room of my own, with a latch inside and outside, for which I came equipped with lock and key. This was not to make sure my valuables were safe (I carried my camera and passport with me) but to have personal space for at least some part of the day and at night.

When my daughter was with me she would invite her girlfriends into our room. They were fascinated with everything we owned: our magazines

---

30   All the girls wanted her for their friend and she, in turn, enjoyed the experience of living there. She hugged newborn lambs and baby goats and climbed trees with the children in search of ripe apricots. We would separate after breakfast and I never had to worry that she was lost or hungry. The first year she was there seemed to her an endless holiday, homesickness notwithstanding. When we went back four years later, there were shouts of Tara! Tara! across the fields.

My husband Ken is a physical geographer who has been going to the Karakoram-Himalaya mountains since the early 1960s. He has always made it a point to be on good terms with his porters, visiting their homes and preferring to eat local foods rather than the canned food favoured by foreign trekkers. Now he was freely admitted into the inner, private spaces where women live, with Tara and me. In order to make him feel at home, Rabia asked me to teach her to say, "Ken, are you hungry?" At the appropriate moment, with much giggling and with her mouth covered, she came out with "Ken, arr ju tingrry?" But the fact that she, a respected, married woman, wanted to talk to Ken in his language is a measure of the ease women felt with him.

31   We remained in the tent for the whole time on our first visit in 1989. After that we lived with a family in their house.

and books, hairbrushes, our jars of moisturizing cream.[32] The toiletry bags were a hit. They would examine the toothbrushes, tubes of toothpaste, small mirror, combs, hair clips, safety pins, scissors, and tweezers. They knew the purpose of everything (some of the wealthier villagers had toothbrushes although they weren't always used daily). Even toothpaste was available to some although the traditional method for oral hygiene is to brush with the frayed twig of a walnut tree. The slightly astringent juice from the bark cleans the teeth and reddens the gums.

Rafia, aged ten, immediately began to pluck her eyebrows, using the mirror. Two of the older girls pored over the coloured advertisements in the magazine. The shampoo advertisement showing cascading hair made them gasp—the woman's head was not covered! A *man* was visible in the background! They talked rapidly in low voices over these daring images.

I would dab cream on girls' chapped hands and sunburned cheeks and let them keep hair ties or clips and smell the hand soap. The first-aid bag, our rucksacks, and sleeping bags were (mostly) left alone. At first, after a while, I would politely ask the girls to leave, or else suggest that we go out for a walk. Something about having them crowd around in my personal space made me feel uncomfortable, out of control, and claustrophobic. This feeling diminished as I got to know them and the language.

Being able to speak directly to people, however haltingly, was important in gaining their trust and friendship. But the language seemed difficult and unpronounceable, so my progress was slow. Baltis tend to speak using gestures and what appears to be sign language as well as silently mouthing the words as if for lip reading. This may be because there are many deaf-

---

32 We did not take any other cosmetics into the villages because their use would have been culturally inappropriate.

mutes in every village.[33] Hence everyone—man, woman, and child—knows sign language in order to communicate with deaf-mutes.[34]

Because my only tutors were women who did not know Urdu, it was inevitable that I would make gaffes. Once, after I had been there three months, I was on an errand with my friend Rabia. As we walked towards the village store we met a woman *stu rdungma*, pounding apricot kernels to extract the milky residue.[35] Of course I knew her so we stopped to chat. She had previously complained about a pain in her lower back, for which I had given her aspirin. "How is your back?" I asked sympathetically in Balti.

Her response was surprising. With a shriek she threw her *dakhun* over her face and started rocking back and forth. A wailing sound came from under the shawl. Alarmed, I turned to Rabia whose face had turned beet red and yes, tears were streaming down her face as she silently—laughed! When they had recovered sufficiently to talk, Rabia explained delicately that I had actually asked, "How is your penis?"[36] She spoke to me in Balti, using gestures and meaningful looks. Still, in spite of my halting progress, the fact that I was attempting to learn their language endeared me to them and I had many willing teachers.

Another way that I gained their affection was by giving people medicine and helping when they were injured. It came about accidentally—I had no

---

33   The reason could either be intermarriage, which can lead to multiple birth defects, or the incidence of hypothyroidism, which can lead to the development of goitres, lethargy, and cretinism if untreated. In one village of about forty-five households, I counted at least twenty babies, children, and adults who had speech and hearing problems. Not unusually, given intermarriage, one extended family, with multiple cousin-marriages, had four. There were also at least ten people with goitres. Some people with these issues can be mentally handicapped. If born deaf, they are generally mute. Men are called *ghot* and women *ghunmo*.

34   I found that chance or new acquaintances would initially speak to me using this method. After watching them in perplexity for a few moments I would say "*Chi zere? Gna ghunmo met!*" "What are you saying? I am not a deaf-mute!" They in their turn were confused that I could not understand the simple signs that even deaf-mutes could follow! Gradually, I began to learn some signals. One suggestively extended forefinger, other fingers and thumb bunched up and shaken from side to side, signifies *plu*, a boy or son; a balled up fist, with the elbow supported by the other hand and twirled like a rattle, means girl or daughter, *bongo*. The sign for going to the *chhu* to bathe is a cupped hand taken to the mouth, as in drinking water. Initially I was puzzled why they asked me if I wanted a drink when they met me on the pathway.

35   *Stu* is used as a substitute for fresh milk in cooking and in salt tea when livestock is in the high pastures.

36   The Balti word for back is *stikpa*. I had said *skitpo*.

intention of pretending to be a doctor, or even of doling out medicines. On our second morning in the village, when we had pitched our tent, we lit the fire and started boiling a kettle for tea and drinking water for Tara.[37] Seeing me outside the tent, one by one, little girls carrying babies almost as big as themselves, followed by boys and women, started congregating on the roof.

They squatted in a semicircle, watching us intently, whispering and pointing. Whatever I did caused comments and exclamations and ripples of excitement. I did not mind this as much as the presence of a cluster of bold-looking young men who stood on the edge, staring and laughing. I felt that they should have known better than to intrude into women's space.[38] But I continued for a while, pretending that it was quite normal to brew tea watched by a crowd.

One woman caught my eye. "*Sman,*" she said, gesturing towards her mouth, as though putting food in it. "*Sman?*" My *Balti Grammar and Vocabulary* was in the tent. "What is she saying?" I asked our host, who had come up to see what was happening. (He was curious as well, but more reserved.) Like most men, he understood Urdu. "She wants medicine," he said. Rashly, I asked, "Why, what is the matter with her?" "Headache," he said after a brief consultation. Without thinking, I went into the tent and came out with a large, foreign-looking bottle of aspirin. There was a rush towards me, with outstretched hands. Women grabbed their babies as they tugged at my clothes to get attention, one little girl held out her baby sister's arm with a boil on it, "*Sman, sman,*" they cried.

For the next two hours, I administered aspirin tablets for colds, fevers, and headaches; shook my head and asked mothers to wash their infants' hands and faces if they wanted me to give them medicine for diarrhea; and asked my host to boil water so that I could clean and bandage wounds. (I realized only later what a big sacrifice that was for my hosts—to use precious fuel to boil water for washing when there was a perfectly good hot spring nearby.)

I was prepared only in the sense of having brought from Canada a supply of medicines for our own use for the six-month stay. There were antibiotics for bronchial infections as well as over-the-counter remedies for diarrhea, painkillers, antihistamines, and anti-nausea drugs. As my reputation spread, people came from other villages in the valley. The basic

---

37   This was before we discovered that water from the hot spring was pure enough for drinking. We cooled it by putting the bottle in an icy channel.

38   But then wasn't I, a stranger, intruding in their domestic space?

first-aid knowledge I'd learned as a mother stood me in good stead. I set up "office hours" when people could come and see me. (This did not prevent people from asking for medicine any time they saw me on my walks or visits to homes and was also the way I made friends.)

Women were especially pleased that I had come to their village, for they had been hesitant about going to see the male dispenser. Unless they were gravely ill, their male relatives would not take them out of the village to the Skardu hospital to see the female doctor and sometimes not even then. They always repaid me in some way—a few precious eggs, a summer squash, apples, a handful of walnuts or dried apricots—and there was always tea and bread when I went into their homes.

Early and late they came. One morning before we were awake, someone unzipped my tent at 5:00 am. I lifted my head groggily to see a little girl pop her head in. "*Sman, baji,*" she said, "*Dana,*" showing me her baby sister's skinny arm that was covered with boils. I had applied ointment on it the day before, promising to do so every day until it was healed, but not at dawn. I told her sternly to come back later. This did not deter her from coming back often.

Another time it was "Come quickly to my house with me, *baji*. Halima is very ill. She has big lumps here," and the woman indicated her groin. This was a woman whose home we often visited and whose little daughter was Tara's friend. It was nearly our suppertime, but I went because she would not have taken advantage of our friendship. Indeed, when we reached her house, I could see that the child was running a high temperature by the look of her flushed face. She was lying on a pallet on the roof in their summer kitchen, with her *salwar* pulled high up on her left leg where a swollen, angry-looking gland in her groin was visible.

What could I do? I wasn't a doctor! I searched for a similar experience in my life and remembered one concerning infection from blackfly bites with similarly swollen glands. An inspiration came from this memory. "Does she have a wound or injury on this side?" I asked. "Yes, she stepped on a rock and cut her foot," her mother replied. "I put *girri*, crushed apricots on it." I looked and sure enough there was a deep, festering wound on the sole covered with dried paste. Anticipating my request, she was already boiling water. When her foot was clean and bandaged, I counted out a dose of ampicillin capsules and gave them to her mother. This woman could be trusted to give them, but generally as a sick person recovered, caregivers and patients stopped administering or taking the antibiotic pills. Often, they "saved" them for another time. "Be sure to give her three a day, for five days," I said. The girl was fine in a few days, hobbling about, in plastic slippers.

After this, my reputation for healing spread widely. However, I would not treat any illness if I suspected that it needed a qualified doctor (e.g., if it could be appendicitis, heart trouble, and once, it seemed, skin cancer) for which I recommended them to go to the hospital in Skardu four hours drive away. Neither did I attempt to treat wounds that obviously needed stitches. A man came cradling a finger which was all but chopped off, wrapped up in a rag. Apart from loosely wrapping it in a gauze bandage, I did nothing more than advise him to go to the hospital on the next jeep.

There were lots of accidents when people worked feverishly to take advantage of good weather. A man came from a village lower down the valley with a smashed finger. With no expression of pain on his patient, wrinkled face, he said simply, "*Rdwa*," indicating that a big rock had fallen on it two days ago. In reply to my question as I bandaged it, he said "I could not come earlier. My sister died the day before." "Come tomorrow for a fresh bandage," I said. He replied, "I do not know what God has in store for me tomorrow." He never came back.

There were other requests that were beyond my scope. An elite man with a family of five sons and two daughters came to see me one quiet morning. "Do you have medicine to stop *hummal*, pregnancy?" he asked, hesitatingly. He avoided my eyes. It was interesting that he came and not his wife or that she had not asked when I visited her at home. She may not have been aware of birth control—women are so sheltered and ignorant of their rights. Or she may also have felt shame because pregnancy is the outward sign of sexual relations, which the code of modesty denies.[39] Another woman brought her newborn son who was ill with whooping cough. Since there are no vaccinations for early childhood diseases in these remote parts, there must have been many more like him. The baby died soon after.

On another occasion, I was invited to the home of a woman who complained of a bad cough and intermittent fever. She was very thin. I suspected tuberculosis because it is common in the north of Pakistan. Since she belonged to a wealthy family, her husband took her to hospital in Skardu, at my suggestion, where there is a good T.B. clinic.[40] Once, a woman asked me to her home, ostensibly for a cup of tea, but really

---

39   For more on this code, see the story called "Mainly Women" in chapter 3.

40   She went there and then to Islamabad to a T.B. specialist. Within a few years, she was cured and gave birth to another son (her sixth).

for medicine. She appeared to be in her late thirties and had five living children. "My flow hasn't stopped since the birth of the baby," she said wearily. The baby, a few months old, looked thin and sickly, as did the mother. "Do you have *sman* for me?" Sadly, being a busy farmer's wife (with no brothers) it was doubtful that her husband would take her to Skardu hospital's women's clinic.

Later, I realized that these incidents showed the acute need for medical care for women (and men). Why else were women waiting for me on my rooftop in the busy growing season, or stopping me as I walked around the village? They are often too busy in the day to even have time to feed children (who have to forage for leftovers). Surely their need for my services must have had to do with a glaring lack of accessible basic health care. But, without health, how could they do the physical work demanded for subsistence?

Chapter 2   THE VILLAGE SCENE

The Four Seasons

Peet, Spring

The growing season officially begins on 21 March (known by Shias as Nauroze, literally, New Day, which coincides with the vernal equinox of the Roman calendar), and ends in mid-October. Throughout this time, women like Rabia are most visible in the landscape. They may be seen in the fields, on the pathways around the village, along the water-courses, and on the rooftops as they go about their work of cultivation, helping with the harvest, cleaning and milling grain, picking and processing fruit and nuts, as well as carrying out their household-related and family chores. As the various crops ripen, the water mill runs continually in some part of the village or the other—from the first harvest of barley in late June, to wheat and beans in July, then to late October when the last of the buckwheat is milled.

The first job is to plough the field. Rabia walks behind a simple, two-pronged wooden plough called a *tshul* dragged by a *dzo*, which marks a deep furrow in the earth. The *dzo* is a curious animal, unique to the valleys of Tibet, Ladakh, and Baltistan. It is a yak-cow hybrid with shaggy fur, black or brown or grey in colour, with long, curved, pointed horns, roughly the size of a yak. Its ponderous and fearsome appearance belies its generally docile nature.

Rabia's daughters pick and toss rocks and stones that were heaved to the surface by winter frost. Their father follows, a leather pouch around his shoulder, and scatters the seed by hand. Behind him another man, usually a *rohmi* (hired help), drags a frame with thorny branches set in it, weighted down with stones.[1] This action covers the seeds lightly with earth. The frame is called *tshalba*.

With the help of *rohmi*, Hamid cleans the irrigation channels as meltwater from the glaciers starts to flow. He deepens the pond, *bearzing*, outside their house, through which the channel flows. It is here they wash dishes so that the grease and debris sink down, and the clear channel continues to the next house, the next pond. The sandy loam the men dig out is piled in the animal sheds, along with straw, and also in the room below the latrines. This will help convert human and animal waste into manure. The composted night soil and manure is placed on people's fields in the spring and autumn as mounds of dark, surprisingly non-odoriferous earth. It is the only fertilizer they will need to use.[2]

Rbyarr, Summer

The months from June to September are the busiest for the family. Their animals are taken up to the high pastures and remain in the care of young and able men, designated from the village to mind the village livestock in return for payment in kind. The shepherds' main occupation is to tend the *hyuk*, *dzo*, *lu*, and *rawak*, yak, sheep, and goat; shear, process, and bring down the goods from the pastures—wool, hair, curds, soft cheese, butter—and take up provisions such as flour, salt, matches, and tea.

Meanwhile, Rabia and her daughters, one as young as five, do the work of weeding, irrigating, and the many tasks that farming and household care involves. Now, as men increasingly go down to the plains to work for cash, women are left as the farmers. Since they are using techniques and technology that have not changed much over the centuries, it means the knowledge and experience of the old and of women are valuable resources.

---

1 Deaf-mute men or women from poor (landless) families are often hired and usually paid in kind. They form a transient group, going from house to house and to other villages in the valley. Although they have no fixed home, they are known by name, are reasonably well-clad for the season, and are generally treated kindly and have a sense of self and self-respect.

2 The combination of glacial-fluvial sediments, which are rich in minerals, and organic manure makes an excellent fertilizer that maximizes crop yields. However, men are beginning to buy chemical fertilizer and pesticides for their wives to apply to kitchen gardens. Unable to read the labels, women use them in onion beds and for other vegetables, in hopes of getting bigger and better yields, without understanding the dangers of pesticides.

Stunn, Autumn

At the altitude of this village (2,800 metres) there are two cropping seasons. The main work of harvesting and threshing starts in late June for barley (after which buckwheat is sown, which will not ripen until early October) and again in September when the wheat harvest begins. Buckwheat is not threshed by *dzos*, but the whole plant is uprooted, *bluy kattal*. Then it is laid out to dry in heaps in a circle, the pods on the inside until the milky, white seed easily separates from the black husk by shaking. The milling is different too; the millstone is raised in the *rinthak* so that remaining husks are not crushed. They are painstakingly sieved by two people holding a large strainer called a *standal*. "*Blo*, buckwheat, is planted last and we eat it and finish it first. We like it best," a villager told me.

As the crops are harvested, the cleared fields become playgrounds. They are happily reclaimed for tag, running races, or flying homemade paper kites by children. The oldest daughter is the main baby-minder but she enlists her younger sisters' help in order to have some free time for herself. Occasionally, a little knot of children will light a fire of twigs to warm their hands as they play. If they can scrounge a few potatoes from their field, they bake them in the embers and hot ashes, running in to the nearest house for salt.

Now too, the animals start coming down from high pastures and Jamal, the oldest son at twelve, is given a man's job to bring down his herd. When the *hyuk* engages in mock battles with the male *dzo*, there is great excitement and young and old flock to watch. Rabia's younger sons knock down leaves known as *longa* from apricot and mulberry trees to feed the hungry goats.

As long as the weather remains clear, Rabia and her mother-in-law work seated on *chharas* on the roof to clean, dry, and store seed in wooden boxes for next season's planting. The results of their labours are evident around them. Red and green chilies are strung on thread and hung around windows to dry in the sun. Orange piles of apricots are spread on screens of dry brush called *burtsa* on the rooftop; heaps of purple and white mulberries lie drying on wicker mats; baskets of little green apples wait to be stored in the cool earth cellar.

Everywhere in the village there is the sound, sight, and smell of grain. Wheat, barley, beans, and buckwheat in jute bags, sheepskin bags, and *markhor* or mountain-goatskin bags, stand around in rooms, and on rooftops and porches, waiting for *zanphapbiksba* (*zanphe*, grain, *spikba*, to be cleaned). The *rinthaks*, water mills, are busy churning, grinding flour night and day. Dwindling piles of wheat stand in fields, waiting for *dzos* for *khuyyun*, to thresh, alongside larger piles of beans.

Rabia looks up in one of the lulls. "*Ishin las*! A lot of work!" she says, shaking her head and kneading her sore shoulder. Children play around her, a reminder that routine chores of cooking and childcare must continue. Around the house's yard, the apricot, mulberry, and walnut trees, which supply the villagers not only with fruit and nuts, but also fodder and fuel, are carefully pruned and tended.

Hamid "winterizes" the house by daubing the woven willow *shuck* walls with a fresh mixture of clay and straw, which keeps the cold wind out and seals the cracks. Big holes made by rats in the mud walls are repaired with plugs of earth, in the hope that it will deter them. It does not.

Rgunn, Winter

Temperatures remain at or below freezing point from November to February, and the daytime high in winter is about six degrees Celsius. According to locals, more than a metre of snow can fall in the winter. The family moves down into the *katza*, the cellar, once the buckwheat has been milled and bagged, all the animals have been brought down from the high pastures, and all the bounty of summer has been prepared for storage. This is their below-ground winter home. Work has finally come to an end. Now it is a time of *aram*, rest. "All we need do is clean and sweep. It's nice! *Plupla tharrat. Khlarrat met, icchat met.* The children love it. We are not tired. We are not bored," Rabia says.

She describes the scene. Baskets of dried apricots and mulberries; dried bunches of spinach, cabbage, and other greens; bushel baskets made of hand-woven willow filled with potatoes, onions, turnips, and radishes lean against the walls. Just off the main room is the storeroom, piled with bags made of mountain-goat hides full of flour—barley, bean, wheat, and buckwheat—for loaves of unleavened bread, the mainstay of the Balti diet.

The fireplace is in the centre of the room almost below the opening in the roof (but not directly, because of rain and wind). "We get light from the square hole in the roof. It's not dark in the day. I sit here on the mat next to the fireplace and I can reach out to pots, spoons, and the cupboards behind me." The dark walnut cupboards are filled with supplies. A bucket stands nearby, with melted snow for cooking, washing, and drinking. To one side, the high, carved wooden cot is piled with pillows, blankets and quilts. "That is the cot where *api* spends most of her time. The children can sleep there too."

Across a raised lintel, a doorway leads into the byres where the animals spend the winter. "We don't have to go out to feed them," but on milder days they are led out. Their warm breath and bodies add to the warmth of the human inhabitants.

This is the time for storytelling, songs, and crafts. Hamid is famous in the valley as a carpenter and woodcarver. He whittles at useful and ornamental objects: *kacchu* or ladles for measuring flour; a round salt-keeping box; spoons for cooking; *thalo*, a heavy platter for kneading the dough; as well as whimsical toys for the younger children. A sturdy *gharry* is a favourite toy. It has wheels that twirl on a wire strung through the body made of wood and becomes a jeep in boys' play. Jeeps are popular—they are the only vehicles that can come as far as the village on the fair-weather road from Skardu. To be a jeep driver is every little boy's ambition.

Rabia uses this time to prepare the sheared goat and *dzo* hair and sheep's wool for Hamid to weave. When the snow is deep and they cannot go outside, that is when men weave sturdy *chhara* to cover the floor, in the colours of the earth; *qar*, a warm woollen blanket; and soft *bal-gosse* for adults and children to wear in the form of baggy trousers and loose-fitting tunics. Rabia unravels old sweaters, winding the wool into balls on the outstretched arms of patient children, and knits them into new ones for the family. She embroiders colourful borders, *tsenmo*, onto her and her daughters' garments, with silk and silver thread, one of the few, precious, cash-bought luxuries. This is also the time when Rabia and her daughters shell walnuts, which together with dried mulberries and apricots, provide them with a nutritious snack.[3]

Who does what and where may vary from valley to valley, but essentially this yearly cycle of activities and routines of Rabia's household is repeated from village to village and in each household throughout Baltistan, and indeed, with local variations, in all the mountain villages of the Hindu Kush and Karakoram-Himalayas.

---

3   I pay attention to food in my stories because hospitality is an integral part of Balti culture, which involves offering food and tea to guests (even a chance traveller). Women's work revolves around it. The cultivation, rearing, and nurturing of cereals, livestock, and fruit trees is every Balti's foremost work and food processing and cook-ing is women's. (See Courtenay, *The Power of One*, 135-36, for related themes on the significance of food and hearth in rural households.)

Bread Is Sacred

It was like a scene from the pre-industrial past of all grain-growing lands. Women, bent in clusters on the field intent on *thimboo*, the act of picking up every last grain of barley with their hands, and groups of young children carried small loads on their backs, *lapke skya*, climbing up the ladder to the top of the growing pile of grain. Old and young helped, even five-year-old boys, who had bundles of barley tied by rope and looped through circles of wood. They worked in temperatures of thirty degrees Celsius, sweat trickling down their faces, prickly straw against their necks, dust in the air and in their mouths and in their hair.

Some carried the barley in *chorrong*s with a leafy willow branch flying jauntily in the air, wound around the top and plaited in, to keep the grain from spilling out of the conical basket worn rucksack-style on their backs. They handed the grain to an old woman perched atop the grain pile who released their ropes and spread the grain neatly on the mound. Other young children, mostly girls, minded baby brothers and sisters, soothing them with crusts of *khurrba* and songs.

Sometimes a mother got up from her work in the field to nurse a fretful baby lying under a tree. Occasionally, a woman, red-faced and hot with sweat trickling down her face, came to sit in the shade of a mulberry tree, dipping her feet gratefully in the cool waters of the *rshka*, or splashing some water on her face and neck from the channel flowing by the side of the field. With cupped hands, she took a mouthful to drink.

Children started up games on the cleared threshing floor. They played tag, always a favourite, mostly among boys, now that there was room to play in the bare field; the girls tossed small stones on the backs of their hand, catching them before they dropped to the ground. Another game involves one stone caught front and back rapidly until it falls to the ground (a favourite with girls). The winner catches the most and must keep adding more. Other games more familiar were tug-of-war with a piece of *dzo*-hair rope, and another that looked very much like postman's knock (but no kissing!), long jumps, and of course, races.

Bread is written in the landscape and in the lives of the people. It is the driving force or energy behind their everyday world. In order to illustrate the significance of bread, here is a recreation of events that were played out in the growing season, year after year, with a few variations, not only here but in villages all over Baltistan. So many of the actions related to the growing, tending, and preparing of grain are performed in unison, rhythmically, but not effortlessly. To an observer they appear to be a dance enacted in the fields or at the water mills. They have at once a specific quality unique to each patch of ground and overworked body and a timeless and placeless quality which suggests the harvest scenes of pre-industrial Europe that were romanticized in paintings.

The Cycle of Bread

In Chutrun, barley is sown in March when the mountain slopes are still covered in snow. The field where I first saw activities related to cereals and followed them through the growing season belonged to Nurbano. Before the sowing could begin, a male calf was slaughtered and its blood was spilled on the field to sanctify the ground and celebrate the first sowing of the year. Nurbano was a handsome woman, not young, but strong, with piercing black eyes set in a brown, seamed face. She always wore traditional Balti dress: a long, full woollen *gunmo* with many pockets, decorated with silver trim at neckline, hem, and cuffs. Her baggy pants fell in graceful folds, gathered in at the ankles. Although not tall, she looked distinctive in a *natting*, the woollen cap decorated with silver embroidery on the rim, under her *dakhun*. She was not someone to be trifled with. Her husband, about fifteen years older, was unwell, so it fell on her to do a man's work as well as her own.

The first planting could be done by a man only, so she had brought her eldest son. With a leather bag slung across his shoulders, the young man cast the seed on the ploughed field as he walked. Two women dragged a *tshalba*, the rake of thorny branches, weighted down by rocks, across the furrows. Little girls ran here and there, picking out stones and tossing them to the edges. There was still some snow on the field then. *Lut,* which had been spread the previous autumn and again in early spring, slowly flushed into the soil as the snow melted.

In time the green shoots of barley showed through the rich, dark soil. The barley grew, fed by irrigation water. Late spring and summer can be very dry, so water from melting glaciers high above must be channelled to the water-starved land. This work is not only arduous but also a feat of skill as water is led along contour lines from glacial streams to drop lower and lower into the village and the fields.

Nurbano and her sons, a daughter, nephews, nieces, brother-in-law, and sister-in-law all watched the crop by turn. The women weeded it to keep it "clean." They threw stones at birds and bold chickens, which ventured in among the tall grain. Despite the watchers' vigilance, hungry cattle, sheep, and goats would break in and eat a path through the grain. When this happened (not often) Nurbano cursed them, loudly calling down dark fates on the owners.

By early July, the grain was ready to be cut by the men of the family. Crouched down in the field, they sliced through the stalks of the barley with short, curved blades. Nurbano, her female relatives, and countless children swept the cut grain into sheaves. These they then tied in bundles, heaved onto their backs, and carried to the corner of a cleared field. Because this was the first field to be cut, it was designated the threshing floor after it had been swept thoroughly, the earth tamped down with water and hardened. Into the centre a pole, three metres tall, was firmly hammered.

Nurbano's strong frame bent under a load of barley was a common sight at that time. Her voice could be heard urging her relatives, "*Shokhmo*! Faster!" in case of a sudden shower of rain. Everyone's eyes anxiously scanned the sky for clouds. When all the cut barley from their fields had been brought to the threshing floor, it was securely covered with old tarpaulins tied on with goat-hair ropes. It lay stacked in neat piles, three by two metres square, to dry out and await the arrival of the *dzos* for threshing to begin.[4] The process of stacking and the stacks themselves are called *herris*. After that stage, and as soon as weather and other work allows, the threshing or *khuyyun* begins. This is men's work.

Nurbano's sons and nephews brought the *dzos* down from the high pastures where, since late June, they had been cared for by a male relative. Six or seven *dzos* were tied with a thick rope to the threshing pole and the men took turns driving the large, bulky animals round and round over the grain. They urged the beasts on with loud and cheering cries, "*Hurr, hurr.*" A boy ran in front constantly raking and turning the grain. When manure was dropped by the animals, it was quickly picked up and deposited to the side so it would not soil the grain. The school is closed periodically to allow for harvest, since teachers and children all have to work. Small children sat around the space, watching and playing. Dust filled the air.

Meals were brought out to the fields and eaten under the shade of a tree. Nurbano disappeared into her house to bake barley loaves and churn salt tea, foaming with butter and milk from their cow. "*Gno*! Take!" A large

---

4   Their large hooves are ideally suited to the task because they do not break the grain. Also, the fissures in the hooves are wide so that the grain does not lodge there.

tin bowl of *paillu chai* with a *khurrba* was thrust in my hands, because I had helped a little.

It is an exhilarating time, repeated year after year in fields all over the village. It is also a time when men and women go to their houses totally exhausted, day after day. Fevers, coughs, boils, cuts, and bruises are common. There is always the fear that the work may not be completed before rain and windstorms spoil the grain.

After the barley had been threshed it was ready for winnowing, *phyarrat*. The grain is tossed up into the air with a *khatze*, a five-pronged rake fashioned out of a single willow branch. The wind blew the chaff into one pile, while the grain fell straight down. The chaff from wheat and barley, *phoongma*, becomes fodder for livestock. Generally the winnowing is men's work, but Nurbano helped her son do theirs, while her female relatives and children swept up stray grains with their hands. Every little grain was picked up out of the dust and flung into the *kharrik*. Her other male relatives were needed to cut the wheat that was now ready.[5]

When Nurbano's grain was carefully heaped up on the threshing floor, ready for bagging, a male elder was called. He hobbled out of his house, an old, stooped man with a grey beard. *Apo* is a landowner and the father of sons. He now lives with his eldest son while devoting his life to reading the Quran. Sometimes he weaves baskets on the rooftop.

As a respected elder, *apo* was often invited to perform this task. He knelt beside the newly threshed grain, facing west towards Mecca. With both hands uplifted and cupped, he murmured a prayer while Nurbano and her son bowed their heads. Then he took a wooden dish in his hands while the son held a bag open for him. With each dishful of grain from the pile that he poured in the bag, he intoned *Bismillah-ir-Rahman-ir-Rahim*, in the name of God, the Beneficent, the Merciful.

When the first bag was full, another one was held up by the younger man. *Apo* took a few grains from the full bag and, in a clockwise motion, passed it over the empty bag, the heap of remaining grain, and finally the dish. He dropped a grain or two in each as he did so. He repeated this procedure three times, then proceeded to fill the second bag, calling down an invocation as before. I was sitting with Nurbano and she motioned me to stay in the background during this ceremony. Being women, we would have "polluted" the grain if we had touched it then.

---

5 Wheat is not an important crop because it is not as suited to the environment or as productive as barley, but it is increasingly grown since its bread is thought to be finer. Eating *khurrbas* made of *tro* instead of *nas* is a status symbol.

As I watched this quiet ceremony unfold, a younger man passing by said disdainfully, "We don't do this any more. It's superstitious nonsense. Only the older folk still believe in it." With the introduction of cash, values are changing and life is speeding up. In more and more villages the threshing is done by hired tractors that travel the valleys and do the work at breakneck speed. This also speeds up the other processes. But it appears that some are still living in the "slow lane," where old people and traditions matter.

The importance of *phe*, flour, defines the place of cereals in the Balti value system. In Baltistan, the traditional grain is *nas*. Flour is held in esteem for two reasons. On the one hand, it is a staple food. On the other hand, it is a sacred or blessed resource with life-giving qualities. Spilling flour or bread carelessly is considered a sin because it becomes *charru*.[6] When a member of the family goes away on a journey, a bowl of flour is brought to the threshold and the traveller's right fist is imprinted in it. The flour is then given charitably to the first needy person that passes by. This act conveys a blessing on the giver while ensuring the traveller's safe return. The ceremony is also done when a baby leaves his/her natal village for the first time.

Due to its sacred properties, flour is believed to have the power to drive out evil spirits, ward off evil, or cure sickness, acting somewhat like a charm. For example, when my hostess was talking to me and kneading dough at the same time, she told me about a deaf-mute boy who was mentally retarded. "He catches mice in the water mills and eats them." As she said this, she picked up a pinch of flour, blew on it, and tossed it over her right shoulder with a prayer to be preserved from a similar fate.

I witnessed a healing ceremony done with flour for a baby who had fallen off the roof onto his head.[7] The child's grandmother took dough and passed it over the baby's stomach (the navel), the top of his head (the patella or "soft spot"), and the soles of his feet, as she recited verses from the Quran. This was done to banish the evil spirit which, it was believed, had "captured" the boy and caused his injury. Later I heard that the father had taken his son to Skardu hospital where an x-ray revealed a fractured skull.

---

6   The word means unclean—more than dirty. It is impure, in a sacred sense.

7   It does happen, but not as often as one would think, given that small children play on rooftops without guard rails.

He was treated for that, but his recovery was attributed to the traditional healing ritual after which the hospital treatment was effective.[8]

Flour is believed to have purifying qualities. It was used to "cleanse" a hand-loomed shawl the first time it was washed in the pond. Flour was sprinkled on the shawl before it was dipped in the water to soak. After soaking, the shawl was beaten with sticks. I was told that this was meant to disperse any bad influences it may have picked up during the weaving process due to the evil eye.[9]

However, *phe* is first of all, and obviously, *roti*—bread, food. The cultivation and harvesting of cereals and the making of bread in its many forms are surrounded by social traditions and practices that have evolved over many centuries and through generations, traceable to their origins in Tibet, Ladakh, and Persia. The sowing, manuring, and irrigating in fields and gleaning and cleaning of grain on rooftops require painstaking effort. However, the work brings with it social interaction, cooperation, and relationships that are forged by helping and sharing; songs are sung and leisure time is enjoyed together; food is prepared and eaten communally in the field before work is resumed.

The *rinthak* is another scene of activity connected with, and reinforcing, the significance of grain. The reciprocal work of grinding flour, bagging, and giving or receiving payment in kind for help provides an opportunity to practise generosity. Again, these are among the many tasks that create and strengthen bonds within a social group.

---

8 The perception is that allopathic and folk (in this case Islamic) medicine are not in conflict with each other. Modern medicine is accepted after evil spirits or *djinns* have been driven away by spiritual healers. On the other hand, herbal medicine (e.g., Chinese, Balti) practised by indigeneous peoples worldwide is seen to be in competition with modern medicine and the latter appears to be winning. One reason is that herbs are slow acting and their effects are not instantly apparent like antibiotics (Giles, "Medical Aspects of the IKP"). So they are falling out of favour with the people too. Moreover, they are rejected by modern doctors (and pharmaceutical firms) as being backward and unscientific.

9 *Nazar*, (U.) meaning "the look," is always used in a negative sense. For example, someone could have looked covetously at the shawl, or wished the weaver bad luck.

Little Brown Hen or Settling In

In Chutrun, a green canvas tent became our home away from home that first year.[10] We had bought it second-hand in Islamabad. The following stories give a view of our life on the rooftop, until freezing temperatures forced us out. The first anecdote is about a hen.

When our tent had been pitched (the earth beneath and around it tamped down and swept with a twig broom by Razia, our host Husain's wife), Husain laid down a large piece of flattened cardboard, carefully smoothing the edges. "Here," he said, "is your kitchen." In the corner was a large can of cooking oil, cans of sugar, tea, and milk powder, salt, a bag of onions, and a sack of flour, all neatly arranged on cardboard, much like in their own kitchen. (Things like matches, cookies, crackers, and oatmeal were in a duffel bag in the tent, prudently away from rats and inquisitive children). The local stove would appear later (our Canadian Coleman stove having failed without the correct fuel).

Beside our tent, there was another little shelter of a sideways-turned tea chest. Husain carefully removed all nails and the precious aluminum lining to be used in his own *thap* in the new room to be built next door. The tea chest served as our cupboard for enamel plates, mugs (two of each), and saucepan (one). Here I also kept vegetables bought or given to me in the village, like potatoes, chilies, cucumber, a summer squash, a cabbage, a handful of small turnips, or radishes.

A little brown hen, a *byafo,* lived under an upturned cardboard box nearby on the roof. The box was loosely covered with a burlap bag to keep the hen warm. Every morning Razia would lift a corner of the bag to look for eggs. Early one morning in October, still snug in our sleeping bags, Tara and I heard a loud clucking from the location of the tea chest. I poked my head out of the tent in the direction of the noise to see the hen sitting in a deep enamel plate among the potatoes. After clucking and squawking busily for a few moments, she got up and wandered away. A hasty check showed, sure enough, a warm, brown egg! Tara and I were delighted. I took it down to our hostess who was below minding her husband's shop.

"Ali! Where did you get that?" she exclaimed. Her hen's egg was in my possession! "I will pay you for it, for Tara," I quickly assured her. She

---

10   On subsequent visits to this and other villages, we lived with a family in their house, since we were more at ease with the language and customs and accepted as friends rather than strangers.

smiled in relief, while at the same time embarrassed that I was paying her for it. This was one of those in-between transactions of neither traditional commodity (because *byabjon*, eggs are sold in her husband's shop, yet laid by their hens), nor a store-bought item (like salt or tea leaves) so there was some ambivalence about how to deal with it. I gave her two rupees for it, which was about twenty cents in 1989.[11]

Thereafter, rarely a day went by when the little brown hen did not lay in our cupboard. She would come clucking and scratching and we would wait, quietly smiling in the tent for her obliging gift. Eggs, plus the daily *khurrba* our hostess made for us, were a staple of Tara's diet, so we were grateful to the little brown hen and she did not fail us.

However, as the next story shows, living simply is a more complicated business than it seems. With limited food supplies and utensils and only a small, smoky kerosene stove called an *ungeethi*, cooking was rudimentary. A big kettle provided us with plenty of boiled water for tea and Tara's drinking water. Beside that, I cooked *dal*, vegetable soup, or vegetable curry for our evening meal. Our menu was meatless.

Our daily comestibles were largely augmented by *namkin chai, khurrba,* and *spacchus,* salt tea, unleavened bread, and stew, eaten in warm, dark kitchens by firelight, surrounded by scuffling, snotty-nosed children and an old *apo* or *api* wrapped in a blanket in the corner. As well, we received a variety of dried fruits that women would pile into our cupped hands as we went on our daily walks. Then there were the gifts of eggs, breads, and vegetables, which we were given in return for medicines. Razia would also cook us meals if we supplied her with a chicken for a special occasion; sometimes we had cabbage or potatoes and onions were always welcome.

One afternoon, in readiness for supper, I chopped up a small summer squash and onion into a saucepan, added water, put it on the stove, lit it, and walked off to visit friends. When we came back, I planned to put the finishing touches to the soup. Due to a lack of experience in rooftop cooking in Baltistan, I thought my "kitchen" was sufficiently sheltered by the *dhurries* around our living space to protect it from little marauders. I also overestimated the proficiency of the smoky, kerosene *ungeethi*.

Alas, when I returned an hour later, a sorry sight met our eyes. As we ascended the stone steps to our roof, there, on the ground was the toppled saucepan, empty except for a dribble of water. The fire in the stove was out. When she heard our voices, the daughter came out from the room next

---

11   At the rate of twelve rupees to the dollar. Currently, the rate is eighty rupees to the dollar.

door. We understood from her gestures and the word *lu*, repeated often that some sheep had clambered up. "*Meh met*," Nargis said, twirling her open hands (the wind must have extinguished the fire, a lesson to me about the fragile nature of kerosene stoves).[12] "The sheep knocked the stove over and ate the vegetables. I tried to chase them away." She showed us how she flapped her hands, saying *chuu, chuu*, but obviously not fast enough (she was five years old). I cannot remember clearly, but I believe we ate dinner with her family that night.

The third story is about a scary experience. After writing in my diary after lunch, I helped our hostess and her sister to *yakpa chakpa*—crack apricot shells for the kernels. Tara helped too, then ran off with a group of girls walking by and I went to attend to a boil that had been festering on a boy's leg for several days. Before leaving I was given a handful of apricot kernels, which I dropped into my rucksack. When I arrived at the boy's house, a stack of rich, sweet loaves were being baked by his aunt to take with her on a journey. She handed me two hot *kultchas*, which I wrapped in some toilet paper (always carried in my rucksack for multiple uses) and placed in my bag.

I went on for a walk around the village until a woman beckoned to me from her roof. It was Nurbano, who was engaged in *chhang bya*, tossing barley in a *phyallu*. The lighter grain falls to the front of the straw sieve and heavier stones to the back. This is the final step in cleaning grain before taking it to the water mill—the *rinthak*. "*Baksheesh*." She stopped to reach into a basket behind her for two eggs and handed them down to me, thanking me for the aspirins I had given her earlier. I carefully placed the eggs beside the *kultchas* and *girri* at the bottom of my rucksack. After chatting for a few minutes, I continued on my way until I came to a *rinthak*. It seemed to be in action as water was running along the flume at the top, churning the big wooden paddle in the stream below. Peering into the floury interior, I saw Josa grinding wheat, her hair and clothes ghostly white with flour, the air sweet and thick with its smell. She gave me a cheery wave as I hastily withdrew my head, coughing.

Soon I came to a clearing under big walnut trees where a young woman sat pounding *girri, stu rdungma*.[13] The action extracts the milky juice from apricot kernels. "Why are you doing that," I asked, setting my rucksack

---

12 Upon later reflection I realized that a kerosene stove left unattended could have started a fire.

13 If the paste is kneaded further, it yields oil, *chuli mar*. The residue is fed to animals.

down to squat beside her. "For *halva*.[14] It's our *bari* to make food for the *masjid*," she replied. "Every household does it turn by turn. We give food to all. I will make three plates of *halva* and two of *chapatis* for *Ashura*."[15] She gave me two handfuls of sweet apricot kernels (they were dropped into my rucksack) and I gave her a cigarette—hardly a fair exchange in my mind, but it seemed to please her.

As I walked along, a woman smiled at me on the path and said "*Salaam*," as she pressed four small apples into my hand. I dropped them into my rucksack and reflected on generosity that asks for nothing in return. Back at the tent I set the rucksack down and waited for Tara who was still out with her friends. She burst in an hour later, "I had so much fun! We lit the fire in Halima's kitchen and roasted potatoes in the ashes and ate them with salt. Then we took the baby to the *chhu*." We sat on the mat and ate our modest lunch of bread and tea. The rucksack, still containing the gifts, was safely beside me.

"I'm making *bles* tonight," Razia said later. "Tara likes rice. Come and eat with us." "*Liakhmo!*" We both enjoyed that not only because it was a change from my limited repertoire, but also because we could sit on comfortable mats by a fireplace, play with the children, and be with people. It can get lonely in the tent at night, when everyone else is inside. At night there was a greater sense of the space around us—our tiny, dark village felt lost in a valley. Naturally, my rucksack came with me into their kitchen, where I put it down behind my back and leaned on it comfortably while I toasted my hands at the fire.

After dinner we came back to our tent and made our preparations for bed. It was mid-October and the temperature had dropped to six degrees Celsius, so Tara slipped into her sleeping bag wearing her snowsuit, gloves, and woollen hat. I sat down in a corner in the tent with a shawl around my shoulders, a lantern beside me to memorize Balti words from my grammar book and practise some of the new sentences I had learned that day.

---

14   A cooked pudding of wheat flour, sugar, and *ghee* or *stu*.

15   The tenth day of Muharram, when a procession of young men goes around the mosque, bearing symbolic replicas of two coffins that contain the bodies of Hasan and Husain, the grandsons of the prophet Muhammad. For Shi'ites, they are the real successors to Muhammad. They were both killed (martyred) at Karbala. Muharram commemorates this time of mourning. After the paper-covered boxes called *tabut* have gone around the *masjid*, where everyone tries to reach out and touch them for a blessing, *halva* and *chapatis* are distributed.

As I unzipped the rucksack and reached for a pen, my hand felt something wet at the bottom. The eggs! I had forgotten all about them, but they were a sticky reminder of that morning. In the cramped space in the tent, there was no room to clean the bag. I decided to take it outside onto the mat and assess the damage. On three sides around our tent there were *dhurries*, and the frame of a doorway. The fourth side, facing our tent opening, was the wicker wall of our hosts' room (they had moved upstairs). Their room was in darkness, as was all the village.[16] I could hear gentle snoring, so very quietly I brought my lamp out with me and started.

Only one of the eggs was smashed but the bread, walnuts, apples, and apricot kernels were lying soggily in the mess at the bottom of the bag, with my camera, fortunately in its leather case. I tipped the contents out onto the reed mat and started cleaning with lots of toilet paper. So busy was I with this work, trying to be quiet so as not to disturb Tara asleep behind me and our friends asleep on the other side of the willow wall, that I did not pause to look up. When I did (was it a slight noise like a murmur?) I went numb with fright. There, crouched in the doorway, was a shadowy figure with his hand stretched out towards me!

I managed to stand up and slide past him (he shrank back) and knocked loudly on the door to the family room. "Come quickly," I hissed, keeping one eye on the figure. Husain opened the door and peered out, a blanket thrown around his shoulders. I pointed wordlessly to the hunched shape outlined by the lamplight. "Oh, it's the *ghot*," he said with a smile, stepping out. "If you give him bread he will go away." He went back into his room and came out with a crust of bread. The boy snatched it and hobbled away into the dark night. "He saw the light of your lamp. Who knows where the poor boy sleeps," Husain said. "He's harmless."

It turned out he was the deaf-mute, the hunchback son whom I had heard about. I had often seen him sitting and smiling vacantly near his home. Rumour had it that he caught mice in the water mills and ate them, but since Baltis are tolerant people, everyone in the village treated him with casual kindness.[17] When I went back to the village four years later, he was dead.

---

16 People go to bed early and get up at first light of dawn with the *azan*, the *muezzin's* call to prayer.

17 Baltis believe they will receive blessing, *sadaqat*, through acts of kindness towards people who cannot return their generosity.

Chhu—The Social Hub

The natural spring is at the southernmost edge of Chutrun. After the *masjid,* this is the most important place in the village and one of its distinctive features. A group of buildings, visible as one rounds the bend on the narrow dirt road from Skardu, are grouped around it. They comprise a series of bathhouses that have been built at the site of the mildly sulphurous hot spring. Below them is a small lake of hot water that empties into the Basha River over the pebbled flood plain. This is one of perhaps a dozen hot springs sprinkled throughout Baltistan.

On a cool May morning, Rabia awoke at dawn as usual. In a basket she collected the dirty utensils from last night's dinner, tied a shawl around her head and shoulders, and stepped out into the still-dark morning. A few other figures were discernible on the pathways between the fields, hurrying towards the bathhouse. As the day began for the women, the number of tasks and chores stretched ahead of them. Rabia hoped to be back, bathed, and with the dishes washed before her youngest children woke up and cried for her. She had alerted her oldest daughter to take charge. When Rabia reached the women's room, she entered, disrobed, and, with her hands modestly folded in front of her, sat down on the concrete edge that encircles the hot pool.

Rabia began to wash her dishes. Taking the utensils, she soaped and then rinsed them in the flowing hot water. There were already other women, either doing the same as Rabia, or bathing themselves. A girl stood in the waist-deep water soaping and rinsing her long hair. Two women sat on the edge, one soaping the other's back. Another woman rested on the side, talking to her friend in the water. A young mother washed clothes energetically, slapping and punching them against the edge, while her little daughter copied her actions.[18] There was a loud buzz of chatter, the rattling of dishes, and the pounding of clothes that echoed in the cement-walled room. The running water carried the soapy bubbles away.

After she had piled the clean dishes back in the basket, Rabia bathed and hurried home. She did not stop to say her prayers in the prayer room next door. As the sky grew lighter she knew that her children would be waking up, her mother-in-law waiting for breakfast. She had still to light the fire to prepare the first breakfast of *chapatis* and sweet tea. In the

18 Little girls learn women's work by imitation. In a few more years she will be helping in reality.

evening, after her farm chores had been done, dusty from the fields, Rabia would come back, this time with clothes to wash as well, accompanied by one or two of her daughters. Afterwards, she would stay to recite her evening *nimaz* in the small *masjid*.

The first time I had ventured to bathe in the communal bath alone I had no idea how this ritual was performed, or even that there were unspoken rules about bathing. I, and sometimes Tara with me, had always bathed in the adjoining private bath, in a room with a lock and key, known as *limik chhu*, key bath. The *chowkidar* thoughtfully suggested that I might prefer it, and indeed I did.[19] Meanwhile, Tara would often join her friends in the communal one.

Now, after removing my clothes, underwear last, I stepped down into the pool only to meet the curious gaze followed by a gasp of the young girl who had been watching me intently from the other side. She covered her ears and her lips moved rapidly, presumably in prayer to ward off evil for having looked at me.[20] I bathed hurriedly and got out, grabbing my towel in confusion. For several days I made an excuse not to bathe while I pondered the next step.

Soon after, Rabia happened to mention that her middle daughter was not feeling well. She looked meaningly at me and said "*Khrak,* blood." I seized this opportunity to find out how women managed their menstrual flow. "Do you have a spare *kaccha,* underwear?" Rabia asked in reply. "We put rags in it. If you have one, please let me have it." I asked her what other women did. "If they can buy one in Skardu bazaar, otherwise—." She left the sentence unfinished and added, "They can also wear it when they bathe." Now I knew! "Is it good to wear it in the *chhu*?" I asked casually. "Oh, yes. It shows *tamiz,* manners," she replied.

Through these conversations I came to understand that while female nudity is acceptable in an all-female gathering, there are still certain steps that must be followed in order to preserve modesty, such as wearing an undergarment or covering one's self discreetly with folded hands when descending into the water.

---

19   On my third visit the building changes had been completed and there was no more "key bath."

20   According to Buitelaar, women "undress completely, covering their genitals with a hand or a washbowl" when they are out of the water as a modest gesture ("Public Baths as Private Places" in *Women and Islamization: Contemporary Dimensions of Discourse on Gender Relations,* ed. Ask and Tjomsland, 118).

Other rules for bathing are that one never sits with legs apart—both legs are kept together, knees touching, when outside the pool.[21] It is permitted to sit outside and soap oneself, rest, or soap a friend's back, as long as these steps are followed. Clothes are not worn, indeed, one should remove clothing before bathing.[22] Much later a woman told me disapprovingly about a group of *jahil,* ignorant women who had come from the Punjab, and entered the pool *fully dressed* (her emphasis). She paid me a compliment when she said, "You know how to bathe like us."

Following that first attempt at bathing in the communal *chhu,* whenever I visit the village and stay in Rabia's house we go to the *chhu* together. Some time after the *muezzin's* call to prayer has finished echoing over the mountains and through the open window of my small room, there is a knock at my wooden door. "*Onse,* Rabia," "I'm coming," I call, scrambling out of my sleeping bag and reaching for my *chaddar.* It is 4:30 am. She carries her basket of dishes, and I bring a towel, a change of underwear, soap, and a flashlight. It is still dark as we hurry along the paths. I stumble occasionally on rocks and hollows and Rabia gives me a steadying hand. We skirt water spilling out of fields, as hens and ducks squawk out of our way. A few minutes later, we push open the door into the steamy darkness of the bathhouse.

I hurriedly take my clothes off, leaving my panties on, after having learned this lesson. Very few wear panties, mainly for lack of owning such a garment, but it gets me approving looks. However, there are still problems in communal bathing for me. While I am welcomed into the pool, some more religiously minded women stay upstream of me because

---

21   See Ask and Tjomsland, eds., *Women and Islamization: Contemporary Dimensions of Discourse on Gender Relations,*
22   Ibid, 103-23.

I am *isai*, Christian, and therefore "unclean." I eat pork.[23] So I have to do some manoeuvring, to be near one of the clean spring sources, and yet not in anyone's way downstream. For my part, I try to avoid being downstream of anyone who is blowing her nose vigorously into the water, spitting, or dandling a baby. Sometimes I dawdle at the edge, until these dangers are past. Because of the women's extreme courtesy, there is no unpleasantness.

We bathe together amicably, although no one offers to scrub my back. My soap goes the rounds of the women. On her first visit to the communal bathhouse (we usually bathed in the *limik chhu* on our first visit), my daughter went with a large new bar of soap, and came out an hour later with a small sliver. She said the soap travelled hand-to-hand through the bathers, but finally came back to her, so there was no question of the women stealing it. They simply asked to use something they did not have and returned it at the end.

Without my eyeglasses I am at a disadvantage and unable to recognize anyone further than arms' length from me, especially in the semi-dark of the room. In a strange way, this also affects my hearing, or at least

---

23   There were other instances when I realized that I was considered unclean by some. For example, my hostess in one village always served me mulberries, walnuts, my food, or other edible items on a separate tray or plate. I never had to put my hand into the communal plate. I thought it was done out of deference for me due to her sense of courtesy. But then I began to realize that the family did not *want* me to touch what they were eating from the communal plate. When I asked for extra salt in this household, the saucer or tin of salt was never handed to me, but whoever was nearest, father, mother, or child would add a pinch to my outstretched plate. When food was served by the mother to all sitting in a circle around her, I was never asked to pass a plateful. It was done very politely as if they did not want to trouble me, so I thought no more about it. But then there was the time when I was plucking and eating mulberries with the five-year-old daughter of the house. She could reach only the very lowest branch, so I picked some luscious ones higher up and handed them to her. She looked solemnly at me as she accepted them with both hands, then without changing her expression, tilted her palms so they all fell out. Suddenly it became clear why they would not let me wash dishes after a meal—why, if I fell, my hostess after helping me up would make an excuse to bend down by the nearest stream and wash her hands; why, when I had wrapped the woollen shawl I was wearing around her shoulders saying, "I want you to have it," she thanked me but took it off quickly. (Later I found it washed and drying on the roof.) There were many such incidents. Even more puzzling was that we were warmly greeted with hugs from everyone when we arrived; when people needed medicines or first aid for an injury, it was all right for me to touch them, even the most religious; and my soap was not unclean in the *chhu*.

comprehension, so that I am enclosed in my own little world, surrounded by noise. But no one seems to mind that I don't talk.

I follow the ritual of bathing—I lie back and soak in the water, sit outside to cool off, soap myself and my hair, then plunge in again to rinse off. I walk back alone in the morning light because Rabia has not yet finished bathing. More villagers pass me on the path to the *chhu*. We greet each other with a smile and exchange some talk. Starting the day with a *chhu* leaves me with a satisfied feeling for the rest of the day. It is not just about cleanliness, but about a sense of belonging as well.

The concrete bathhouse is weather-stained and lichen covered, in the usual style of government architecture for Gilgit-Baltistan. The buildings have corrugated metal roofs with squares cut in them for light and air which also means rain and snow can fall in as well, but that is welcome when one is basking in hot water. Where the roof meets the wall there are airy gaps, but unfortunately (for the women inside) this is also where *changchang* or naughty boys can get a boost up from their friends to peek in. The floor of the bathing pool is sandy and not unpleasant to tread on except when one steps on someone's lost garment, or a chicken bone. These small discomforts may be drawbacks for citified visitors, but the hot spring is beloved by the villagers and indeed by people from the entire Shigar-Basha valley.

As I lived there I began to realize the value of the *chhu* for the villagers, I could identify four main uses. First, as might be expected, is its value in promoting cleanliness. Men, women, and children bathe in it. The water is forty degrees centigrade, so even in winter, when there is thick snow outside, people have the luxury of a hot bath. They also wash clothes in it and mainly women and children wash utensils as well.[24] The men bring sheep to the small pool outside the men's bathhouse and scrub them before shearing. The sheared wool is also soaked in the hot water to make felt rugs.

Second, the water has medicinal uses. The villagers are well aware of its healing properties for cuts, bruises, and skin ailments. They soak their aching limbs in it after a hard day's work in the fields. Bathing is believed to cure headaches and fevers.

Third, the bathhouse provides the opportunity for recreation. It is a place for relaxing with members of one's own gender, rather like a sauna

---

24 Boys accompany their mothers until they begin to see women's nakedness with "knowing eyes." Then they are banished to the men's room, usually after age two. See Buitelaar 112-13.

in a private club. Women groom each other's hair, massage backs, or just lie silently together in the hot water. Children play in and out of the water around them. It is one of the most enjoyable times of the day, and no one is in a hurry to leave at the end of the day's work.

Fourth, it is a social meeting place. Whether sharing confidences, telling of good fortune, or relating their problems, much talking goes on in the bathhouse. Issues are discussed and advice is given from the old to the young. Sooner or later, everyone meets everyone in the bathhouse, so there can be no secrets. For example, no one can hide a pregnancy in the communal bath.

Here the women gossip about the everyday.[25] Gossip, which strengthens bonds and defines who belongs and who is an outsider, is also a way of exchanging information and news. In such a face-to-face society where the written word is absent, the role of gossip cannot be dismissed as trivial.[26] Because women share confidences with each other, they also feel their secrets will be safe with bathers who in turn have told theirs.

Most adults go daily; children may go several times a day. Groups of children can be seen splashing in the pool with younger siblings who are in their charge. Seeing babies in the care of quite young girls of seven or so is not unusual in traditional societies, where not just the nuclear family but the whole community is responsible for the nurturing and safety of the children. In the bathhouse, all the grownups keep an eye on the children, regardless of whose they may be, reprimanding unruly behaviour, but also helping, soothing, and chatting with them.

In the autumn, when work in the fields and water mill is over, groups of men, women, and children flock to Chutrun from other villages in the valley: from Shigar, Alchori, Dassu, Gulabpur Tissar, Hamesil, and Nyasilo they come, looking for the benefits of the water. They may stay a day or a week, lodging with friends or relatives. Sometimes they arrive as strangers, certain they will not be turned away, as that would go against

---

25   Men gossip too, but I could not be privy to that.

26   See Illich, *Gender* and Ladurie, *Montaillou—The Promised Land of Error*. In *Veiled Sentiments: Honor and Poetry in a Bedouin Society*, Abu-Lughod writes about the sense of *us* versus *them* that is conveyed by talk known only to people who are on the "inside" (20). She refers to this as being "central to social relations."

the unspoken code of hospitality.[27] The pools ring with chatter, laughter, and the rub-a-dub-dub of clothes being slapped and thumped, from dawn to dusk.

The bathing arrangements at the spring have gone through many changes in the last three or four decades. In the first decades of the twentieth century, the hot spring emptied into a natural lake where men and women bathed separated by a rough fence, woven out of willow. The willow partition must have filtered noise, laughter, and gossip, from one side to the other, so there was not the same strict segregation of men and women as there is now. The *chowkidar* who was about thirty-five years old in 1989 remembered it as a child.

There was also, according to early European visitors like Vigne and Dainelli, a separate enclosure for honoured guests 150 years earlier.[28] About thirty-five years ago, the construction of a fair-weather road from Skardu

---

27 The desire to be hospitable, and to be *seen* to be hospitable, can create awkward problems for kind hosts. Here is an example. Tara and I were relaxing on the rooftop of Rabia's house one afternoon. She was away for the day in the neighbouring village with her children and her husband was in the high pastures. Perhaps anticipating social complications, Rabia had told me to lock the door when I went out and bar it from the inside when I returned. Soon after returning from our walk, I heard voices and looked down from the roof. A group of women and children, perhaps eight in all, accompanied by one man, were standing below asking for Rabia. "She has gone to visit her mother," I said. "Open the door," one of the women demanded, but I shook my head. "She will return in the evening—come back then." While I was speaking, a young boy grabbed the ladder that was lying on the ground beside the house and clambered up to the roof. In a flash, he ran past us to the opening in the roof, down the other ladder into the kitchen, unbolted the door, and let them in! Tara and I also came down and retreated into our room and locked it. In the face of this resistance and entry, we felt out of our depth. Rabia returned half an hour later followed by her husband. The "guests" had unrolled their mats, opened up their food bags, lit the fire (using their host's wood), and were busily preparing supper, helping themselves to pots and pans out of Rabia's cupboard. Rabia came into our room, full of concern. Hamid explained to the others that they really had no room since I had come from a far country and was staying with them in their only spare room. But the visitors were unconcerned and said the kitchen would be fine for them—they had come for the waters and planned to stay a week. I thought surely they must be relatives because of their familiarity in the home, but no—they were the relatives of a family who had put Hamid up for a night when he was working as a porter in another valley. He had generously said, "Please come and stay with us when you come to Chutrun!"

28 Vigne, *Travels in Kashmir, Ladakh, Iskardo*; Dainelli, *La Esplorazione Della Regione Fra L'Himalaja Occidentale e il Caracoram*; there are photographs that attest to this.

brought government officials, tourists, and development agents into the valley. This road passes directly above the baths, and gave the visitors a view of the bathers. Some objected to what a non-governmental official described to me as "the villagers disporting themselves like ducks in water." So, because of an objection and a need expressed by outsiders, changes were made to an activity of vital importance to the cultural and social life of the village.

The changes have been cumulative. First, at the time of road construction in the 1970s, the government built a cement bathhouse consisting of three rooms: one private with key, *limik chhu,* one women's, and one men's, each containing an individual tank. The water from the private one spilled into the women's room and from there into the men's. Each also received a fresh channel directly from the spring. The effluent then flowed into a small lake at the southern extremity, which drained into the river.

Most men prefer to bathe in the outdoor rather than the indoor pool. They are still visible from the road, but being male this is considered acceptable. Only men can enjoy the open-air pool. The women were confined to one small room, where the practice of washing greasy dishes and laundry with soap (which women do more than men) contributes to the growth of algae in their pool.

The key to the private room was with the *chowkidar,* who had strict instructions to give it to visitors to the resthouse only, who have made the booking from Skardu. He very kindly included us in that category, although soon Tara preferred the fun of bathing with her friends in the communal pool. This was the situation when I arrived in 1989.

In the summer, a Kuwaiti foundation donated a sum of money to the village to build prayer rooms adjacent to the bathhouses (separate ones for men and women) and a walled, gated bathhouse for their delegates when they visit once a year for a day.[29] The construction of this private bath had just been completed (in summer 2000) when it was discovered that because the builders had dug too deeply, the flow of the natural spring has been disrupted. Not only has the spring's flow diminished in quantity but it is also cooler in temperature.

The key of the new marble-lined room stays with the agha, who obviously then is the only one with access. The wall between the men's and women's bathhouse was knocked down as part of the renovations and the two tanks were left in what became the enlarged women's room. With

---

29   The Kuwaitis also gave money for metal filing cabinets to be installed in the agha 's house to store historic documents which were being chewed up by mice.

the decreased flow of water, the second tank in this room (previously the men's) is often without any water or with very little, which means it is lined with algae and lichen. Very few women want to bathe in it.

Meanwhile, the private, or *limik chhu* has been left awkwardly placed behind the new prayer rooms. Its bolt and lock have been broken and the door hangs loosely on its hinges. Now anyone can bathe in it, which means men, because no woman would bathe in an unguarded room in public space (except at dawn—Rabia and I used it daringly once, each looking out for the other).

The lake outside was enlarged and made into a men's pool, with a roof over it and a half-wall around it, making it more secluded, but still airy. All this means that there is a loss of pleasure in bathing for women, which is one of the few luxuries in their lives. Older women, who remembered when times were better, would try to go when they thought it was empty. "It's too crowded now," one said. "The noise hurts my ears. Besides, it's dirty, there is no time for the water to get clean." They sympathized with me for having to bathe there. "*Baltilog troktrok yut*," they said in embarrassment, covering their mouths, calling Baltis *troktrok*, dirty. (Since this is a gendered activity, I have only written about women in the *chhu*.)

Chapter 3 THE PEOPLE

Mainly Women

One sunny morning I went to Dubla Sar, a promontary on the Hushe River, overlooking the confluence of the Shyok and Saltoro rivers downstream where I was staying in the village of Haldi.[1] We set off along the jeep road from Fatimbegum's house. With me were Syeda, Fatimbegum, and two little girls who tagged along. Syeda is a quiet, thin woman, tall for a Balti. She was dressed in the typical Balti *gunmo*, a wide flared shirt of homespun wool dyed a traditional green, with a *natting* atop her head. Fatimbegum, her younger sister-in-law, and my hostess was plump and eager to please. Her husband, a busy mountaineering guide was away all summer. In his absence, his wife did all the farm work on their considerable lands, as well as caring for his elderly parents and their children. She wore an ordinary, rather grimy suit of *salwar kamiz*, because she had no time to care for herself. Fatimbegum tucked her arm into mine. Since we were walking on the main road, the young women's *dakhuns* were drawn tightly around their heads and tucked in behind the ears with not a hair escaping, to show that they were respectable women. But still it was hard to conceal the joy and anticipation that we felt on this outing. The occasion was lunch at Fatimbegum's aunt's farm.

For me, the best part of the outing began when we had finished eating and feeding the children—once the dishes had been cleared away we women went for a walk. We were going to the point overlooking the meeting of the rivers. As we sauntered through the fields, various sights were pointed out to me, houses and their inhabitants identified as we

---

1 These mighty mountain rivers are loaded with detritus. They are known to flood and are constantly changing their courses, running close to one bank as they undercut it and leaving sandbanks on the other side. The sandbanks may be reclaimed for cultivation, to compensate for lost land, only to be inundated years or months later.

stopped to pluck and eat apricots. Occasionally someone would crush the apricot stones on a smooth rock and pass the kernels around. The grain was lush and high, so it was difficult to find a foothold on the narrow paths. The women with plastic slippers were at an advantage over me, because they could step into the wet field, whereas I, with leather boots, had to find a dry foothold.[2]

We reached our destination and sat down on a grassy bank to admire the view. My companions proudly pointed out landmarks and neighbours' houses, gratified by my pleasure. The brown and grey of the rivers and sandbanks in the vast floodplain below us contrasted with the rich greens and golds of fields and trees. Brown roofs were splashed with the orange of drying apricots. In the background stood steep, angular peaks and range after range of snow-capped mountains, blurring to purplish brown in the distance. Some peaks were lost in clouds. "India is there," they said, waving their hands to the left, looking south along the river.

Then we started back to Khati's house. We walked through her vegetable garden where she picked a nosegay of sweet-smelling purple *kali-mar* flowers (a herb which I cannot identify, but the leaves smell like basil), another herb which resembles spearmint in flower, called *samik*, a rose, as well as fragrant, small-leaved, pink flowers that grow on a low bush "only in the *bluk*," that Khati's son had brought down from his trip to the high pasture. She presented the flowers to welcome me to her house for the first time. Balti courtesy always overwhelmed me. I admired the neatly edged vegetable beds with poppies, marigolds, and hollyhocks growing among herbs like mint, coriander, and fenugreek.

We went into a comfortable room with a big window that had a view of the river and the fields below. The floor was covered with coarse, homespun rugs of *dzo* hair. Big bolsters and cushions were scattered around the walls. In a corner was a pile of blankets, quilts, and pillows for nighttime, when the room's function changed from being a social space to their sleeping area. With sighs of contentment the women flopped down; *dakhuns* were loosened or thrown off; one woman leaned her head in her neighbour's lap, who began to search for nits. Although there usually are nits, having one's head examined is very soothing, rather like a gentle scalp massage.

Khati's daughter-in-law was with us, a fresh-faced girl of sixteen with henna patterns on her hands. "Zohra *la hummel yut*" Fatimbegum whispered loudly, patting her stomach meaningly. Zohra had become pregnant in the first week of marriage after which her husband left for work

---

2   However, as much as possible, I tried to dress simply.

downcountry. There was teasing and laughter about her quick pregnancy. Being so young and newly married, Zohra admitted that she missed her husband, which was accepted with a tolerant smile. She appeared to have an easy relationship with her mother-in-law who was also her maternal aunt.

Syeda, the one with five children, announced that she'd had a contraceptive loop (an IUD) inserted because, she said, "I don't want any more *plupla*. I'm finished with that." Now *this* was shocking! The other women turned to me in horror and asked, "What is she doing with that? *Tshelba onget!*" at the implication that she enjoyed sleeping with her husband. But they were laughing.

A younger woman then boldly announced that she had asked me to take her to the clinic in Khapalu, "I want the loop as well!" The other women covered their mouths with their *dakhuns* and said, "She wants *that*? She's got only two sons! She sleeps on one mattress with her husband, that's why!" Her husband is a mountaineering guide who spends the summer working with climbers and tourists. The young wife blushingly denied it. They joked that she could only be "safe" with a contraceptive.

It was remarkable to hear such frank talk from women who are cloistered from strangers and even, for the most part, from their men. One asked me teasingly, with a sly look at the others, if I missed my husband while I was travelling. "Do you sleep in one *sembu* with *ashipa*?" "No, we each have our own sleeping bag," I replied, in mock indignation. Our hostess joined in the laughter but nudged the inquirer reprovingly for being too bold.

As usual, even though we had just had a big lunch, the laughter and ribbing was accompanied by snacks and tea. A basket of apricots, freshly picked, was brought in with a plate of *pokhstrun nas*, roasted pea flour. A flask of *paillu chai* with a tray of small china cups accompanied it. Syeda split the *chuli* to remove the *girri* and passed the apricot halves and kernels around to us on a saucer. I copied the women as they dipped the succulent orange fruit in a plateful of flour before biting into them. Babies and small children sat in their mothers' laps, helping themselves, or cried until their mothers popped morsels into their mouths, juice dribbling down their chins. Cups of tea and the flask were handed to young and old alike. All this was done without a break in the talk.

"Dipping apricots in flour prevents gas," Fatimbegum explained to me. Then, "Zohra is so full of gas, she should eat it." There was much laughter, in which Zohra joined. A slight diversion was caused when a baby, crawling bare-bottomed around us on the rug, had an accident by my feet. The women shrieked with laughter as I drew in my toes. The mother went off to get a rag to clean up the mess. No one was upset, least of all the hostess. The pregnant girl crinkled her nose up fastidiously. "Wait till it's your turn," they told her, "You'll soon be doing this." "I'm going to teach *my* babies manners," Zohra said. "What manners?" they scoffed, "Babies are babies!"

We talked about education. The women, who were aged fifteen years and older, belonged to a generation and a village for whom there were no schools for girls. "My daughters go to school," Syeda said. "I didn't. *Gna la jahil yut,* I'm illiterate," she added regretfully.[3] Whenever I wrote in my diary, she would peer admiringly over my shoulder.

Cleanliness and *tamiz* were discussed. "We're *jungli,* barbarians. All we know is giving birth to children, and working in the fields. Baltis are dirty. Don't you find that?" Khati asked. Yes, I did think their children had snotty noses and dirty faces, but the women were scrupulously clean in the preparation of food. Also, their graciousness to guests belies the first part of the statement.

As for having too many children, it seemed to me that it was their husbands who needed more education! It is they who want sons, and in order to have at least three (in case one dies in infancy so two will remain to help each other) women may have seven or eight children. The mother-in-law abets in this process, just as her mother-in-law did.

As the sun dropped lower in the sky, we got up and prepared to leave, regretfully, but not hurriedly. Once on the path and heading for home, we did not face a direct journey back. Syeda still had to pick up the apricots that the wind had knocked down from their tree in a field close by. We helped her pick and pile them into the *chorrong.* Little girls were put in charge of crawling babies. Then, with Syeda weighed down by about twenty-five kilograms of wet, heavy apricots in her conical basket, we set off again. Fatimbegum's son began to cry, so, with a baby already tied on her back, she picked him up and carried him in her arms. Playtime was over for the day.

I experienced another special "ladies only" day in another valley, another village, Chutrun. "Tomorrow we will go *sehrla,*" Rabia said one evening, when we were sitting around the fire. "*Bustryn sehrla.*" This

---

3   For more on women and education see the chapter called "Asking for Moon and Stars: The Social Context for Women's Desire for Literacy," in Horseman, *Something in My Mind beside the Everyday: Women and Literacy.*

literally means "women go for a stroll." At this time of the year in mid-June, she explained, there is a lull in women's work. Weeding is over, fruits and nuts are not ripe yet, and only irrigation continues, which is not a daily activity for women. "*Chhutti yut*! It's a holiday!"

Our destination would be a meadow in Hamesil, the village where she was born. We would stop at a relative's house for refreshments on the way before continuing with our walk. We would return in the evening. She explained all this to me while getting ready to make a cake called *shahi* to take with us.

Almost all the ingredients were homegrown.[4] As she worked, I followed her. She sieved the flour, added eggs, milk, butter, sugar, and pinch of soda; then she mixed it well all together. Rabia then melted more butter in a small pot in hot embers, poured the mixture in, and covered the pot with a tight-fitting lid. She placed clumps of burning *burtse,* artemesia roots, on the lid to form more embers and create an oven effect. Half an hour later, Rabia lifted the lid to check and said the cake was rising. Forty-five minutes later, presto! A rich, delicious, sponge-type cake was ready.

After an early breakfast the next day we left for our walk. Our group consisted of Rabia, her eighteen-month-old son slung in a *dakhun* on his mother's back, three daughters aged twelve, nine, and six, Tara, and me. The old mother-in-law, hearing of our plans, left home early to visit friends. "*Api* was afraid I would leave the baby with her," Rabia said with a wry smile. "She never helps me." The two older daughters carried cloth bags of sugar, dried milk powder, tea leaves, and a blackened tea kettle. Rabia herself carried the cake in a tin.

At the next house we picked up three girls married to three sons of the family, then the married sister of one of the girls from another house. At each house I was welcomed by the women, while children came out to stare at me. "*Shukhs, shukhs*, come in, come in. *Chai thuns*? Will you drink tea?" Two of the young girls were Rabia's husband's nieces. The older one brought along her two little boys aged three and six. Both sisters were pregnant. Of a necessity, our stroll was haphazard, with many meanderings and stops for children crying, falling, being picked up, running ahead, disappearing, and being scolded when they were caught.

We crossed the barren rock- and boulder-strewn land between the two villages on one of the narrow paths worn down by countless feet. "Once upon a time the fields and trees of Chutrun came up to the *nallah* and the

---

4 Everything I ate in the villages, with very few exceptions, was homegrown or home processed.

two villages were separated only by the stream," Rabia told me. "But floods carried away the soil as well as the fields on our side." Now, sun-bleached limestone rocks covered the ground. An occasional tree trunk stuck out its leafless branches dangling like broken arms.

We crossed the narrow and fast-flowing stream on a slippery log. It did not do to look down. The light drizzle changed to steady rain as we hurried through the fields on narrow paths through dripping barley stalks. "We'll go to Sajida's house," Rabia panted as we ran, "*Chharfa ishin*, rainfall is heavy." It was about noon and since we had to wait it out in Rabia's sister-in-law's house (the home of the nieces) we would eat our *shahi* there.

It was a big log house. Inside there was a stiff and formal atmosphere unlike other Balti homes I had visited. We were shown into a large room, with fine carpets and cushions not found in farmers' houses (except the agha's). Obviously, this was a room where important people sat. I had heard that the sister-in-law's husband was a rich landowner with business connections in Skardu.

We sat down on the soft carpet as we waited for our tea. A serving-man (not the hostess or one of her daughters) brought it on a large silver tray. Even though it was our own tea, sugar, and milk powder (as Rabia pointed out), we were suitably awed. Rabia opened her tin, sliced the cake, and passed it around as she poured the tea. There was still no sign of the hostess.

"His sister did not want her only brother to marry me, *baji*, because I was not rich. *Nnongo*, his older sister and *api* are always trying to get him to leave me, to give me *talak*, divorce," Rabia whispered, as soon as the man left. "They say I am a bad woman, I am lazy, I don't work." "But Rabia, you have all these children, what would you do?" I asked, shocked by what she had told me. She shook her head. I had heard that Rabia's mother-in-law was unkind to her. She sometimes refused to eat with the family when her son was not there, under the pretence that Rabia would not feed her. Days would go by without *api* speaking to Rabia, a fact which depressed the young wife.

When I lived with them, *api* would often sit down next to me and complain about Rabia's so-called laziness. I remembered once when Rabia had just returned from a long, tiring day at *yurma*—the children also tired and complaining of hunger. Her husband was down from the high pastures at the same time. *Api* immediately seated herself next to him and started complaining that his lazy wife had not fed the family yet; it was late, the children were hungry; the clothes hadn't been washed; the floors were unswept. I knew that Rabia was ill with dysentery and feeling weak, especially after her day of weeding in the sun.

As she started preparing dinner and nursing the baby, Rabia looked at me sadly. "A mother is not honoured in her own home," she murmured. "There is no justice in this world." Now, in her sister-in-law's home, we spoke in hushed voices about that and other incidents. Finally, the rain stopped and the sun came out. We were all relieved to get out into the open air again. The sister-in-law had not joined us at all. This was taken as a slight by Rabia not only towards herself, but as an insult to me, an invited guest.

As we proceeded on our way, our lighthearted mood returned. I began to realize that this was indeed a special time for women who were free to play with no men to watch them. We walked on further, leaving the houses behind us to reach a certain place where they always go on these jaunts. It was a wide grassy meadow full of flowers, with a stream running through it and a big, smooth, sloping rock sticking up in the middle. This became a natural slide and with shrieks of delight even the pregnant girl ran to slide down with the children. They played tag, threw their *dakhuns* aside, flung themselves down on the grass, and literally let their hair down. The younger children picked flowers to put in each other's hair.

"Look at these plants, *baji.* Watch." Rabia plucked the plant, crumpled and wet it in the stream, and rubbed it between the palms of her hands. Frothy green suds formed. I took some and found it to be soapy and silky. Rabia explained that the plant grows in sandy, pebbly soil close to water. It had rows of tiny leaves like a fern and small purple flowers, resembling vetch. It is aptly named *chhu chhu dacchal.* Rabia and some of the others hitched up their *salwars* to the knees and stood with bare feet and legs in the stream washing with it, laughing and splashing their faces and each other. They dried themselves on their *dakhuns,* warmed by the sun. Contented children rolled around in the grass near them.

Peace reigned. No chores, no mothers-in-law to nag them to work! I have a photograph of the women to remind me of that pleasant day and best of all, many memories. In the photograph, the women and girls, heads hastily covered for the photo, are holding bunches of wildflowers, smiling and looking curiously into the camera.

In this and the other stories about women, one of the main issues is the segregation of women in order to maintain their honour. This is a central concept in traditional Islamic and other societies.[5] The code of honour is mainly concerned with women's honour but it is enforced by their male kin, since it is really men's honour that is at stake. When a woman "loses" her honour, it affects her husband/father/brother—in other words it affects the family name. Once a woman's honour is lost, it can never be regained—she and her male kin are forever disgraced. Because honour can only increase in value, it is jealously guarded by the menfolk in her family, even to the point of death (usually hers).

Honour and modesty are preserved by segregation and/or *purdah,* or veiling. This means that women spend most of their public lives as groups defined by gender. Paradoxically, or perhaps because of segregation, women's conversations among themselves are usually about men—their relationships with husbands, experiences of love, anticipation of marriage, loneliness, misery, or happiness regarding these relationships.

Once women are past menopause and no longer involved in sexual relations (whose outward sign is childbirth), they become the guardians of young women's honour. Through reproofs and reprimands veiled as jokes, older women chastise younger ones if they are seen to "become bold." Abu-Lughod remarks, "Much of the frequent teasing among women serves to highlight societal standards ... for example, women often tease each other about sexuality, which above all else violates concepts of propriety."[6]

Another issue is women's work in subsistence societies, well-documented in social science literature. Indeed, their work has been called the cornerstone of the economy. They work hard not only because it is their role to provide sustenance for themselves and their families, but also because their husbands demand and expect it, since marriages are primarily economic unions and the work they do complements men's work in the traditional economy. More importantly, without women's work, men would not be able to enter the modern cash economy. Even though cash is desirable or needed, men still want their traditional lives to continue on the land and women are the keepers of tradition.

Women also work because the elder women (in-laws) in their extended families compel them. Most women live in homes where there is a mother-in-law who was brought into the household as a young bride herself and "trained" by her mother-in-law. Now she repeats the pattern with her

---

5   Ladurie, *Montaillou: The Promised Land of Error*; Illich, *Gender*; Abu-Lughod, *Veiled Sentiments: Honor and Poetry in a Bedouin Society.*

6   Abu-Lughod, "A Community of Secrets: The Separate World of Bedouin Women," 646.

daughter-in-law.[7] Depending largely on the mother-in-law, women can have a difficult or easy married life.

Other issues that are commonly associated with women are hospitality and communality. In the absence of government aid, villagers depend on each other for their very existence. There are no nuclear families here. While the household is the social and subsistence unit of survival, the environment and living conditions in these high mountain valleys are too harsh and demanding for families to be able to survive in isolation. This explains the mutual aid and reciprocity that are features of village life and especially of women's, based on family bonds and neighbourly connections. An observer from the affluent Western world would be surprised to see such seemingly poor people feeding uninvited guests, but not to do so would threaten future relationships and survival. It would earn the reputation of being *kamina*, miserly, the opposite of their ideal of generosity.

Stories about women have to include stories about children. Balti women bear many children, a fact of which they are only too aware. A young woman remarked to me, "You have so much freedom. You are fortunate in every way. I only have *las, plupla,* work, children." Advocates for effective birth control believe that while education for men (and women) is important, it has to be accompanied by an improvement in women's lives generally. According to social science experts, development is the best contraceptive.[8] But women's invisibility to development officials in Islamabad and the West has resulted in a lack of programs geared for them, which ensures their continued low status, high birth rates, and high infant and child mortality, which in turn maintains the need for many children.

Tea in Loqpar

Whenever we are feeling low, or at a loss for something to do in the village, or when my friend Rabia has an hour or two when nothing much needs to be done, there is a special place where we go. Rabia packs a basket with a small, soot-black kettle, a few handleless china cups, and some leftover *khurrba*. Into the kettle she puts little paper twists of tea leaves, sugar, and milk powder and ties a box of matches into the corner of her *dakhun*.

---

7   Ibid, on the relationship of young women with those in authority over them in the marital home.

8   Hartmann and Boyce, *A Quiet Violence: View from a Bangladeshi Village*, 120. See also Hartmann, *Reproductive Rights and Wrongs*.

These preparations done, we are invited to tea in their nearby lower high pasture.

Rabia is the mother of seven children. She is about thirty years old (we worked her age out from her remembered age at marriage, and my estimate of her eldest daughter's age). She is slim and beautiful with thick-lashed brown eyes, and long, curly black hair, which she keeps neatly plaited underneath her *dakhun*. She is also one of the hardest-working women I have ever known: her fields are always cleanly weeded; her house is well kept, swept, and tidied. She prepares delicious meals for about ten people every night and morning. Yet she is always patient with her children and her lap is ready for the child who needs it wherever she is—by the fireplace, weeding in the fields, or processing grains on the roof.

Loqpar has fields of wheat, potatoes, and beans, surrounded by mulberry, walnut, and apricot trees, all conveniently close to the village. We can get there in just five minutes' walk northwest from Rabia's house. Loqpar means "opposite side," because it is on the other side of the jeep road from the village. After clambering up the slope across the road, we continue on a very narrow path westward, sharing it with a water channel at times that hugs the side of the mountain above the gorge of the glacier-fed Phuchhap *nallah*. This is a stream that causes the villagers misery when it floods, but generally it flows harmlessly at the bottom of the deep gorge. The depth of the gorge hints at the swollen, raging river it can become—big boulders lie in the ravine, carried down and tossed there by the flooding river.

Rabia's husband Hamid told me how he helped his father create the beautiful pasture and fields as a young boy. He and his father laid claim to the land simply by working on it, uncontested.[9] They cleared rocks and boulders, slowly built up organic soil with the careful application of manure, and then planted potatoes and saplings that allowed for the build-up of further soil. Then they put in fruit trees and finally, sowed barley. "Was there water here already?" I asked.

"No," was the reply, "We had to dig channels from the *nallah* to bring it here. There was nothing, only sand and rocks." Now little channels of clear water crisscross their fields as their cow grazes peacefully on the lush grass.

---

9 This process of claiming land is called *taqsim*. People sometimes claim the flood-plain of a river, if it has not flooded for several consecutive years, or any land lying unused near the village.

Hamid also helped his father build a little shepherd's hut of squared timber and stone, with a well-packed roof of turf and logs. Upstairs there is an airy room for shelter from the sun or rain and downstairs, the byres for animals kept there in early summer. He took me down to see a small room with a fireplace and little window. "We stay here when we are working late at harvest time," he said. "Sometimes we work late into the night and start again at dawn." The earth floor was covered with *chharas*, and a few pots and pans hung by the *thap*.

The roof of the hut is supported by a polished walnut wood pillar, which goes down to the cellar floor. It is embellished at the top with two stylized ram's horns. Such decoration is thought to bring good luck. It is called a *ghobus*, and is found in only the older homes of men who are skilled as carpenters. There is one in their main house as well.

The current baby would be tied to Rabia's back with a *dakhun*. Was it Rahim? Or Rehana? Holding her finger, or Tara's or mine, a three- or four-year-old child would walk beside us. Or Tara would give the child a *hachhu*, a piggyback ride. When we have stepped over the many rivulets, climbed over big boulders and a stone wall (stopping to pick mulberries on the way), and passed their stone hut, we arrive at our destination—a grassy corner, shaded by apricot trees and bordered by a small stream.

In the lee of a large boulder Rabia prepares to light a fire. We all help to gather dried twigs, branches, and pieces of bark. Someone scoops out water from the stream and balances the kettle carefully on three flat stones. Rabia sets the baby down to play in the grass and bends to alternately blow on the fire, heap more twigs, or steady the kettle. She takes out four cracked china cups, without handles, *karols*, and a hunk of bread from the basket.

The sweet, hot tea is ready surprisingly quickly and tastes delicious after our walk in the fresh air. The only sound is the gurgling of the water and the bleating of goats grazing on the mountainside, on the other side of the wall. Occasionally, a rock clatters downslope as the goats skitter about. The others take turns waiting for a cup to be emptied and washed in the stream, but as a *mehman,* a guest, I am given the first cup.

We pass an hour or two in tranquility. Tara teaches the older children a song in English as they climb into the branches of the apricot tree.[10] Girls can climb trees without disapproval because they have to climb to pick fruit. When there is no fruit on the branches, there is another delicacy for

---

10   I asked Tara what song she was teaching them. It was something by the Back Street Boys, popular among young teens at that time (1993). They did not learn the words, but they hummed the tunes.

the children: the sticky resin of the apricot tree, which has oozed out onto the bark, called *thhanchu*. They peel off clumps of the sap and chew them like gum. The resin has a pleasantly fragrant flavour.

The baby plays in the little channel with stones and sticks. Rabia wanders off to open a channel to irrigate a field. She removes a clod of earth from the side of the channel to divert the water into the field. When the field has been flooded it is closed in the same way. She pulls weeds here and there. For a farmer's wife, there is always work to do.

Once, when I had gone back to the village without my daughter and we were having our customary picnic in Loqpar, Rabia said, "Show me pictures of Tara. I miss her so much whenever we come here. This place reminds me of her," which is exactly what I had been thinking. The pictures were passed around, with exclamations and comments. They were old ones that I always carried in my purse, which Rabia and her children had seen many times, a little frayed and soiled, but the group still loved looking at them. Some of my homesickness vanished. I did not feel as if I were far away from home.

Ei'la—Celebration

For busy farmers, feast days stand out like islands of fun in a dull sea of routine—convivial times when people dress up, meet, and eat buttery, sugary, spicy foods. Most celebrations in the village are for weddings and religious holidays. Wedding celebrations last several days, even weeks. Friends and families get together to shop, sew, cook, and prepare for the big day. Relatives come from far-away cities in lowland Pakistan and even abroad from Saudi Arabia, Iraq, and Iran. They must be accommodated, fed, and visited by the other villagers. The rituals and activities stretch out pleasurably.

Religious feast days, whether joyful or solemn, are other times when people meet in mosque and home. Two such days are *Eid-ul-Fitr* and *Eid-ul-Zuha*. The first, known as the little *Eid*, commemorates the revelation of the Quran to Prophet Muhammad at the end of Ramadan, the month of fasting. The second *Eid* is a celebration of Abraham's faithfulness to God, recalling the occasion he prepared to sacrifice his son at God's bidding and was given a ram instead. The pilgrimage to Mecca called the *Hajj* precedes it. *Eid* is an occasion when relatives and friends get together, give and receive gifts of food and money, and wear new clothes, shoes, and jewellery.

The sound of male voices singing religious songs (the only kind of public singing permitted in the Basha valley) pours out of open windows.

Today is *Eid-ul-Fitr* after one lunar month of fasting. During Ramadan, no food or water may pass a person's lips between sunrise and sunset. When Ramadan falls in the summer months, with work to do outdoors in the sun, men and women who observe the fast are particularly tested. At the anticipated time, families gather on the rooftops to look for the new moon. When the faint sliver is sighted, signalling an end to fasting, there are joyful hugs and exclamations of *Eid Mubarik*! Feasting takes on a new meaning, marked as it is by satisfaction at having stayed the course. (Most adults in these valleys are devout in keeping all the fast days.)

By the time I came out of my room, *api* and the two oldest children had gone off to celebrate at their relatives' house in Tissar, a village just over three kilometres to the south. It would take them about an hour walking downhill on the rough dirt road that winds along above the Basha River. In places the track is broken and breached by channels of water, which make their way down to join the river. *Salwars* need to be hitched up and plastic flip-flops are removed to navigate the icy, pebbly runnels. *Api* and the children left before the high sun could turn the streams into rushing torrents across the track, taking some of the so-called road away. Since the fun continues late into the evening, they plan to stay the night with relatives. The rest of us had a fine breakfast of *parantha* and sweet tea.[11] This was my first breakfast but for the family, their second. As a treat, Rabia had brought up a bowl of *cha-phe*. This is a flour made of soaked, dried, roasted, and then ground barley. It is sprinkled on *paillu chai* as well, or simply rolled into balls and eaten. It is similar to Tibetan *tsampa*, and has a pleasantly nutty taste.

After eating the rich, flaky bread, I decided to go for a walk and then a bath. The bathhouse was still relatively empty because visitors from other villages were attending the service in the mosque. They would almost certainly go there after prayers. This village is home not only to the religious leader of the valley, but also has a hot spring, so it is a focal point for local visitors.

When I came back to the house, Rabia seemed not to have left the fireplace at all, because now a third breakfast was underway. There was more tea, cold *parantha,* and a new addition, *chuskoo*, brought down from the high pastures by her husband for the holiday. *Chuskoo* is a refreshing,

---

11   The tea is commonly called Lipton, even though the brand is not now Lipton. This distinguishes it from salt tea.

creamy drink, a cross between buttermilk and yogourt. Some relatives from another village who had come to visit them unannounced were also sitting around the fire, sipping out of tin bowls and scooping up *chuskoo* with their fingers.

On a religious holiday, everyone is free from work. The women do not go out to weed or irrigate; the men stay at home instead of climbing to the high pastures or else they come down from them (one or two "regulars" stay with the animals in each pasture). Those who are away in the plains try to come home. No harvesting or threshing is done and the school is closed.

I looked out the window at the deserted paths between the fields. Everything was quiet outside. Everything? No, not quite. Into this silence a very loud noise was projected by means of an ancient, crackling loudspeaker attached to the *masjid*. "Modern" technology was bringing the agha's message to the ears of those who were not attending (mainly women who were busy in the kitchen), carrying it across the fields, cutting through the silence.

When the last visitor had departed, Rabia cleared away plates and bowls for the third time and sent the younger children to wash their face and hands. She disappeared into the storeroom off the kitchen and dug out their best clothes from a deep tin trunk. "We are going *Ei'la*,"[12] she explained, putting a few drops of apricot oil in the palm of her hand and rubbing it over the baby's soft hair. "*Gunchas badal, sang gwit.* Change your clothes, we'll go together."

Rafia, aged seven, ran and got a small wooden box out of the storeroom. She pulled out the key on a string around her neck from under several layers of clothes and opened the lock. "*Amma*, look what I have. Which one shall I wear?" The box was full of gilt and silver rings, broken brooches, gaudy plastic earrings, and some necklaces.[13] She selected a pair of earrings, and a necklace of big, flat stones, interspersed with silver beads, strung on braided thread, which ended in tassels and bobbles. I helped her tie the necklace around her neck. "*Rgasha*," I said when she proudly turned around to show me. She did look beautiful wearing the *phallu* made of two kinds of turquoise stones, one green flecked with brown and the other, sky blue. The green is the true Ladakhi turquoise and the blue is from Iran.

Entering into the spirit, Tara took out a new *chaddar* from her rucksack, which we had been saving as a gift for the next village we visited. But Rabia

---

12 Visiting on Eid day.
13 Jewellery made of gilt resembles silver in design, but is cheap.

was pleased to see that we were honouring their special day so I, too, put on something fresh. I combed out Zahra's tangled hair and plaited it. The five-year-old solemnly arranged her little gauze *dakhun* over her head. Her big eyes were outlined with *kohl*, giving her round face an owlish look. We set out attired in our finery.

We crossed the fields to their neighbour's big house, which consisted of two structures. One was the house and the other smaller, newer one adjoining it was a guesthouse in which the men sat. The women and children were sitting on *dzo* hair mats on the roof of the big house. The men sang religious songs, the sounds of which floated out to us through the open window. The songs they sang were *qasida*—joyful songs telling of the birth of imams and prophets; *tawwara*, mournful songs about Husain's martyrdom; and *marsia*, recording the misery and troubles inflicted upon prophets and holy men by kings in days gone by. The women chatted while babies crawled, fell, cried, and were comforted. While toddlers, babies, and girls were up on the roof with their mothers, older brothers stayed in the fields around about the house, playing tag or hitting targets with stones.

We found a spot for ourselves and settled down under the shade of a big mulberry tree overhanging the roof. The women greeted us as they shifted to make more room. "*Thar thar yut, aram yut?*"[14] The hostess came out of the house with her daughter-in-law, each carrying a big *deg* or large cooking pot. Out of one they handed out *chapatis* and out of the other spooned dollops of semolina *halva*, sweet and greasy, onto a *chapati*, on outstretched palms. It is considered a blessing or *sawab* both to give and receive this food, called *tammaruq*.

The greasy *halva* was crumbled into the mouth, scattered on the goat-hair *chharas,* and trampled down by babies, who picked up bits to eat with their little fingers. With much lip smacking, the women wiped their oily fingers in their hair, *dakhuns* carelessly pushed aside in this women-only gathering. From the silence in the men's room, it appeared that they too were eating.

A group of younger women had been whispering together in a corner. Now, prodded by the others, one said with a laugh, "*Baji, fotoo chik!*" I was often asked to take a photograph. *Dakhuns* were adjusted, and babies' caps straightened. A few of the older or more serious-minded women turned away, so that only their backs were visible.[15] A hush fell on the group as I

---

14   "Are you well, are you comfortable?"

15   I noticed that unless men were present (they always forbade the photographing of women), women used their own discretion about being photographed.

positioned my camera because a photo-taking session is a solemn occasion. For some, it was the first time. Some still believe that the camera takes away a little of their identity.

On my return to Islamabad I would have the film printed and mailed to one of the families. The next time I came, whether it was in two or five years, the photo would be produced, frayed and a little grubby now from being passed from hand to hand many times over. They loved any kind of pictures, but especially ones of themselves.

My host family and I were now invited into an adjoining room by a smiling Khair-un-nissa. "Come and have *namkin chai* and *khurrba*," said our hostess. "*Bara zan yut*," because it was now midday. We were being especially honoured because the two families were related through marriage. Their oldest son, Mosa, was married to Rabia's husband's niece and Rabia's daughter was engaged to Mosa's younger brother. I took pains to unravel these relationships, which sometimes crisscrossed generations and made aunts into sisters-in-law.[16]

By this time I'd had as much bread and tea as I could manage in a day, but the others tucked in heartily. No one refuses *Eid* food! Most had observed the month-long fast while working in fields under the hot sun, which was evident by their sunken cheeks and thin arms. The fast is especially hard on women who are already worn out by childbirth and prolonged nursing, because it is these young, able-bodied women who do most of the fieldwork. Men and women in the mountains are generally lean anyway, but after the month-long fast, they are noticeably thinner.[17]

We stayed for an hour or so until Rabia looked up at the sun. It was late afternoon. She motioned to me to get up. "*Gwit*, I'm going," we said as we took our leave in the customary abrupt manner and hurried home. Rabia still had one important task to perform. She had to make a pile of *paranthas* to take to the agha's house. The purpose of this visit was twofold: *Ei'la* plus a *skyazan* visit.[18] The agha's sixteen-year-old daughter, who was married to his deceased brother's son, had given birth to her first child and Rabia had

---

16 This happens because of the huge age gap between siblings. The oldest daughter may be twenty-five years old when her youngest sister is only two. It is not uncommon for mother and daughter to be pregnant at the same time. Then the mother will try to hide her pregnancy due to a feeling of *tshelba*.

17 However, fasting is excused for travellers; pregnant, lactating, and menstruating women; the sick; and the elderly.

18 Taking food as a gift after childbirth, from the verb *skyespi*, to be born, and the noun *zan*, meaning food.

not seen her yet. Since they were neighbours, it would have been considered a slight by the agha's family if she had not made this formal visit.

Rabia kneaded the dough, punching and flattening it until it was soft and elastic. "Halima, *burtsa khers*," she instructed her oldest daughter to fetch kindling from the roof. After several puffs the wood caught fire and Rabia sat back, wiping her watery eyes on her *dakhun* as she balanced the pan on the stones. Soon the *paranthas* were fried to a crispy, bubbling brown. Then she slipped down into the cellar with a bowl and milked their goat into a tin bowl. Rabia delicately fished out a fresh goat dropping from the bowl as she poured the milk into a clean plastic bottle. When all preparations were complete, she wrapped the gifts in a cloth bag, picked up her baby, and we were ready.

First we went to the agha's cousin's house, which was attached to the agha's house in an L-shape. Here more *halva, chapatis,* and tea were being passed around on a tray to the guests seated in a circle on a carpet. There were also china bowls of *samik*, too tempting to resist. *Samik* is a savoury concoction of green coriander, salt, and hot green chilies ground to a paste, then mixed with *chuskoo*.

We took our leave despite many more urgings to *duk*! *duk*! (sit! sit!) and hurried along a winding, mud-floored passage with many doors and smaller passages opening on it, until we reached the agha's quarters. (I thought with amusement that this house was like a rabbit warren, or as Topsy would say, it "just growed.")[19] Men and women were sitting in the formal room, the *rafsal,* to pay their respects to the religious leader, the women clustered at the back by the door.

We walked past them into an interior room where his wife sat in the *angun,* the kitchen. Reclining on a bolster on *Farsi* rugs, *ascho* was threading a *phallu* with silver trinkets and small coral and turquoise beads. "Zakia *la*," she said with a smile as she rose and greeted us warmly in the traditional way with an embrace three times on each side. "*Duk*! *Duk*!" she ordered, patting a cushion beside her. The new mother came into the room carrying a tiny baby in swaddling cloths when she heard our voices.

Zakia was a fair-skinned, plump young woman, her loosely worn *dakhun* barely covering her curly, light brown hair.[20] She was dressed in a *salwar kamiz* of satin with a big floral print, as befits a new mother from

---

19   Topsy is a character from *Uncle Tom's Cabin, or Life among the Lowly* by Harriet Beecher Stowe.

20   Being fat is considered a sign of health and wealth, hence it's desirable. Hard-working peasants do not carry excess weight, unlike high-status men and women.

a prestigious household. "*Barkat*" she said graciously, as she accepted the fried *roti* and bowl of milk from Rabia and promptly drank the milk.[21] Rabia also dropped twenty-five rupees into the baby's lap.[22] I did the same with a hundred-rupee note. One of the *rohmis* sitting by the door nodded approvingly at me that protocol was being observed.

The baby was tightly wrapped in blankets in spite of the hot, stuffy room. Newborns are always completely covered here, whatever the weather, to avert any danger of chills.[23] I cradled the baby, admiring her. "She's sweet, Zakia. She looks like you," I said, uncovering her face. The baby actually looked like both her parents, since they were cousins with the same aquiline nose, long, light-coloured eyes, and fair skin. "*Baji*, look at her stomach," Zakia said. She unwrappped the baby and pulled up her shirt to show the baby's protruding navel. "Ever since she was born, it has been bleeding." Then she added reproachfully, "I was waiting for you to come, *baji*. Why did you take so long?" I unzipped my *jholi* and took out the first-aid pack.

Over the years, I had treated several members of this family for boils, bruises, and mild fevers. "You should have sent someone to get me, Zakia," I replied, as I cleaned the soft navel with antiseptic lotion and applied antibiotic ointment. Then, under their watchful eyes, I wrapped the baby's tiny stomach with a pad of cotton wool and gauze bandage.[24] It is true I had not gone when I heard that Zakia had arrived with her new baby. But I had become more cautious about helping in women's affairs.[25]

We were offered tea (again!) and then directed to a courtyard outside the big, rambling house where women were gathered to listen to men singing inside, hidden from view. Everyone was dressed in obviously new

---

21 Fresh milk is scarce in the summer when all the animals are in the high pastures, so it is considered a luxury. It was a generous gift, because by giving the milk away, Rabia deprived her own children of fresh milk for that day.

22 Again very generous— that is a lot of money for cashless farmers. Her husband would earn that in a day by carrying a twenty-five-kilogram load for an expedition (in 1993).

23 The high infant mortality rate may be a reason for extra precautions.

24 These are things I would normally never presume to do with any baby. But there is no alternative when one is hundreds of kilometres away from any possibility of medical assistance, especially for women and babies. Sadly, on my next visit a year later, I learned that the baby had died after a few months. By then Zakia was pregnant with her second child.

25 See chapter 7, "Rumours and Resistance."

or best clothes. Some of the poorer women had simply covered their shabby clothes with a pretty *dakhun*, or worn a piece of jewellery.

At all such gatherings, the village women sit close to each other regardless of rank or wealth, chatting, nursing babies, listening to religious songs—and, of course, eating. In big firepits dug out behind the big house, men had been cooking *halva* in iron cauldrons all morning, stirring the sticky pudding with giant ladles, and making mounds of thin, fragrant *chapatis*. Now a man came out with *chapatis* and *halva* on tin platters, which he passed around. No one refused the food, but I noticed that if they did not eat it right away, they put the little parcels he offered into the pockets of their capacious garments, perhaps for later consumption—or for absent ones.

A breeze was blowing as we sat outside under the trees. Occasionally, one of the men would lean out of the window and get a request for a song. Little children climbed across laps or sat down wherever they were, regardless of whom they were near, their faces smeared with *ghee* and sugar. Zahra leaned her head on my shoulder as she did at night when we sat round the fire at mealtime. No one was in a hurry to leave. But finally, at sunset we rose, saying, "*Gwit*," to our neighbours, and turned homewards. Songs and the day were over and some tasks simply could not wait, holiday or no.

Rabia went to water her kitchen garden while I sat on the roof with the children, enjoying the evening breeze and the view of the village at dusk. On the paths down below, crisscrossing the fields, we could see groups of people hurrying home to their chores, to water and feed animals, lead the milk cow back to the *phingkhan* from the grassy meadow, and shoo the mother hen with her chickens inside (and count them just to make sure).[26] The children chattered away sleepily, reliving the holiday. Later that evening after she had bathed and said her prayers, Rabia cooked dinner for the family. Even though we had spent the day snacking, farmers need a square meal.

As I lay in my sleeping bag, I looked back drowsily on the day. The musical sound of water came through the open window and the dark shape

---

26 Rabia taught me the different sounds to make to shoo or call different animals.
Ahhiye, aahiye for *rawak*
Chhoo, chhoo for *lu*
Toosh, toosh for *byango, byafo*
Hurr, hurr for *ban, dzongo, dzo* (in a deep gutteral voice. You can't do this if you have a sore throat, I discovered).

of the mountain was visible through the cherry tree, making me realize anew, but not unhappily, that I was very far from home. Even the sound of *api's* snoring through the wall sounded friendly. The thought of the beetles and centipedes I was sharing the floor with did not spoil my mood either. It had been a satisfying sort of a day.

Child Bride

One sunny July morning, after my morning tea, Khadija looked up from rinsing cups. "*Baji*, today we will visit my relatives. *Shukhs*, Let's go."

"Don't you have to work today?" I asked in surprise.

"No," she replied. "*Chuli sputz chham, herris chham.*" There was a lull in her work—apricot-picking and harvest were finished and her two small sons were with relatives for the morning. It was not often that she was free. I accepted eagerly because, sad to say, I had been grumbling that she never had free time—when she would have liked nothing better than to have a day off!

We walked in a direction I had not been before, finding our way along narrow paths between houses so close together that it was possible to stretch my arms out to touch the walls of houses on both sides. The smell of damp earth, goats, and cooking was carried faintly in the air. Somewhere a child cried. This was the old part of the village, she told me. Often, we had to leap across wide channels that ran across the path. We reached her cousin's house at the other end of the village. It was beautifully constructed of squared timber and stones daubed with mud and surrounded by fruit trees and fields. It stood a little apart from the other crowded houses in the alleys we had passed through, as befits the home of a landed farmer. We crossed through a muddy yard where a channel was overflowing its banks and climbed up to the living area, on wide stone steps that had been worn into hollows by countless feet. A carved wooden railing ran around the airy room upstairs, open to the yard.

We were warmly welcomed by a small, pleasant-faced woman who had been waiting for us. (How did she know we were coming? People often seemed to be expecting us—how did they know, I often wondered? There were no telephones!) After seating us on a *chhara*, she disappeared through a doorway and reappeared carrying glasses of cold buttermilk on a tin tray.

Our hostess watched intently as I sipped it. Her round face beamed with pride at having me as a guest—someone from outside was a change in routine. It would give her something different to talk about with family and friends for days after. She plied Khadija with questions about me. "How did Khadija know me? Why did I come alone? Was I really Pakistani?" I had discovered that rather than speaking to me directly, the villagers spoke to my companion about me. Since very few outsiders know Balti, they simply did not expect me to understand. She was delighted when I answered for myself.

Two little girls who looked less than ten years old hid shyly behind her. "*Sung! Baji la chuli khers.*" At the mother's request, the older one ran out and presently came back bearing an enamelled tray of freshly picked and washed apricots. As soon as I had eaten a few, the little girls took the apricot stones to crack them and presented me with the milky-sweet kernels on a saucer.

As we talked, I learned that she had four living daughters. Her three sons had died in infancy. While the parents were still fairly young (under forty) and healthy, they were worried that there were no male heirs. "We have a lot of land and we're getting older," the mother explained. So their two older daughters had been married as soon as they reached puberty, in order to ensure sons. The two girls sitting with us were also engaged to be married to two cousins. Actually, according to Muslim custom, *nikah*, or the marriage vows had been performed by a *mullah*. "They will go to their own homes," the mother said.

"When?" I asked, looking at the childish faces peeping around her shoulder.

"Oh, whenever we want. The groom's party will come. We call that ceremony *seremosing*, farewell."

The little girls listened without any sign of embarrassment about their impending marriage. In fact, not to be married as a teenager would be more problematic for them. They were engaged to boys who were closely connected by blood ties, so they were not strangers to each other. In all probability they had been playmates when they were younger. This also ensures that divorce will be difficult, since it involves the extended family rather than only the husband and wife.[27]

We chatted comfortably as we reclined on pillows. This was one of the few times Khadija had no work in the middle of the day since the start of

---

27 It can happen however, that when the time comes for the wedding, the girl or boy objects to the chosen partner. In theory, they can break off the engagement, but in reality it seldom happens. The parents of the two children would lose face. The girl's reputation would also suffer, thereby preventing other possible unions.

the growing season. She yawned and closed her eyes. But as the sun rose higher in the sky we got up, gathered our belongings, a bag of *pharring* and *starga,* dried apricots and shelled walnuts for me, even as we were being urged to eat more. "*Gwit.*" Khadija had planned another visit. We walked down the steps, going back part of the way we had come. Now we walked in the shade of huge walnut and mulberry trees as the sun was high in the sky. Khadija explained we were going to Maniza's house, the younger sister of the woman we had just visited.

Maniza, a tall, good-looking woman of about thirty-five, had five daughters and two sons. She greeted us at the door of her narrow, dark kitchen with a fireplace at one end, dressed in good clothes—a suit of matching *salwar kamiz,* with a brightly printed *dakhun* covering her *natting.* She wore an armful of glass bangles. A younger woman sat by the *thap* stirring a pot, another sister who had been asked to help prepare for the "important" guest. The steamy kitchen smelled of spices, onions, and boiling rice. Children belonging to various relatives were perched around her hungrily, waiting for this special meal.

In the middle, a long, low table had been laid down (a concession for the *shahri* visitor)[28] with a jug of water, spoons scattered around, and in a tiny glass, some purple and yellow flowers that grow by the roadside. Normally, the family gathers around a *dastarkhwan,* a cloth, spread on the floor, which is shaken and folded away for the next meal. "*Duk,*" I was told, so I folded my legs awkwardly back at the table, while children crowded behind us. Soon, the savoury-smelling *sonma spacchus* (spinach stew) was ladled onto plates and passed around. "*Baji, zos,*" the cook urged, as I protested at the large helping.[29]

There were also plates of *salat,* on the table, finely sliced green tomatoes and raw onions sprinkled with salt, and plates of lettuce leaves likewise sprinkled with salt. I copied the women who picked up lettuce leaves and wrapped them around morsels of the spinach stew like bread. As always, there was a mound of freshly baked loaves, some barley, some wheat, and a few, heavier darker ones of a mixture of beans and barley. Bread made from beans and barley is considered more nutritious, but also not "fine" enough to be offered to a guest.

The bigger loaves were for two giggling teenage boys who burst into the kitchen to have a look at me, then carried their plates, scuffling and

---

28　Citified.

29　I often amused my hosts by saying "*Las bya met, za met,* I don't work, so I don't eat," when refusing large food portions.

whispering, to eat in another room. When we had finished we were given cups of salt tea. Mine was in a handleless china cup, but all the others had big tin bowls called *mungurr* into which they crumbled more bread. They scooped up the soaked morsels with fingers of the right hand, sipping the tea from the bowl. Only the tips of fingers were used and then licked clean.

At the end of the meal, a young girl of about eleven came into the kitchen. "This is Zainab, my oldest daughter. *Lapko min*," Maniza instructed, leading her daughter forward to shake hands with me. She was thin and fair-skinned, but despite her childish appearance she wore bright red lipstick, a heavy silver necklace, and rather fancier clothes than is usual for girls her age. The backs of her little hands were covered with faded henna patterns. Her small, stubby nails were also dyed red and on her middle finger was a huge silver ring with a blue stone. Khadija leaned over and explained, "She has just been engaged to her cousin. *Bakhstrun byas*, she will be married." Perhaps Maniza feared one or both of her younger sons would die, because her sister had lost all her sons. Soon, this daughter would be ceremoniously leaving for her husband's home.

The young girl appeared remarkably composed and self-possessed for all her youthful appearance. She arranged her *dakhun* carefully on her head, sat soberly with the women, not scuffling or whispering like the other little girls. Her bracelets jingled on her thin arm as she ate. When she had finished, she rose and rinsed her plate off with a ladle of water from a bucket in the corner where it sat on the mud floor. "*Barkat*," she said, carrying one of the crying babies out, as if practising for the day when she would be doing this with her own. Clearly, she was preparing to become a wife and mother.

Like weddings on the Indian subcontinent, Balti weddings are extravagant, last several days, and demand months of planning and preparation, at least for the bride's family. Accommodation and food has to be arranged for all the relatives who will congregate there, as well as food for the wedding guests (for several consecutive *dawats* or parties), to say nothing of getting the trousseau together. If the family can afford it, a resident tailor (who must be a relative if male) is installed in the house. He or she can be found in a room at all hours of the day, plying a hand-sewing machine, surrounded by bales and rolls of cloth, along with pins, scissors, and needles as piles of garments mount up.

Mehndi is bought and applied to the hands of young and old. Even grown-up men dye their finger-tips, thumbs, or nails bright red. In the *nallahs* it is customary for brides to dress in traditional *seino-gunmo* and *dakhun* with a *natting* under the *dakhun*. The bridal cap is covered with a filigree of silver, set with stones, ending in a peak at the top, called a *tomar*. Because of its dome shape, it is also referred to as a *masjid*. "Only in the *nallahs* is proper Balti dress worn," I was told. In Skardu, the wedding dress and rituals are similar to those of the Punjab (i.e., lowlands).

When both sides have agreed to a marriage, the boy's family gives one thousand rupees, twelve kilos of *ghee*, two *maunds* (about 35 kilos) of *nas* flour, and twenty kilos of *azzuk*, sweet, fried bread. The wedding is set for a date when the moon is either waxing or full, both considered propitious for marriage. When the bride leaves for her marital home, she carries with her 1800 rupees for the boy's father, and a woollen *qar* or blanket. For the mother of the groom, she takes several suits of *salwar kamiz* and *dakhuns*. For his brothers, one hundred rupees each or fifty if they are small; for the sisters a set of clothes each, for cousins and father's sister, a *dakhun*.

A *baraat*, or wedding party of thirty people accompanies the bride to the groom's house, spends the night, is fed, and then each person given one kilo of *girri* and fifty rupees. After a week, the groom takes his bride back to her natal home for a week. The bride's father then gives him a thousand rupees and their married life begins. The material goods are in keeping with the family's status and not ostentatious, as farmers in a mainly subsistence society cannot afford to live beyond their means.

I was lucky to be in a village when Fareba's wedding took place. The bride was seventeen, the optimum age to marry according to recent Balti tradition in well-to-do families, so she was not quite a child bride.[30] She was married in July. Since it was a wedding of two elite people (Sayyids) and the bride's father and paternal uncles were schoolteachers with important roles to play in the ceremonies, the schoolchildren had been given a holiday for about a month.

The whole village buzzed with excitement. Clearly, it was the main topic of conversation: who was invited from outside, what the trousseau cost, what the bride would wear, who had gone to Islamabad to buy the cloth, who was going to cook for the *dawat*, what kinds of food, and so on. When an elder aunt arrived from Iran after many years of absence, there was a steady stream of people to and from the house, most content just to sit on the edges of the room, to watch and listen to her stories. The focus

---

30   With the opening up of the mountainous northern regions, roads that bring visitors and increased awareness of the world, as well as the building of girls' schools, child marriages are decreasing.

temporarily shifted from the wedding to Iran. In a sense, everyone in the village was involved. Close friends of the family invited the bride-to-be and her female companions to lunch in the days preceding the wedding (for women-only meals). The bridegroom, in another village accompanied by his teenaged friends, was similarly feted.

The first day of the wedding involved the religious ceremony to which I was not invited (as a woman and an outsider) and the second day there was a formal dinner to which only prestigious men closely connected to the family and their wives and/or children were invited. Since Baltis have many children, only the eldest child from each family accompanied his or her parents. Women and girls were seated in a room separate from the men.

The last day was the formal leave-taking ceremony, *seremosing,* when the bride departs for her husband's home. I went to this function with the women of my host family. The whole process took three hours, from dressing and grooming the bride, listening to religious songs, and watching as she formally took her leave from her older male relatives, to the final departure when she tearfully climbed into the jeep that took her away to her husband's home, more than six hours' drive away.

The long upstairs room of the house was packed with women and children, some perched on the wide window sills for fresh air. At one end, Fareba was seated with cushions behind her back, with her paternal aunts, her sisters, and girl cousins around her. As women entered the room, those who were close friends to her family came and sat beside her for a few minutes. Graciously, because I had been a friend of the family since she was seven, I was ushered to this place. Fareba bent her head very low as I held her hand for a few moments. She said softly, "It's good of you to come."

The women attending her began with her hair. Since she was going to be a married woman, fashion demanded that she change her hairstyle. Two locks of her long black hair were cut to ear level on either side. The rest of her hair was drawn up and clasped at the top of her head with a large, gaudy clip, then gathered at the nape of her neck in a round, red plastic comb. Finally it was plaited with red silk tassels called a *parandah* which adds thickness and colour to the plait. We all sat around and watched, calling out helpful suggestions to the young married woman who was grooming her.

When her hair was done to their satisfaction, two women led the bride out. "They are taking her to visit her *nanas'* graves," Rabia explained. She sat with me on a windowsill, giving a running commentary. Fareba was going to the small chapel next door which housed the graves of her paternal grandfather and granduncles, religious leaders in the village before her uncle. When she came back half an hour later, supported by the women on either side, it was obvious that she was overcome by the sadness of impending departure.

The heat in the overcrowded room was oppressive and I reflected that Fareba did not have to feign that she was feeling faint (as "good girls" are supposed to do at their wedding). Women were wiping their faces with their *dakhuns* and someone was fanning Fareba. She whispered something to her aunt who sat beside her. "*Fareba la guin sett*," she said and sent a child to get aspirin for her headache. Now the process of dressing her began. A large *dakhun* was held around her for *gunchas badal,* changing her clothes.

Two men came into the room and sat down discreetly at the back. They were the only men in the room. One carried a harmonium that he proceeded to play. They were well respected in the community, men who often took part in special occasions as singers of religious songs.[31] The melodies they sang in high-pitched mournful voices were poignant, even though I could not understand the words. While a wedding is a joyful occasion, at one level it is sad, for the bride's party at least (who are losing a daughter) and for the bride, who is leaving her home.

The singer was my host. He had told me previously that he had been assigned a special role in the wedding party as well, as a *ghiopa*. This name signifies that not only is he a trusted male escort (*propha*) for the wedding party, but is more than that, somewhat like an uncle, who will personally hand over the bride to her groom.

When her garments had been changed, the sheet was lowered and the next step started: makeup. This is one time in a woman's life when she must wear nail polish and makeup. I examined the jars. The blue jar contained moisturizing cream called "Tibet Snow" and there was a small brown bottle of cover-up as well. Both creams were made in Pakistan, inexpensive, and easily available in the bazaar in Skardu. There would be little need of them after the wedding. The used lipstick and nail polish were bright red, probably from a previous wedding.

The bride wept silently but was comforted by relatives and friends around her. When all was complete, we were able to see her resplendent in her purple going-away outfit. The long loose shirt and baggy pants of her *salwar kamiz* were made of velvet, heavily embroidered all over in gold

---

31 There was sobriety at functions because this was a valley where the agha lived.

thread. Over it all she was draped with a white silk *dakhun* covered in small purple flowers.

As the final touch, glass and gold bangles were slipped on her arms, a watch was fastened on her wrist, and gold and silver rings were slid onto her slender fingers. Her nails were painted to match her lipstick. Black *kajal* outlined her eyes.[32]

"*Chham, ma'gnuss'* stop, don't cry," her attendants consoled her, but every so often a black streak ran down her cheeks. Two or three necklaces were fastened around her neck along with some coloured beads, but one was a beautiful *phallu* of silver set with green turquoises, probably a family heirloom. Finally, a fancy silver nose ring or *chhargul* was inserted into her pierced nostril.

Fareba sat passively and as the inevitable time approached, more calmly. At last, she was ready, pretty, but somewhat overwhelmed by her ornate apparel. She had always been a friendly girl who never gave herself airs in spite of her elite status, playing with younger children, bringing special herbs and food on visits to her mother's *rohmi* who was sick. Everyone was fond of her and that is why her *rukhsati* had been so well attended.

"*Liachmo*, we're ready. Let them in," her aunt called out. The door opened and into the already crowded room her father, two uncles, and older brother filed in. A space was hastily made for them in the centre of the room facing the bride. Fareba prostrated herself in front of each one of them in turn, crying again. "*Baksheesh*," she said, thank you. It was a sad moment and I had a lump in my throat. Her sister and mother, as well as several women, were openly crying.[33]

Her father, brother, and uncles wiped their eyes with large white handkerchiefs and blew their noses. "It's alright, get up, get up," they murmured. Her father leaned forward and stroked her head. At this emotional moment, as if by an invisible signal, it was evidently time for her to leave. The room emptied while the bride was helped to her feet by her aunts who escorted her out.

---

32 *Kajal* is an eyeliner made by burning a wick soaked in castor oil, then collecting the resultant soot on a saucer held above it. It is considered to have therapeutic as well as aesthetic value. It is available in the Skardu bazar at a *hakim's* shop.

33 Women use these occasions when tears can be shed to cry about life's hardships—mother-in-law troubles, hard work, the memories of dead children, marital problems—there are many things women can cry about. So, when they peel onions they sniff and wipe their eyes without comment or criticism for being "weak" (seen as an undesirable trait from the standpoint of in-laws).

Four jeeps were waiting to take the *baraat* to the village where her husband, who was her father's older sister's son, lived. His father was the agha of that valley. They had played together as small children and he was also seventeen years old (often, grooms are older). Even so, for a young girl, to leave her natal home is a traumatic event.

Symbolically, Fareba was leaving her home for the last time. She would never again be a daughter of the family, because she had become a wife in another one. For this reason there was care and nurture involved in sending her away with specially appointed people. Their task was to hand her over safely to her in-laws and see that she was well established in her new home.

She was going to be accompanied by an older woman who had served her family as a helper at times of harvest and other events. This woman's own wedding had been arranged by Fareba's family, so she looked up to them as patrons. Her role was as a *lemma*, someone who renders service. She would stay two weeks with Fareba, getting her used to her new home, helping her to dress, and bringing her meals in her room away from other eyes. The bride is expected to be unable to cope alone and the *lemma*'s job is to anticipate her needs and act as a go-between, even in her aunt's home. She would sleep outside the door of their room.

Also going with her was her best friend and paternal cousin. She was going in the capacity of *gniopa*, a daytime companion, who would stay two days. I was told that Fareba would be back in two weeks with her husband, when a big welcome dinner would be given in their honour and food distributed to all in the village. But I was not there for that.

When I visited Fareba in her husband's home a year later, she was the proud mother of a small son and no longer a shy bride. She sat by the fireplace, confidently cooking and serving food while her baby lay beside her. Her clothes were simple, her face serene. She reminded me of her mother, when I had first met her ten years ago.

From a stereotypical outsider's point of view, it might seem that with marriage, a young girl will surrender all the fun and freedom of childhood. But my experience showed that work and play are not sharply separated as they are in the Western world. Rather, women of all ages manage to combine the two. They work incredibly hard, but generally there is time to stop for a cup of tea, sit down in the shade of a tree for gossip, teasing, laughter, and play with female companions. Since they own the means of production, the work they do is for themselves, their husbands, and families, not for an employer, so they are not rigidly bound by time or place.

If the girl's husband and mother-in-law are good to her, in all probability her life will not change markedly from when she lived in her parent's home. Instead she will achieve the independence of an adult as a married woman and mother. Her worth will increase even more if she gives birth to sons, which continues the tradition of very young girls being given in marriage in order to bring a son into the family.

As long as this attitude continues, the value of girl children will not increase. To break the vicious circle requires the combined efforts of the larger community, the immediate social group, and the parents, to recognize a girl's worth, treat her as an equal to sons, and, among other things, educate her.[34] The marriage of very young girls in poor countries is deplored as a barbaric practice in Western development literature. Islam is usually blamed, but there are other religions that sanction early marriages, including Hindu, Buddhist, and Roman Catholic.

Tradition and labour requirements are more likely at the root of this practice. For example, son preference is one reason for child marriages: the need to marry a daughter so that she will produce a son. Here, sons are valued more than daughters due to inheritance laws and patriarchal norms. Muslim inheritance laws dictate that a daughter can inherit land, but only half her brother's share. In Gilgit-Baltistan, if land is scarce, a girl may inherit a fruit tree or two. By contrast, Hindu girls do not have any rights of inheritance at all.

Even though women can theoretically inherit land, there is often a gap between theory and practice.[35] In reality, sisters will give up their share of the land to brothers in return for having the (unspoken) promise of their care and protection in times of need. For example, if a woman

---

34   On the topic of education for girls, some caution is needed. The idea and the school building should come from the people themselves, with ideally a local teacher. If outsiders are involved, especially foreigners, not only will there be poor attendance (only richer families might send their daughters) but male elders can be hostile to the venture. An extreme example is the burning of girls' schools in Swat by the Taliban recently (2008). In the context of a patriarchal subsistence society on the margins of capitalism, the reason for opposing female education is not Islam, as generally accepted, but the control of female bodies (their labour and reproductive abilities). See Mies, *Patriarchy and Accumulation on a World Scale: Women in the International Division of Labour*, 48.

35   Hewitt (Farida), "Women in the Landscape: A Karakoram Village before 'Development.'"

is abandoned (a rare occurrence, but it does happen) or widowed and without sons, it's desirable to find sanctuary in her father's/brother's home, given that respectable women do not live alone. To be sure of receiving this protection, many women relinquish what by Muslim law is rightfully theirs—their land.[36]

The son inherits the family home. If there are many sons, the oldest or most favoured son will inherit it. If there are none, the home could go to the oldest daughter and her husband (who would prudently be her first cousin on her father's side, thus maintaining the family name). The parents continue to live in this home until death.

Another reason for the value of sons is that marriage laws in Baltistan are patrilocal. Because the bride moves to her husband's home, her labour and value are lost to her parents. Not only that, she carries with her a dowry of money and/or material goods, as a gift to the groom's family, to increase her worth in their eyes which in turn, increases the cost of raising daughters.

The gendered division of labour is yet another reason for the desirability of sons. In Baltistan generally, in common with most traditional, subsistence economies, men and women perform different economic tasks. According to this division, men have the more prestigious roles. While women are involved in essential work for everyday living, men are heads of families and house owners who make important family and community-based decisions (at least outwardly) and have a voice in the public, or official world. All this means that without sons, there is no assurance that land and family home will remain with close blood relatives who would carry on the name after the death of the parents.

Finally, the code of honour may influence parents to marry their daughters early, before they have reached their teens, even if they have sons. There is always a fear that a young, unmarried girl's name and reputation will be spoiled (since the code of honour is about what people say) making it difficult to find a "decent" husband for her. Even a rumour about a girl's character is enough to frighten off the parents of eligible suitors.[37]

As an interesting aside on how young girls themselves may desire marriage, I will recount my daughter's experience. It showed me that sometimes marriage is indeed not forced on very young girls. On our

---

36   Hartmann and Boyce, *A Quiet Violence: View from a Bangladeshi Village*, 92.

37   While this applies to rich, or high-status families, the poor are less constrained by societal rules, simply because they cannot afford the luxury of being segregated. Their labour is too necessary.

second visit to the village, we stayed for three months. As usual it was exciting to meet our friends again, to visit their homes, go on familiar walks, bathe in the *chhu*, and catch up on the news. We immersed ourselves in life: so many marriages, so many new babies, and sadly a few deaths. I always enjoyed the first few days thoroughly, even though later there were unavoidably feelings of exasperation, irritation, impatience, loneliness.

Tara was thirteen years old at this time. She was welcomed by her friends who were also teenagers—one was married, one was engaged, and like young girls everywhere, they giggled, whispered, talked—and discussed boys. We had been there over two months when Tara unexpectedly expressed a wish to get married and settle down![38] She even mentioned a boy she thought she would like to marry. I could not get over my surprise since I knew of her longing for Canada, peanut butter, chocolates, television, her sisters, and her house (to name only a little of what she had articulated to me). I tried to explain how she would feel if she gave all that up and stayed behind. "Well," she replied, "You could do your research from *my* home, if I married someone here." Time passed and we returned home and forgot about it.

On several occasions after that, whenever she went back to the mountains, Tara never referred to or repeated the wish. Recently (in 2006) during a conversation with friends in Toronto, she told us why she had wanted to marry in the mountains. "We had been living there for awhile. All my friends were married, engaged, or talking of getting married," she said. "Mahjabeen who was fourteen and just married, opened her trunk and showed us all her silk suits and *chaddars* and jewellery. I thought if I got married I would be like a princess with beautiful things too—that's why I wanted to be married to one of the boys in her family." When I remembered how we had travelled in the mountains, her explanation made sense. In order to be as like them as possible, we wore simple, everyday clothes and certainly had no jewellery or silks. Of course, being travellers, what we carried was all we had—unlike they who had boxes and cupboards and cellars full of stuff!

"Did you know, Mahjabeen didn't have a room of her own until she got married?" Tara said. "Where did she sleep then?" I asked in surprise. "Anywhere she could, in the *rafsal* sometimes or the *angun* with her girl cousins." "Where did she keep her clothes?" "In boxes in the passage and

---

38   Here I should explain that we had been in Islamabad for eight months already. Tara had attended school with her cousin and was immersed in Pakistani culture. Perhaps this throws some light on the reason for her inexplicable wish!

in her parents' room," Tara replied. "She said only sons have a room, when they are grown up. Girls go away to their husband's houses."

I realized that in the Balti world, getting married gives young girls importance, recognition, a time to be centre stage, have fine clothes and ornaments, feel pampered—all the things they crave in their busy, practical lives. The reality of married life— babies and sickness and work (and mothers-in-law)—must pale in comparison.

Dre chatphe phonse (Buddha carved on stone). Manthal, Skardu.

Shigar Masjid, seventeenth century, showing Buddhist influence on architecture; pagodas instead of minarets.

View of Chutrun, 1989. Bathhouse in foreground.

Girls in field. Loqpar, Chutrun.

Women and girls weeding.

Tara standing beside a ghobus in the katza.

Man ploughing field with shul and dzos (simple wooden plough harnessed to animals).

Boys threshing grain.

View of fields and rooftops, Tallis.

View of Hushe's terraced fields looking south.

Dzos.

*Carpenter making window using tongue and groove
joints with a starrey (adze). No nails are used.*

Building the roof of a house. Large logs are placed first, then thinner ones crosswise. Finally burtse (artemesia) is laid over them, and daubed thickly with a mixture of clay and straw.

A salleh, rooftop (summer) kitchen, showing khurrbas baking on a to (griddle). Kitchen implements including a carved wooden kacchu in L. foreground.

Shepherd shearing sheep with a chhadma (metal shears).

Men twisting ral (goat hair) with a thap (twisted wooden stick)
into a rope. Only men can handle goat and dzo hair.

Woman pounding grain in wooden tanus bus (pestle and mortar, a phyallu (sieve) beside her.

Women processing grain.

Man with markhor bags full of grain.

Tara trying her hand at churning, Damsum.

Two shepherdesses, Alling.

From R. to L. Author and daughter Nina on Barpu Glacier, with porter

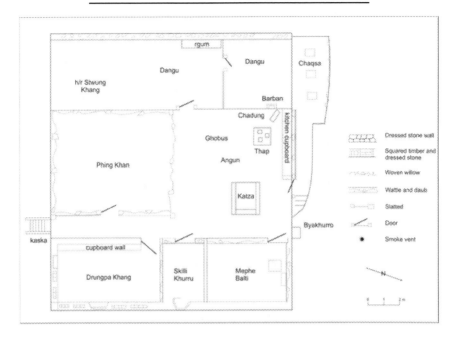

Floor plan of a typical Balti home

Diagram 01: Main Floor: key:
kaska: ladder; angun: kitchen or family room; thap: fireplace; chadung:
tea churn; ghobus: carved pillar with ram's horns; barban: window;
dangu:storage room; rgum: box for flour: stwung khang: closet or larder
for edibles; phing khan: room for baby animals; katza: opening for ladder
to cellar; drungpa khang: Large room for assemblies or guests; skilli
khurru: small spare room; mephe balti: family room for sleeping, with
stove (mephe:fire and bread); byakhurro chicken coop; chaqsa toilet.

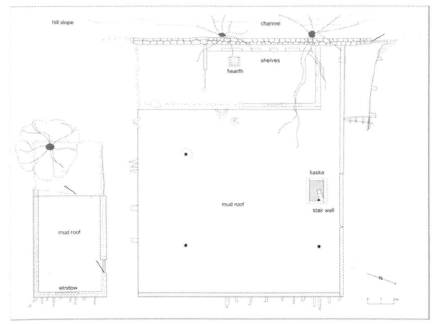

Diagram 02: mud roof: key:
handoq, with salleh: summer kitchen and living space.
To the left, rooftop of small adjoining room. The swirls with
black dots represent three fruit trees around the house.

Chapter 4   WORK

All in a Day's Work

As we walked home after a day's work in the fields, Rabia stopped by a heap of *hrstwa*. "*Le, Rafia, khers,* here, bring it," she called to her daughter, who obligingly picked it up and bundled it into her *dakhun*. The grass and weeds, a valuable byproduct of weeding, would be fed to the animals at home. Some are too young or too old to be sent up to high pasture, or a cow is kept to provide fresh milk over the summer months for little children.[1]

Weeding or *yurma* is one of the main activities in spring and early summer for women who, together with children, work in their fields for the larger part of the day. This is where they also eat, rest, and play. "What are you doing today?" I would ask my friend in the morning, over my cup of tea. The usual reply would be followed by my response: "I'm coming too." These were pleasant days (for me). They included visits with neighbours as they passed by our field, meals eaten picnic fashion, a chance to gossip with the women who were working alongside, and freedom (again, for me) to wander away, read under a tree, or just sit. Initially, of course, I tried my hand at weeding.

Weeding is difficult work for a novice. It is hard to distinguish some weeds from grain when the plant is immature, because weeds mimic grain so closely.[2] I pulled out only the easily identifiable ones. Zahra, aged six, can recognize the more subtle differences. She taught me that the red-veined plants growing amidst the wheat are weeds. They are poked out with a pointy metal tool with a wooden handle, called a *phurrpa*, and

---

1   Households with cash buy powdered milk from village shops to use in tea, but not to drink as milk.

2   Whiteman, *Mountain Oases: A Technical Report of Agricultural Studies (1982-1984) in Gilgit District, Northern Areas, Pakistan.*

tossed aside on the verge. Zahra watched as I tried my hand, wiping her runny nose on her *dakhun*. "No, not that one. It's *tro*," as I dug out a wheat seedling. Later her mother told me how to distinguish between them. "*Tro* is in *purdah*, the seed head is closed; weeds are open." It was tiring dusty work, squatting and moving forward in the rows.

I was slow compared to Rabia who did five rows to my one. Each *shuu* or bed is about half a metre wide. My back ached, my knees were stiff, and I had to keep standing up to stretch my legs. The sun beat down on my head which I'd covered with only a thin *dakhun*. It had not rained for several days and the hard, dry earth hurt my fingers as I tried to dig. Dampening the soil with jugs of water helped. Even so, because my fingertips were not calloused like Rabia's were, I soon had cuts and blisters. Rafia sprinkled the ground for us while she carried her baby brother on her back. As she rocked him, Rafia sang a song in a childish, reedy voice. I recognized the words *plupla* meaning children and *kaka*, elder brother. The song had a plaintive sadness to it.[3]

I soon discovered that *yurma* is not easy when it is windy. Sometimes in the late afternoon a strong wind blows down the valley. As you dig with the stick, dust flies up into your face. That would explain Halima's eyes, red and itchy, from rubbing them with muddy fingers when she came back one windy day. There are many problems with *yurma*—headache, aching legs, bruised knees, sore eyes, sore back, sore arms, and sore fingers!

Everyone works fast, looking at the sky anxiously. If it should rain, the work stops, while the women and girls shelter under the trees; if it looks like the rain will continue, they go home. Rabia says it is essential to weed or the harvest will be dirty. Weeds standing up in the field when a crop has matured are also the sign of a "lazy" woman, which implies loss of respect for the head of the household.

Around midday, Rabia looked up at the sky to judge the time by the position of the sun, then got up to light a small fire under the pot of *namkin*

---

3   According to Kazmi (The Balti Language), the songs women sing while they are working or weeding in the fields, called *yurmi-glu* are not composed spontaneously, but are traditional and familiar melodies, referring nostalgically to childhood and other experiences good or bad, concerning relationships. We can compare them to the poetic recitations by Bedouin women described by Abu-Lughod, in which they express longings for, or sadness about men (*Veiled Sentiments: Honor and Poetry in a Bedouin Society*, 238). The singing appears to be an outlet for women, a way to reveal private sentiments in song in the company of other women. If they are challenged, they can say, "It's only a song." The skill, according to the author, is in choosing the song which best expresses their mood.

chai she had brought. "*Ya Allah!*" She stretched her legs, closed her eyes, and lay back, cradling her head in her hands. When the tea was ready, we drank it out of *mungurrs*, crumbling *khurrba* from a pile loosely tied in a cloth. Rabia nursed Rahim and laid him down asleep under a tree, wrapped in a *dakhun*. After this brief rest, I walked home with the younger girls but Rabia stayed for another four hours with her eldest daughter and baby.

They came back when the sun had set, *gniwa phonget,* and before the rain started. Their eyelashes and faces were coated with a film of dust. Halima flung herself down on some cushions and fell asleep immediately by the cold hearth, but Rabia gathered up clean clothes and went for a *chhu,* her only chance to relax before the evening chores began. She took the baby with her. The other children, tired and sleepy as they lay or sat on the *chhara*, waited impatiently for her to come back.

When she returned, the little ones clung to her, complaining, pulling her clothes, and crying, "*Ayo, tokhs yut, zan min, zan min,* Mother, I'm hungry, give me food." Without answering them she sat down with a sigh. Tiredly, from the cupboard behind her she reached for matches, pots, and a sharp knife, as she started preparations for the evening meal.

I sat opposite her by the fire, writing in my diary. The six-year-old flung herself beside me, dusty and tired. Wordlessly, she leaned her head on my shoulder and was soon fast asleep. I shifted her weight and gently laid her down, with a bundled *dakhun* for her pillow.

When the pot was simmering on the fire, the mother went down into the *katza* and milked their goat. She gave each of the two younger ones—who were still crying and rolling on the rug—milk in tin bowls. They sat down with pieces of stale bread and wolfed it down to the last drop, scooping it up with little fingers. With stomachs full, they too fell asleep beside the fire.

For dinner that night, which was later than usual (at about 9:30 pm) we had *ballay.* This simple dish of shredded dough, rather like dumplings, dropped into a simmering sauce of onions and spices, is pleasant and quick to prepare, but it's normally not considered adequate fare for a hard-working family.

Tired as she was, Rabia had to finish her chores before she could go to bed. She collected the dirty dishes and piled them into a *kharrik* to take to the hot spring at dawn, put away spices in the cupboard, and dumped scraps for the chickens into a pot with a lid (because of rats).

Then, glancing at me as I sat warming my hands at the hearth, she asked, "*Baji, chai thu'nwerra*? Will you drink tea?" and, with a little smile she put a small pan of milk and water to boil on the fire. She sprinkled tea leaves into it. "I know you like tea before going to sleep, *baji*. So do I, now." We could hear the rain on the roof. With everyone else in bed, we sat talking about her girlhood and marriage.

When she was fifteen years old, Rabia married Hamid who was twice her age. I gathered that his first wife had died and his second wife had left him because of "mother-in-law troubles." Hamid was the only son of a landowner who had been famous in the valley as a carpenter and calligrapher. He had inherited his father's house and land, as well as his talents. It was considered an honour for Rabia to have received this eminent man's proposal, because she herself was the daughter of a widow. That is, she would not have much wealth to inherit, since one brother lives in the parental home and works their land and the other lives and works in Karachi. A fatherless family is considered a poor family.

We drank our tea as we sat with our feet close to the dying embers in the cool of the night. "I'm glad you are here," Rabia said. "Before you came I was always alone at night. I had no one to talk to—just work, work." She banked the fire with ashes, and balanced her mother-in-law's aluminum water pot on stones to keep it warm for *api's* early morning ablutions. It was 10:30 pm. She had been up since 4:30 that morning.

One rainy evening we two sat on by the fire after granny and children had gone to bed. Her husband was away in the high pastures, as he often was in the growing season. It had been drizzling all evening—summer rains which are welcomed by the farmers. A light spray came down into the kitchen through the square hole in the roof and made a wet patch on the earth floor. This opening was necessary for light and to allow the smoke from the fire to escape, but we were dry because it was not directly above us. A sturdy ladder was propped up to allow a way out onto the roof and to the road at the back of the house.

As we sat talking and drinking tea, three things happened simultaneously: a centipede ran diagonally across the wall behind me, driven out of the thatch roof by the rain. "*Haboo!*" I cried. There was a flash of lightning followed by a loud crack of thunder, *khrok barrik, blok bosset!* And a man descended the ladder from the dark night. To say that we were surprised is an understatement but Rabia remained calm. The man exchanged a few words with her and sat down at a slight distance from where we two women sat. Rabia drew her *dakhun* closer to her head, but it was obvious that she was not the focus of his attention.

He turned to me and, speaking in Urdu, fired a volley of questions, his manner belligerent. "Who are you?" "Why do you come here?" "What does your husband do?" "Where has he gone now?" and then the most important question from his perspective, "Does he collect gems?" So that was it. Rabia and I exchanged glances as I told him that my husband was interested in rocks, but not of the precious kind.

While he was questioning me I had a chance to take a good look at him. He was dressed in the traditional *salwar kamiz*, but over it he wore a western men's jacket, a peaked cap with the Pakistan army emblem, and good hiking boots. As Rabia put it dismissively later, he was a "*shahri mi*, a citified man."[4] We instinctively distrusted him and Rabia did not offer him tea.

The mountains are rich in precious and semi-precious stones: deep blue lapis with creamy veins, pink Himalayan rubies, malachite, tourmaline, agates both bottle green and brown, garnets like pomegranate seeds, carnelians, and turquoise, to name only a few. In Gilgit and Skardu bazaars, every other shop is a jewellery shop—small, dark, dusty, and pokey, where the best is hidden behind heavy curtains and the shopkeeper will bring a tray out only if you ask for something special. In every tourist spot men loiter hopefully outside hotels with pockets and bagfuls of gems. This man had probably got gems by dynamiting rocks, somewhat like a gold prospector.

We sometimes heard distant explosions in the mountains, when the villagers would look up knowingly and with a grim expression, say, "They are looking for precious stones. It would be dangerous to be up there now." Understandably, shepherds in high pastures do not like their hills to be dynamited. Once the visitor was satisfied that I was not to be feared as competition in the search for precious stones, he left as abruptly as he had come.

We listened for the rasp of the gate as he pulled it behind him and turned to each other. "*Jiksett*—I was afraid, Rabia," I said. She pursed her lips as she damped the fire. "*Onn'wa, liakhmo met*—Yes, it's not good. I have often asked Hamid to put a lock on the gate, *baji*. After all, I am alone at night when he is away." While I had been physically afraid, I understood that she was afraid for her reputation. Nothing could be worse for a young woman than to be alone with a strange man in her home. That night we went to the latrine together carrying the lamp between us, before retiring to our rooms. The desire for privacy had suddenly deserted me.

---

4   Locals use the term in a derogatory sense because these men have left their home, family, and land. They are rootless.

Only Half a Home

> A home without a woman is orphaned and land without a man is orphaned.—Local Balti saying

> The labour of men's and women's bodies and hands is complementary.—Ivan Illich, *Gender*

The goats are bleating all day. They stand up in their small stall in one corner, confined behind a crudely woven wicker fence. Their strange yellow eyes shine in the dark interior. I pick up stray wisps of grass and leaves from the earthen floor and feed it to them through the fence as I pass by. After lunch they are given the slops such as left-over tea and rice with pieces of bread broken into it. Do they get this every day? Yes, but they are still hungry for green fodder. However, there is none, not even in the *shakhang*—in the storeroom in the cellar where every household should have a ready supply.

In the evening, desperate for food, the goats crash through the fence and trot around the house. They are rounded up and led onto the patio outside my room. A visiting neighbour breaks off branches from the overhanging mulberry tree and the goats munch rapidly. He explains to me, "They want *chara*."

"Safura has gone to get grass for them," Syed Abid, my host, replies. But Safura is nine years old and she has gone out to play. Normally, this is work young children would do in their homes, but Safura does not live here. When she visits her father's house, she is left to her own devices, and seldom does chores

Syed Abid lives in a different village from his wife. She is his third wife. The first is dead and the second, a "commoner" (i.e., not a Sayyid) lives in the same village in her own house. He may or may not support her, but he has kept the son from that marriage. Syed Abid is the headmaster here while his third wife lives in the new home he has built for her in a village where he also owns land. It is across the river and lower down the valley. Normally, his own household consists of two young sons aged ten and four and himself. He and his older son cook tea and simple meals, but for the most part they eat their evening meals at friends' homes. There are many hospitable homes open for them since not only is he the headmaster but as a Sayyid (an agha) he leads the Friday prayers and is a respected figure in the village.

He and his sons live comfortably, but there is no woman to do the work that women do: keep the fire going, the hearth warm, and the kitchen welcoming with warm smells of bread and stew; fill the water pots with drinking water; arrange utensils neatly on the kitchen shelves; see to details like making sure there is a curtain across the door of the *desi* toilet (women need it, but not a household consisting of males only); keep the rooms swept; fold bedding away every morning; wash clothes (their room, when I peeked, was a jumble of rumpled clothes, unmade bedding, empty cups, crusts of bread, torn exercise books, plastic slippers, and other discards). Most important of all, women collect fodder for the milk goat and her kid by weeding, then storing the grasses in the *shakhang*, in the *katza*.

Syed Abid has given over the work in his abundant fields and the care of the considerable number of fruit and nut trees to various families in the village in return for a share in the harvest. His livestock is also in the care of others who give him a portion of the butter, cheese, and curds from the high pastures. "Do you lose in this arrangement?" I asked. "I only get about a quarter of what I should," he confessed, "but I am not a farmer and could not do this work myself, or even oversee it. I am a *talibilm*, a scholar, more interested in books and learning. I collect books and want to start a library in my village, where others can come and read."

In the other village his wife *ascho* Arifa (she is a Sayyid) lives with their youngest daughter Safura. This is Arifa's second marriage. She is a small, delicate woman prone to headaches and maybe, depression. For days on end, she will lie in a darkened bedroom, sighing "*Ya Ali*"! while Safura, a bright, precocious girl, assumes a lot of responsibilities due to her father's absence and her mother's frailty. When I stay with them, the child is eager for company and a chance to walk around the village and learn about the world outside. "Tell me about Canada, show me a picture of your daughters. Do they go to school? Tell me a story about Tara. I wish I could meet her."

"Do you want to go to school?" I asked her once. She nodded, but out of loyalty to her mother, did not complain. Instead, "I can read Mohsin's *quaida*," she said proudly. "Abba has taught me to read and write Urdu." Indeed, in conversation, she was more articulate than her school-going brother.

Syed Abid's younger, married sister *ascho* Nafisa, also lives with them with *her* three children.[5] They are from the Chorbutt region on the border with India and are refugees from the Siachin war.[6] Having his sister live with his wife fulfills two obligations for Syed Abid: one to his younger sister, by providing sanctuary as a brother should in times of trouble and second, to his wife by giving her a companion (according to Balti custom, a "respectable woman" must not live alone).

His sister's husband is a schoolteacher who lives and works in the town of Khapalu, so he too is away most of the year. *Ascho* Nafisa is a strong, tall woman who, with some help from the children, does all the hard work of weeding and irrigating her brother's fields, knocking down apricots, and fetching water from the communal well. She laughed at my alarm when I saw her balancing the heavy clay water pot on her shoulder. "Yes, it's heavy, but who else can do it? *Gnis bustryn, chicpa, azab yut!* Two women alone, it's hard!" Meanwhile, *ascho* Arifa and Safura keep the house clean and swept and the two women take turns in cooking. The cow and goats have enough to eat—they are given water and tied in the shade in the day.

But there are other things lacking. There is no man to collect and chop firewood for them. Without firewood they can cook on only a kerosene stove which is often out of order. A male neighbour comes to fix it, but it is not dependable. "We have to eat rice again, *baji*, but I will make *chapatis* for you—I know you like *roti*," *ascho* Arifa says with an apologetic smile. "*Thap met.*" Without a fireplace, the women cannot make the traditional *khurrba*, which requires embers and hot ashes for baking.

There are other problems. Without a man in the house to climb their mulberry trees (taller than apricot trees), much of the fruit falls and rots on the ground. Boys and men climb the tree, while girls and women hold an outstretched sheet under it to catch the shaken fruit. It too could have been collected, dried for their winter use or fed to the animals. The animals are never led out into grassy fields to graze, which is usually the work of men or young boys. The house is cheerless and empty because not many visitors come where only women and children live. It is only half a household.

---

5   Due to the shortage of Sayyid women to marry Sayyid men, there are unusual marriages. Nafisa is married to Arifa's younger brother, Manzur who is both her husband and her nephew. Nafisa's oldest sister married Arifa and Manzur's father, after their own mother died giving birth to Manzur and raised him from birth. This means that Nafisa's oldest sister is his sister-in-law as well as his stepmother.

6   This was ongoing in 1999.

As happens so often in such cases, the man has a better deal than his wife. Syed Abid has a busy social life since he lives in his natal village in the house inherited from his father. He was born here forty-four years ago. The day he was born a poplar tree was planted at the corner of the house and now it is the tallest poplar tree in the village. One could say that like the tree, he is firmly rooted and grounded in his birth village. His wife, on the other hand, lives far from her own village. Also, as an elite woman, according to the code of honour, it would not do for her to go out for meals or indeed, to be seen visiting many houses, or to receive many visitors. Perhaps her isolation adds to her depression. These two strangely divided households are incomplete parts of a whole, evidence of the beginnings of breakdown in traditional living.

In these high mountain villages which are largely outside a monetary economy, the gendered division of labour is one of the most powerful principles governing material life—everything depends on the labour of people's bodies and the work of their hands. Men and women perform different tasks and have different responsibilities. At the risk of derision or dishonour, a man will not do "women's work" any more than a woman will engage in man's work. Ivan Illich, although he is writing of medieval Europe, could almost be describing a Balti point of view when he says "If someone does what we consider the other gender's work, that person must be a stranger. Or a slave, deprived of all dignity."[7]

The division of labour roughly matches the two main spheres of Balti economy. Livestock rearing is men's work and cereal production, based on irrigation, is women's work. In some villages the division may be changed or even reversed, but there always is a division. For example, in the villages of Arindu in northwest and Hushe in east Baltistan, women not only work in the fields but they also gather fuel and take animals up to high pasture, while their men are responsible for all the large-scale work like terracing, house building, and digging irrigation channels in the village.

But change is coming. In many villages, portering seems to be the chief male activity due to geography—their proximity to large glaciers and high mountain peaks. Men are leaving their villages to work for cash, not just as guides and porters, but also in the army or downcountry in the service trade. While who does what differs from valley to valley in the traditional economy, it is still true that the interdependent work of men and women supplies the main resources they need for living. That is why a marital

---

7   Illich, *Gender*, 68.

union is based on more than love: it is first and foremost an economic and strategic alliance between clans, families, and finally, individuals.

A Season for Everything

> To everything there is a season and a time for every purpose under the heaven. —Ecclesiastes, 3:1

Every home has them—soft felted mats called *phingma*, large enough to cover a room, small enough to spread on string beds, or in squares just big enough to act as seats. They are in earth tones of rust, beige, gray, charcoal, and black, with colourful patterns pressed into them, geometric or flowery, in muted shades of red, blue, or brown. Durable and thick, they are a pleasure to look at and touch. Knowing that her husband is a master craftsman, I asked my hostess if I could buy one from them to take back to Canada with me. "We don't have one ready," she said slowly, but that set the wheels in motion. I thoughtlessly added, "I would love to help make one." This was in mid-June when farm work was in full swing.

A few days later, before the animals were taken up to high pasture, a neighbour came by with a large pair of shears in his hands. He sat down in their kitchen by the fireplace where Rabia had just finished baking a stack of *khurrbas*, covered them with a cloth, and disappeared down the ladder into the cellar. Shortly after, she and her eldest son led sheep in by the front door, held by their ears, baaing in protest. Pushing a sheep firmly down on its side, the man pinned it with his knee and proceeded to shear it expertly, watched by an audience consisting of me, Rabia, the baby, old *api,* and the son. The shears were large and sharp, but not a nick or mark was made on the soft grey skin that was exposed as layers of wool, matted, clumped, and dirty, fell away.

When it was finished and all the shorn sheep had been penned up, the wool was bundled and piled into a box. Jamal carried it down into the cellar. Rabia swept the hearth with a twig broom, then blew on the dying embers as she put on a big *deg* of *paillu chai*. The shearer and everybody in the kitchen were handed *mungurrs* of salt tea and piles of *khurrbas.* (By now more neighbours had dropped in, five or six; shearing appears to be one of those landmark events, signalling another stage in the growing season). It would have been unthinkable to have guests in the house without offering them something. Obviously, Rabia had been preparing for this all morning.

A week passed by. When the morning meal had been cleared away, Rabia brought up some sheared wool from the cellar. "What are you going to do?" I asked, having forgotten my earlier request. She had not. "*Yeri phingma la*, it's for your *phingma*," she answered with a smile. She weighed the clump in a small tin scale with a round rock, then separated a small portion to dye and set it aside. The dye was in paper packets of pink and green. Taking a little powder from each, she mixed it in small pots of water ladled from the bucket and soaked the twists of wool in them. The pots were placed on the fire, one by one, and stirred with a stick.

While she did this, she nursed a sick baby but also found time and hands to give some *chuskoo* to an old man from the neighbouring village who had come in and sat down by the fire.[8] "*Sman?*" he asked hopefully, gesturing to his mouth. I sometimes felt it was a reflex action whenever a stranger saw me and usually treated it as such, with a shake of the head (unless something further developed). When she had squeezed the water out of the wool twists, Rabia carried them up to the roof and hung them out to dry on a stack of *burtsa*—all done with a minimum of fuss.

The next step was called *balpo mal*. *Api*, Rabia, and I did that after breakfast the next day, when the children had gone to school, sitting by the dying embers. It consisted of picking up handfuls of the undyed sheared wool and teasing it between our hands to remove lumps and foreign material like stones and sticks. They were twice as fast as I, my fingers not being as pliable and dextrous. "You are helping with your *phingma*," Rabia said encouragingly, ever courteous. *Api* muttered something darkly under her breath. I still had not understood the implications of my request.

The next step in making a *phingma* is *bal rdab*, beating the wool. It happened a week later. I insisted on helping Halima and her friend (it was *my phingma* after all). First, they selected a sandy spot between houses at the northern edge of the village—perhaps it was sandy due to an old flood. They swept the place clean with a *phyakma*, a twig broom, before putting the pile of wool down. Then the girls started to rhythmically beat the wool armed with two long, smooth, willow switches—whack! whack! whack! Dirt and other debris flew out of it as it got fluffier.

After I had watched for awhile, I asked if I could try. It looked easy. But my weak, citified arms had a tough time beating when the sticks were placed in my hands. A crowd gathered. A woman felt my biceps pityingly. "*Shargo*, poor thing," she said, referring to my physical fitness.

---

8   It is normal for visitors to arrive unannounced. They also leave without ceremony, saying "*Gwit.*" "Going."

My shoulders and arms began to ache and I soon gave up. After watching them for a while I retreated to the house to read, leaving them to bring the fluffed-up wool home.

At this stage, work on the *phingma* suddenly came to a standstill, because three of the children fell sick with fever and chills, meals still had to be prepared, and all the burden of the extra work fell on Rabia. So the next step, known as *thalba malba* was continued eight days later by *api* and Rabia as we sat in the kitchen. I helped. The beaten wool is teased into soft thick strands called *khirtee*. "Come up to the *handok*," Rabia said when we had finished, carrying the fluffed wool loosely wrapped in a sheet under her arm. We climbed up the *kaska*, ladder, onto the roof and went out of the gate to the back. "Now we will make your *phingma*." Rabia spread the sheet on the ground by the channel behind their house, under the mulberry tree. Her husband Hamid joined us, now his help was required.

Rabia and Hamid spread the clean wool evenly on the sheet to form a slightly smaller rectangle. Rabia handed twists of dyed wool to me. "Make whatever pattern you want," she said. "You do it first. I don't know how," I replied. Following her example, I placed swirls at the four corners, while Rabia cleared a circle in the centre which she filled in with the rest of the coloured wool. When the pattern had been laid, Hamid poured tumblers full of water on the entire surface. "Now *baji*, press it down like this," Rabia instructed, so we went on all fours, pressing and patting the wet wool down evenly with our hands.

They soaked it thoroughly, then Hamid and Rabia carefully rolled the sheet with the soaked wool on the inside, around a smooth pole, stripped of bark and placed along one end. Finally Hamid wrapped lots of string around it tightly and stood it upright against the tree, to allow the water to drain out. "We will leave it here for the day," he said. We went down to the *balti*.

That evening Hamid took the rolled-up wool to the men's pool where, he told me, he and a companion trod on the wrapped bundle back and forth in the hot water. Eventually, the wool begins to mat and separate from the sheet. This stage can only be done by men in their *chhu*. It needs their weight.

When it was brought back home and peeled from the sheet and the pole, Rabia folded it, tied into a tight little packet, and left it out overnight on the roof to dry on *burtsa*. Two days later, Rabia opened the packet and spread it out. She trimmed the edges, announcing, *"Yeri phingma tayyar yut."* It was ready, nice, but decidedly amateurish, rather uneven in texture for one thing, being thin in some places and lumpy in others. Some of the coloured twists had slipped, giving it a lop-sided look. This was probably due to my input. I decided there is more to traditional crafts than meets the eye.

What I did not realize until much later because of my hosts' innate courtesy, is that June is not the month for rug-making. In order to fulfill my desire to make and to have a *phingma*, a lot of temporal sacrifices had been made in what is for them the busy growing season. Their activities are carefully planned following an age-old pattern of seasonal, routine tasks.

All work in spring, summer, and early autumn is geared towards providing them with the material resources necessary for daily living, plus a surplus, not only for the long, winter months but also for weddings, for barter, and for emergencies like medicines, when they may need to sell their produce for cash. Crafts are made in late autumn and winter, when outdoor work is impossible. While she had obligingly worked on my *phingma*, Rabia was actually preoccupied with farm work. Since we, in the West have learned to live out of harmony with the seasons and the boundaries they set, my unthinking request had been *bewaqt!*—untimely![9] I still had much to learn.

Seasonal Rhythms

As the calendar progresses through the seasons, there is a change in activities. The spaces people occupy change as well. The traditional old-style houses in Baltistan generally (but not always) have three levels: the main floor, the cellar below it called *katza,* and the flat mud roof above, the *handok.*[10] These constitute three different living spaces for the seasons. In the late autumn in mid-November, the family moves down into the *katza,* where they are warm below ground for the duration of winter, since

---

9   For example, in the northern industrialized countries, we can eat fresh strawberries in December.

10   Some newer houses built in the last four decades, or those belonging to "newcomers," *methip,* have only two levels. Instead of the cellar they have a snug setup on their main floor for winter living—smaller rooms or no windows, a bigger iron stove, lower ceiling. But having a well-established *katza* is like a status symbol— for example, in Rabia's *katza* there are beautifully carved dark walnut-wood cupboards and a raised cot. There is also a *ghobus,* the walnut pillar going through the ceiling to the next level where a carved ram's head supports the roof. These days, even the agha's house does not have a *katza* or *ghobus.*

the house has been dug into the hillside to afford protection. Snow can reportedly be a metre deep.

The family stays in the cellar until the third week of March, then moves up to the middle level as snow melts and cultivation and work for the new season begins. The final move is up to the *handok* in the third week of June, after the livestock has gone up to the highest pastures, where they remain for the rest of summer and early autumn. I have lived with the family in the two upper spaces. This story is about life on the roof.

The preparations for moving upstairs to the *handok* started in the middle of June. One morning when she went up for kindling, Rabia looked around the untidy littered floor of the rooftop room called a *salleh*, which had been abandoned last fall. The wooden lattice door hung broken on its hinges, old clothing was flung in a corner, and the dirt floor was littered with last year's debris: apple cores, apricot shells, dried mulberries, kindling, torn paper, and goat droppings. As well there were torn plastic bags, one broken plastic slipper, a cracked tea cup, a rusty can, and an empty container of flea powder.[11] Rabia picked up the rubbish and set to with a bucket of water and a twig broom, a *phyakpa*, first sprinkling water on the dirt floor to keep the dust down, then sweeping with long, firm strokes.

These preparations meant that the family was moving up into their summer living quarters, where they would remain until cold drove them back down. "Halima and Mahjabeen will make a new *thap*," Rabia said. "Mahjabeen *la mahir yut*, is an expert." Halima and her young married friend sat down beside the broken fireplace that snow and winds had crumbled. With a metal bowl of fresh clay mixed with straw, they fashioned the new one, moulding, smoothing, and patting with their hands. The friend was indeed a craftswoman in this work, as she chipped and hammered at rocks to fit in the *thap*, embedding them smoothly into the soft, wet earth. As a finishing touch, she added attractive embellishments to the facade of the fireplace with clay twirls—a half-moon and some flowers growing on a vine.

---

11 These appear to be fairly new additions to garbage in the village. Hence, the means for disposal are unsuitable and even dangerous. Setting fire to litter always worked previously, but plastic bags and insecticide containers that cannot be reused (and there is very little that people's ingenuity cannot find a use for) are another matter. I have seen black toxic-smelling smoke issuing from a small pile of garbage on fire, near a small child.

When it was finished, the fireplace set in the wall was deep enough for two pots to be placed one behind the other. They also mended the chimney wall behind it from the outside. "Now we must test it," Rabia said, bringing a packet of matches and some crumpled paper. But when she lit a fire in the still-damp hearth, smoke billowed back into the room. This meant that the chimney was blocked higher up with fallen mud from the winter. "We will have to wait for *atta* to fix it," Rabia said, referring to the father who was up in the pasture.

So it was not until several days had passed that the family was able to move upstairs. Then, Rabia laid several overlapping *chharas* on the freshly swept floor and proceeded to carry up their bedrolls, pillows with coloured flowers embroidered on the covers (which had become rather greasy with use), pots and pans, tin bowls, matches, salt, tea, and all the other things they would need. She arranged the kitchen items in the brand new pine shelves her husband had made for her last autumn. The *tsungma* and *chadung*, paddle and tea churn, were placed in a corner and china cups were carefully arranged on an upturned tea chest. A solid wooden log was rolled in by the fireplace to make a seat.

"I'm too old to go up and down—just leave me here—I'll be all right," the old mother-in-law mumbled from her bed downstairs, while all this activity and excitement was going on. No one paid any attention to her. "Farida, are you going to sleep upstairs?" she asked when we were alone. I shrugged. "Perhaps once or twice." Her family knew that, when the time came to make up their beds the first night, she would allow herself to be persuaded to go up. Sure enough, when I carried my sleeping bag upstairs to sleep on a rug placed outside the room for me (at my request) *api* was triumphantly there, sitting up on her bedding, right in the middle.

When the move was complete, Rabia arranged her bright and airy kitchen. Flour, spices, sugar, dried milk powder, and other dry goods were arranged in a big wooden box that could be padlocked. Soon, our first meal of the season was being prepared with much to-ing and fro-ing downstairs to bring up forgotten items. There was a picnic-like atmosphere about eating and sleeping in the same space. This was going to mean much less work for Rabia. The younger children tumbled and jumped on the bedding that was piled up in a corner, enjoying the change from the cramped dark room downstairs. They had no memory of last summer.

The first time I had slept with the family *handok la* was with my daughter. After supper, Tara and I carried our sleeping bags up the ladder and lay down at the edge of the row of bodies in the *salleh*. We felt like sardines in a can. Tara was afraid she would not be able to sleep because of the snoring (we had heard granny snoring through the wall in the room below) but I looked forward to the experience.

The order of bedding down for the night reflected family hierarchy by gender and age. The father slept on a slightly raised pallet in one corner. In the opposite corner the eldest son slept with the grandmother, also on a slightly raised mattress. At right angles and between them, all the little children were arranged, mother and eldest daughter at the outer edge (next to us). There was a lot of coughing in the night. Often, the baby would wake up, cry, be nursed, and get hushed back to sleep by Rabia who slept with him between her and her eldest daughter. At some time in the night, the husband summoned Rabia to his bed and I understood why the baby slept between her and the oldest daughter.

The air was fresh and cool on my face, but I could feel fleas crawling about my body and was I bitten all night. Early in the morning, the sun awoke me to find Rabia already by the fire making *chapatis* and *meethi chai* for the first breakfast at about 6:00 am. It had been an interesting experience, but after that first time, I always placed my sleeping bag on the open portion of the roof outside the lattice wall, under the pretext of wanting to see the stars (which was true).

By sleeping upstairs with the family, I was able to understand their early morning rituals and family life more intimately than when sleeping in a room alone. There was no lying abed, except for the two smallest children. By 6:00 am everyone else was going about their morning chores. The parents had been up since dawn and bathed in the *chhu*, where the father also said his first prayer of the day. After the first breakfast, Hamid went off up the mountain to his herd at the lower, intermediate pasture and returned at sunset. In a cloth bag he had tied up two or three *khurrbas*, some tea leaves, and sugar to share with the shepherds as he shared their curds and boiled barley porridge for *bara zan*.

The older brother and sisters took care of the animals penned up in the cellar before getting ready for school: they tied the milk cow up in a grassy meadow near the house and fed the baby goats and young calf. The girls went up the hillside to collect brushwood for kindling. *Api* wandered off to feed the ducks and chickens with dry left-over bread and let them out of a tiny room downstairs for the day, to peck and graze around the house. These tasks done, everyone gathered around the fireplace for their second breakfast two hours later. This meal of *khurrbas* and *paillu chai* was more substantial and would last them until *bara zan*.

In the absence of her husband, Rabia expertly churned the *chai*, pouring it frothing back into the pot on the fire, and ladled it out for everyone. We sat around the cloth with a pile of *khurrbas* on a tray. "*Gno,*" Rabia said as she passed the *mungurrs* around to her daughter. *Api* was given hers first as a mark of respect, on a small salver with two fat loaves on it. Then I was served mine in a china bowl, also on a tray, and then the rest of the family was given tea. The children, hungry after their morning work, ate rapidly, breaking the bread into tea. Through all this activity, Rabia held or nursed the baby.

The second youngest child woke up, crying. Rubbing her eyes sleepily, she stumbled up to Rabia who hugged her. "*Sung! Lapko truss, odong truss,*" Rabia sent her to wash in the channel. She came back wiping her damp face on her little *dakhun.* "*Salaam,*" she said to *api* and her mother. "*Bismillah,*" her mother handed her a bowl of tea. The little girl took it with both hands, saying, "*Barkat.*" When the older children had eaten, they slung their home-made school bags on their shoulders and left with their friends who had gathered at the doorway. A day in a Balti household had begun.

A staple of the local diet, *paillu chai* is to the Baltis what tea is to the British. It defines them. The region was directly ruled by Tibet until the eighth century and the religion of Baltistan was Buddhist into the late thirteenth century. Tibetan influence is still evident and *paillu chai* maintains that ancient connection with Tibet and Ladakh.

It appears to be the same beverage that G.T. Vigne drank in his travels in the Karakoram mountains in the early nineteenth century. His detailed description of their *chai*-making method applies even after more than a century:

> Tibeti cha, or tea as made in Tibet is a very different concoction from ... (ordinary tea) for which the following is the recipe for a party of five or six people: A teacupful of the finest green tea is put into three pints of water, and upon this is strewed a large spoonful of soda, and all three are boiled together. About a half kilo of fresh butter or ghi ... and a pinch of salt, are then placed at the bottom of the milling churn, and part of the boiling contents are poured out and milled like chocolate; a little cream or milk is then added to what has remained in the saucepan, and on this the milled tea is poured and boiled again, and part of it again transferred to the churn, and so on til (*sic*) it is all

properly milled ... much depends on the quality of the tea, and the manner of making it.[12]

Like Vigne, my daughter and I learned to distinguish between well-made and indifferently made tea, and to find it "quite palatable." In fact, we soon learned which household made good tea and tried to drop in there at strategic times. *Paillu chai* does not taste like tea at all. It is stronger, with a hunger-satisfying richness, and of course it is salty. It is one of the foods (for it's more food than drink, due to the addition of butter) that men take a hand in preparing. Churning it in a cylindrical cedar churn, a *chadung* with a *stungma,* wooden paddle, attached with leather straps, is a male task, although women will do it if the man is absent.

It is one of those ancient customs that reflects a gendered division of labour. To churn is considered prestigious work (unlike weeding) perhaps because it concerns a traditional staple of their diet. I was never invited to try my hand at it, although that may be because I am an outsider (or *kumzor*, weak—it is strenuous work). *Paillu chai* is always made with *dzongo* or *ban* milk, never milk powder. One may, however, use *stu* as a tasty substitute for *dzongo* or cow's milk, or ground *lamgan* seeds, which also produce a milky residue.

---

12   G.T. Vigne, *Travels in Kashmir, Ladakh, Iskardo*, 265.

Chapter 5   THE OTHER WORLD

Exodus!

As the snow melts on the mountain slopes, people drive their livestock up and away from fields where the first shoots of barley, beans, and alfalfa are beginning to appear. At first, the animals are led daily to meadows close by but still at a distance from the village. Young boys take charge of the herds of two or three families. In the next stage animals are taken up for longer, to intermediate pastures, where some owners stay with them, taking turns for the night. In the final stage, the livestock stays in the highest pastures for the season.

One June evening I was sitting by the fire in my usual place in Rabia's kitchen, propped up against the wall, writing in my diary. The youngest children were playing with a broom and piece of wood that they swept around the earthen floor. It was dusk and Rabia was peeling onions for our meal of *sonma spacchus*, stewed spinach. The month of June is a lean time of the year—it's just before anything begins to ripen in the kitchen garden and winter food supplies are scanty. Wild spinach, which grows on the edges of fields and channels, is the first green vegetable of the season and is eaten every day.[1] Suddenly we heard shouting and clapping from above.

Quickly, we put down what we were doing and scrambled up the ladder to the roof. Many children, including the neighbours' and Rabia's

---

1   At the end of winter, there is a real hunger for greens. My daughter and I experienced this craving ourselves. In an effort not to cheat but to live the way the villagers do, I brought no vitamins—not a wise decision, because we did not have the benefit of dried fruit in the cellar. We arrived in late May and soon had very itchy palms. Remembering stories about sailors with scurvy, we followed the example of locals by eating unripe apricots and mulberries, as well as plucking young alfalfa shoots as we walked through the fields.

own, were excitedly jumping up and down and pointing to the mountain slopes behind and above the house. I looked up and saw a giant bonfire and dimly heard the answering shouts. At first I thought it was a forest fire, but the children explained that the *blukmis* had arrived with the livestock at the lower high pasture called Skinsar and this was their way of celebrating.

The shepherds had gathered all the dead brushwood they could find and lit the fire to signal joyfully to the village that they had made it to the first stage. It is a landmark event in the calendar. They will stay for a week or so in this lower pasture, and then go up with the animals to the highest areas.

This is the final stage when all the animals go up to the highest pastures for the entire growing season. They are accompanied by *blukmi* who are in charge of the village livestock and paid in kind for their work—*ghee, bal, ral*, perhaps a kid or two—at the end of the season. The move to high pastures occurs yearly in the traditional cycle of activities in mountain villages. The timing coincides roughly with the summer solstice or Midsummer's Day. Since the locals follow the lunar calendar, the actual day can fall anywhere in the third week of June.

Now I understood why, the day before, Halima had been baking a mound of *kultchas*. Notebook in hand, I had followed her as she worked. First we went down into the *katza*. In the small room, with its thick stone walls and low wooden beams, the air was heavy with the smell of urine, dust, and straw. I sneezed and covered my mouth with my *chaddar*, while she raked together wood chips and straw on the floor mixed with dry goat dung and carried it outside their house to a clearing, where she lit a fire. While it burned, she went into the kitchen to make dough.

She measured out three wooden scoopfuls of flour with a carved wooden cup called a *kacchu*—each scoop is equivalent to about 300 grams. Then she cracked eggs, added milk and sugar, and mixed them together in a tin bowl. She balanced a frying pan on the fire with a lump of *dzongo mar* in it. While it was melting she sieved flour into a *thalo,* then poured the melted butter and egg mixture into it, adding cold water and a pinch of soda. Her strong young hands kneaded and punched the mix into a smooth dough. When it was done to her satisfaction, she divided it into little balls and expertly shaped them into bell-shaped cakes between the palms of her hands.

Halima carried the platter out to the fire, which by now had burned down to bright embers. She put three stones in the fire to support the cast-iron griddle that lay nearby and arranged the cakes on it in two concentric circles. She covered them with an inverted metal pot, then laid burning straw and brushwood over that to create an oven effect. A lot of smoke enveloped the young cook who wiped her eyes on the end of her *dakhun*. If the fire is kept smouldering, Halima told me, the cakes will be done in half an hour. Her three-year-old brother squatted patiently by her side, to be sure of getting the first one. *Kultchas* have a light crunchy texture, are nutritious, and keep well, so they are good for travellers and shepherds. They also have a distinctly smoked-goat aroma.

I felt I had to go up to a high pasture to see it for myself, but it would mean finding someone who was free at this busy time to go with me. After asking around, I found a young girl who had recently been married to someone who worked in Karachi but came up to visit the family home. Zarina and her husband agreed to take me up for a night. A few days later I was up at dawn as arranged, warmly dressed with my small rucksack packed with toothbrush, pen, diary, and camera. Zarina is a small, sturdy girl, dark and sunburned from her work in the fields. Her husband is short and wiry, more citified than his two older brothers. They own land, large herds, two houses, two shops, and—an advantage from my point of view—Zarina and Mahdi have no children yet.

We climbed for two hours on a well-worn track, crossing violent, muddy streams. As we went higher, the scenery became more rugged, rocky, and wild. The hardest part was fording the streams, which in places were wide, and my companions had to place large boulders in the icy, rushing water and hold me steady as I balanced on the wobbly stones. After climbing steadily we finally arrived at our destination, a level expanse of grass. By now we were approaching 3,000 metres so, out of breath, I sat down on the nearest sun-warmed rock and looked around.

A narrow stream trickled around my feet. To the west was a snow avalanche that had come down after heavy snowfalls last year. Mahdi pointed out the land that was lost to it. The avalanche engulfed the willow trees at the base of the gully, which were only now starting to stand up again. But the shepherds' low stone huts visible at a distance, with their turf roofs were left intact.

"You sit here and rest," Zarina said. "We will go further up and tell the shepherds they have *mehman* tonight." As I sat, little birds, red with brown-black wings, flitted and hopped around me fearlessly, looking for insects in the grass. A solitary *dzongo* wandered past on the path that comes down the mountain. I am not used to seeing animals roughly five times my size come close, but there was no need for alarm. The female went and stood in her thatched shelter, patiently waiting to be milked. Zarina and Mahdi returned, Mahdi looking for pheasant with a small rifle in hand. Just after he passed, a pair of pheasants came pecking up right in front of me, but he did not see them.

As the sun travelled lower in the sky, I began to feel hungry. My friends had eaten a hearty breakfast before leaving, as busy farmers do who often must make do with one meal in the morning and one at night. But I had been too excited by my trip to eat. Now I took a small omelet folded into a *khurrba* from my rucksack that Rabia had made for me. It tasted delicious, washed down with spring water from my water bottle.[2] The long walk and fresh air combined to make me sleepy. I lay back on the soft, cushiony grass and closed my eyes, enjoying the silence and the gurgling water.

The shepherds returned before dusk, leading the rest of their herd. For awhile they were busy, penning and milking the animals, feeding them a mixture of buttermilk and roasted barley flour. The air was filled with sounds of deep lowing, snorting, and the coaxing *Ush*! *Ush*! of the shepherds. At last, with their chores finished, we were invited into the shepherd's dark hut where we had to stoop to enter. It smelled of dung, tobacco smoke, and butter underlaid by the smell of human sweat. Aside from the low door, the only other opening was a small window without a pane. Dust and soot clung in floury clumps to cobwebs on the stone walls. A small oil lamp burned in a niche in the wall, a small fire in the *thap*. "Come and sit by the fire," a shepherd said genially, spreading a *chhara* on the ground. My companions sat down on either side of me. It was not long before I started itching and scratching my legs furtively, as I knew I would—*kisik!* fleas!

The shepherds were in a jovial mood, enjoying a change from the monotony of their lives. They were dressed alike in heavy woollen shirts with heavy ropes made of *dzo* hair tied around their waists and thick plastic boots on bare feet. On their heads, each wore a traditional woollen cap. "How do you like this? Isn't it better than your city? Here you have clean air and as much milk and butter as you want!" Then, as I expected, his friend said, "I get headaches all the time. Give me some aspirin, sister." I wasn't surprised that a shepherd would have headaches, considering the hours spent out in the bright sun. The shepherd tucked the handful of tablets into an inner pocket as he poured me tea cooked with fresh *dzongo*

---

2   Mountain streams may carry *dzo*, goat, and sheep dung. Sheep dung contains liver flukes (which does not seem to affect the locals. Or perhaps it does?).

milk. The milk is like cow's milk in taste, but richer and creamier. The sweet, hot tea went very well with the *kultchas* Zarina had brought.

For themselves they boiled a big pot of *zan*, stoking the fire with the abundant firewood. "We're hungry for real food, *baji*, *blukmi* work is hard," one said with a laugh. "It is not for gentlefolk like you."[3] His face shone red in the firelight. *Zan* is made of roasted barley flour boiled in water. When it was ready they melted butter in a small pan. Scooping up the thick porridge and moulding it into cone-shapes with their fingers, they dipped the morsels in *mar* before stuffing the large package into their mouths—very nourishing and satisfying, I was told.

A shepherd's day begins at dawn, so after supper the men began their preparations to bed down, burying the embers in ashes to keep hot all night, and rinsing plates with water ladled out from the bucket. At my request, they spread a *chhara* on the ground outside the hut for me. While this was as a precaution against fleas, it was also my wish to sleep out in the meadow, edged by dark mountains. Zarina and Mahdi generously agreed to stay with me, although being superstitious Baltis, they prefer to be securely inside four walls with door and window shut against the Outside at night.

We laid out our bedding in the lee of a huge boulder, and within minutes a heavy snoring told me my companions were asleep. I should have been too, after the long climb, but the sky was bright with stars when we lay down. I found I could not shut my eyes but kept fishing my glasses out of my shoe to look at the incredibly brilliant sky. There were no electric lights to dim the stars. Then, as I was falling asleep, the moon sailed over a peak exactly like a silver boat. I was wide awake in an instant and sat bolt upright with my glasses on again. Finally, I fell asleep as the sky lightened. I have a hazy memory of a hunter going by in the stillness of dawn, rifle in hand.

We were up at 6:00 am and had tea with the shepherds. By the dim daylight that was filtering in, I could now make out smoke-blackened walls, wooden implements hanging from the rafters, piles of brushwood by the fireplace, and scrubbed utensils behind the cook's raised seat—a bucket for water, large wooden ladles, and big brass and stone pots. There was a rough wooden box from which the shepherd took out essentials like tea leaves, sugar, and matches for our simple meal of stale *khurrba* dipped in sweet tea. The men had already done their chores of watering and feeding the animals, milking, and churning the butter.

---

3   He said *sahiblog*, a colonial word to refer to the British.

Now they prepared to take the animals up the slopes for the day. Zarina, Mahdi, and I were going to go up to the next pasture too. The shepherds had gone higher still by the time we arrived at the settlement, but there were ten cows and a *dzo* left behind for the day since they had not calved and were not in milk. It was very peaceful with only the sound of running water and birds.

The young couple went off to forage for herbs, something they always do when they come up here. An hour later, they returned with armfuls of fragrant wild thyme, *tumphloo,* and Zarina had picked bunches of a green, leafy plant like spinach which she called *janjere.* "We eat it like a vegetable." They searched unsuccessfully for *khol* or wild rhubarb, but it was too late in the season to find it. "How do you eat it?" I asked. "We just suck the juicy stalks. It's sour, but it's good for the blood."

Mahdi had a bundle of birchbark. "We use this for many things at home," he said, as he tied it up with long grasses. It works like wrapping paper. "We wrap *ghee* in it and bury it underground in a cool cellar. We leave it there until it's needed, maybe for a wedding." Strong-tasting, aged butter is considered a delicacy in *paillu chai* and *zan.* "*Chuskoo* is also carried down to the village in bark. There are many uses for it in the pastures."

Each village has its own high pastures, generally above an altitude of 3,000 metres. Chutrun's pastures lying above and west of the village are, in order of altitude, Goshilo, Skinsar, and Matinturro, which is nearly 4,000 metres high. All the adult animals go—*lu, rawak, ban, dzo,* and *hyuk.* Hamesil's pastures, a little to the east are Bolla, Boltorro, and Siltorro.

The *brangsa* is the site of many activities related to livestock herding. The way of doing things has been handed down over the generations without changing and without being affected by the outside world.[4] *Bans* and *dzongos* are milked into wooden vessels called *dzua,* carved out of cedar. The shepherds carve other things—spoons and utensils for their homes—and spin goat and *dzo* hair after shearing. They churn the milk into butter, curds, and cheese. They shear the animals for their wool and

---

4 See "*Montaillou— The Promised Land of Error,*" by La Durie.

hair. Each *brangsa* belongs to an individual family and may be used by kin from the same village only. Grazing rights are jealously guarded.[5]

The high pastures are more than grazing grounds. They are sources of many materials necessary for life below. While *ghee* is the main product of the high pastures, other resources are valuable too, such as *ral* and *bal*, wool and hair which are woven into patterned blankets and rugs respectively, in soft earth colours, warm clothes for men and women, and strong rope and twine. Then there are herbs and flowers for culinary and medicinal uses. One such flower is a small violet known as *mindoqskar*, sweet-scented, rare, and highly valued for its healing properties for stomach ailments.

Firewood is plentiful from broken or dying trees that are carried and rolled down the ravines by men who come up just for that purpose each autumn. Hardwood trees like cedar, oak, birch, and plane yield wood for babies' cradles, storage boxes, utensils, and house construction. These trees grow only in the high mountains. Added to this bounty is wild game such as *markhor* and *phurrgun*, which for many cashless households is the only way they can eat meat.[6]

Finally, the pastures' recreational and spiritual aspects must not be forgotten. The villagers appreciate the beauty, open spaces, and freedom of the pastures. Every year before the frantic rush of work for the growing season begins, young women go up with their husbands and brothers, for a *sortie* into the serenity of the mountains. "I used to go with Hamid when Halima was a baby," Rabia told me with a sigh, "Then when the other children came it was too difficult, *azab yut.*"

Schools (boys and girls separately) have an annual outing, *sehrla* in midsummer. Teachers and students gather in Hamid's low high pasture for a picnic and then, bidding farewell to envious younger sisters, brothers, and mothers, climb higher and higher until they are out of sight. The mothers, who have prepared the food in big *degs*, slowly gather up all the stuff left behind: the *chainaks* and spoons and debris of feasting—chicken bones, pieces of *khurrba*, torn paper, and their reluctant small children.

---

5 For example, a feud between the two neighbouring villages of Chutrun and Hamesil thirty years ago resulted in these rights being drawn up on paper. The files are kept in the government offices of Shigar. They are dusty from lack of use by illiterate villagers, but they symbolize official authority and the villagers have knowledge of their existence.

6 Another way is by slaughtering sickly animals or the unwanted progeny of *dzongos*. The young of hybrids do not yield enough milk, are not good draught animals, and consume too much grass to be economical.

The villagers hold the high pastures in awe because they believe *strinjao'n, dre,* witches, ogres and fairies, *peris,* live in the high mountains. Stories about these mythical beings are told and retold in song during the long winter nights and days. These folktales date from pre-Buddhist times and while Muslims say their power has been dimmed by the coming of Islam, people do not disbelieve in the stories. For these reasons, the high pastures are valued and there is an attitude of caring and concern for them.

This will change and is already changing, as more and more young men are being drawn to the towns and cities of the plains for monetary employment. The traditional method of managing the commons communally is supported by strong tribal sanctions. But as Michael Dove and Abdul Latif Rao have argued, "when the traditional institutions for common property management are removed, the people abandon a balanced use of their natural resources and begin to over-exploit and indeed destroy them."[7]

When fewer young men are available to go up to pastures with their herds, their absence is reflected in diminishing herd size, less organic manure for cultivation, and fewer animal products (chiefly butter, hair, and wool), all of which results in a loss of well-being and prosperity, since this is a dual economy of herding and cultivation.

There is a postscript to this story. Twenty years later, on my most recent visit to the village, I took part in a charming ceremony called *ot kallat,* making fire. I was staying in my friend Rabia's house as usual. In the morning, while she showed me the *drumba,* her young daughter who was "cook of the house," plucked bunches of *oosoo* and *gniarma,* green coriander and chilies.

Later that evening, preparations for the meal seemed more elaborate than usual. Hamid went down into the cellar and came back with two *thalos,* one of heavy, dark flour and one of fine white flour. Amina kneaded the first into a soft dough and baked it into loaves similar to *khurrba.* Then she made buckwheat pancakes out of the white flour, pouring the mixture onto the *to,* the griddle. In a tin bowl she melted *ghee* and set it by the fire to keep warm. She doled drinking water from the bucket with a ladle,

---

7   Dove and Rao, "Common Resource Management in the Junglat," 3. Michael Dove, in his study of Baluchi herdsmen, argues that the breakdown of sanctions occurs during the transition from a traditional to a money-based economy. This is what has been happening in Baltistan since the 1970s. One example is that instead of only using dead and rotten trees for firewood, healthy trees are being chopped down.

mixed that with ground onions, the green chilies, and green coriander she had picked that morning, then added salt, stirred, and tasted. Dinner was ready.

We were not going to have our usual meal of *spacchus, bles,* or *khurrba.* I had learned to keep quiet and watch until things began to make sense. Rabia, who had been helping Amina with the cooking, came and sat down beside me. "Samina, *mez khyonse,*" she instructed the youngest daughter, who obediently dragged a low table over and the family seated themselves around it. The platter of dark, soft *khurrbas* was placed in the centre with the bowl of melted ghee. Rabia passed small china bowls of *gniarma chhu* to each one and they started eating, breaking pieces of bread from the platter, dipping the morsels into *ghee.*

Rabia broke a piece, dipped it, and passed it to me. "*Bismillah! Zos, baji!* We are having a special meal to welcome Rahim back from the *bluk.*" So that's what it was: a celebration, because their son had come down safe and sound, after a season up in the pastures. "They are dangerous places. He is alone, there are wolves, snow leopards—he could fall from a high place...*Gna la ishin fiqr yut,* I worry a lot."She was also thinking about the supernatural beings that inhabit high places.[8] Her voice trailed off as she looked fondly at the son who had replaced his father as the shepherd. "He has a very good heart, *sningpo liachmo yut,*" she continued, "There is no *chalaki,* cunning, in him whatsoever."

The *khurrba* was sweet and moist inside like *halva.* It is called *stapkhurr,* made of *tro* and *nas* combined. The grains are soaked in water for a week until they sprout and then are ground into flour. The buckwheat pancakes called *kissar* were also dipped in *ghee,* accompanied by sips of the fiery soup of *gniarmi chhu.* It was a hearty shepherd's meal.

When dinner was finished, a child was sent to the storeroom to bring a sheet of thick paper. Hamid ripped it into strips and fashioned four cones. The parents each took one, dipped it into the flames, and held the burning cones on Rahim's shouders. "*Mubarik!*" they all shouted. Then they held two on his head. "*Mubarik!*" rang out again and this time I joined in. You can make a lot of noise with six children in the family. Rahim sat quietly and smiled the smile of one unused to the company of people. I understood that they were mimicking the bonfire *blukmi* make when they reached the first high pasture and they shouted *Mubarik!* for his safe return. The circle was complete and another season had begun.

---

8 The year before, a fifteen-year-old boy had fallen off a cliff and died while searching for his goat.

After my experience of that first high pasture, I went to others in other valleys. While the focus is still on animal husbandry, one very vital difference is that in some pastures it is *women*, not men, who are in charge. But that is another story.

Veils and Dzos

I peer out of my tent in the early morning as an apple-cheeked, black-haired girl comes striding past. She looks about sixteen. She has a *chorrong*—a large conical basket— strapped on her back, the typical carrier for men and women. As we exchange greetings, her bright eyes look curiously behind me into the tent. A little baby sitting on top of the stuff in the *chorrong* bobs her head up. The baby is under an old black umbrella tied onto the basket—shelter for both mother and child from the bright sun.

We were camped south of a *brangsa*, in a meadow dotted with boulders and flowers, at an altitude of 3,000 metres. An icy stream separated us from the squat, mud dwellings of the *brangsa*. To the north, beyond the settlement, we had a view of snow-capped Masherbrum's symmetrical peak, rising 6,000 metres above sea level. Around our tent amongst the boulders there were clumps of buttercups, clover, harebells, and purple and yellow flowers belonging to the pea family.

Beside the stream and in our view of Mount Masherbrum, a graceful *oombu* tree grew, its Balti name and appearance giving it an *Alice in Wonderland* quality. The tree had small, feathery leaves of a distinctive sage-green colour, with waving fronds of pale pink flowers. The flowers scented the air with a raspberry-jam-like fragrance in the evening. Later, I saw this tree or bush in many other places and valleys in Baltistan, sometimes growing in or beside icy streams, sometimes in rocky, sandy soil. But for me it will always be associated with this meadow: Damsum, the meeting place of three valleys, at the foot of Mount Masherbrum.[9] As I watched, small birds, grey and red with black hoods, flitted about in the willow and juniper.

After setting up camp, we went to visit the *brangsa*. It felt as if we were kidnapped! A group of young girls descended on us and literally dragged my daughter and me up to their settlement, hanging onto our

---

9 Since then I have seen it growing wild in the Camargue marshes in the south of France and as a cultivated plant in southern Ontario (Canada). It belongs to the tamarisk family. In temperate climates the leaves are tightly curled and smaller, as are the flowers.

arms and laughing and jostling us along good naturedly. We crossed the channel stepping on stones, then walked across a grassy slope dotted here and there with large *dzo* patties until we reached the huts. They were low and square with narrow doors, clustered close together for shelter from the strong winds.

It is not often that a strange woman and young girl set up camp near these people's houses, wearing their kind of clothes, and trying to speak their language! Social interaction is dear to them so they were eager to talk to us. As one woman remarked, "If we do not meet well with our neighbours, what is the point of living at all?" News of our arrival had travelled fast through our porters who were all local men.

The brangsa comes alive as the sun sinks behind the mountains, *gnima duet*. Women begin to come back from Hushe, with *chorrongs* full of *hrstua*, blankets, *khurrbas*, and babies, and the animals start coming back from pasture. The women (about a dozen in all) came out of their huts or from the sheds and small barns where they were feeding their animals, to greet us, wiping their hands on their *dakhuns* to shake our hands. Many girls sat on the low rooftops, calling to their *dzongos*, to milk them, *onga tsirrba*. "*Thar thar yut? Liachmo yut?*" Their sun-burnt faces broke into smiles and they nudged each other excitedly, when we replied in Balti, "Yes, we're fine! How are you?" "*Tsaring mohtstung! Balti seremoso!* May you have long life!" they replied

"*Shukhs*," Sakina beckoned, inviting us into her hut. She was the red-cheeked girl we had seen earlier. She sat by her *khling*, the churn, her baby daughter lying beside her on a pallet on the ground. We went in and sat down opposite her after squeezing through the low doorway. The swish! swish! sound of churning and the smell of wood fires filled the air as other young women did the same in their huts. Some were calling to their *dzongos* to come and be milked, making soft *aosh! aosh!* sounds.[10]

Another girl poured curds into the pot of milk in front of Sakina, who was pulling the strap around the churn paddle, the *khlia khling*, rhythmically, to make butter, *mar phyungma*. After five or ten minutes, she stopped. Dipping a wooden ladle into the pot, Sakina took down china cups from a niche in the wall beside her and poured us each a bowlful of *ooshoo*, buttermilk, on which creamy drops of butter were beginning to form, (*oosho* means the same as *chuskoo*. There are some differences in the

---

10   Female *dzos*; may also be pronounced *dzomo*. The suffix *-mo* or *-po* makes the noun feminine or masculine when the word ends in a consonant, e.g., *rgyalmo* and *rgyalpo* (queen and king).

language, between west and east Baltistan). She lit a small fire of sticks beside and just under the big pot to gently warm the milk. The butter thickened as the churning continued, separating from whey.

Once my eyes had become adjusted to the smoky gloom, I looked around the tiny room. We were sitting on a quilted mattress edged with a wooden frame that was piled with a few pillows and folded blankets. Higher up, opposite the door was a small hole or window in the thick mud wall, with bars running across it. Under it were ledges and shelves simply made by wedging slabs of wood between the stones on which cups, platters, and cooking tools were lined up.

Among the empty tin cans, which serve a variety of purposes, was the only way of lighting the tiny room— a *shkumbu, or ot* —a woollen wick inserted into a clay pot filled with apricot oil. If people can afford it, they use tin cans filled with kerosene oil, called *bamba*. The presence of the *shkumbu* meant that either my hosts could not afford kerosene, or that in the high pastures, it is more convenient to use apricot oil from their village.

The wooden churn was attached to a pole in the corner, with leather straps ending in thongs around the churning paddle. Sakina sat on a low stool behind the churn. She continued churning steadily, occasionally turning to smile at us and ask questions. "What is your name? Is the *bongo* married? Do you have sons? Where do you come from?" She paused to wipe her face with her *dakhun* and touched her baby's forehead. "*Guin sett*, headache," she said, pointing out the door at the sun. Her *salwar* was pulled up above the knees and she pointed to show me a bruise on her knee from that morning, when she stumbled and fell, carrying the heavy basket. She salaamed and smiled her thanks when I offered to put ointment on it. It was no big deal though—bruises were all part of a day's work.

When the yellow dots of *mar, ghee*, appeared on the surface of the churning cream, the fire was pushed away with iron tongs. Sakina put a dollop of the fresh, sweet butter on my palm. "*Mar*." Delicious! Her sister brought cold water in a tin canister and poured it into the *deg* while Sakina continued churning. Then Sakina stopped and scooped the butter into another container, disconnected the churn, and cleaned the paddle by drawing the side of her hand down each blade, wiping it on the edge of the *deg*. The remainder of the liquid is *darba*, whey, which gets divided into different pots for their *dzos*.

We went out and chatted to other women as they did their chores. As shepherds these women appeared to be better off than many women in the villages below. Even the children had strong plastic shoes instead of cracked and broken or mismatching ones. People looked culturally and physically more Tibetan in the higher Hushe valley. Their features were Mongolian and their hair was braided into tiny plaits, Tibetan-style. They wore little black woollen caps underneath their *dakhuns,* which all married women in Balti villages wear, but here some just wore the *natting,* so their heads were covered, but not as completely as in the lower villages; some dark hair was carelessly allowed to show. After all, I reflected, this is an all-female world.[11]

A few women wore more "modern" clothing like store-bought *salwar kamiz* and made-in-China machine-knit cardigans. Most wore woollen blankets pinned cape-style lengthwise around their throats against the cold of the mountains.[12] Perhaps their wealth comes from large herds which provide them with butter, hair, and wool—all valuable commodities that can be exchanged for cash in the bazaar.

As their *dzos* came down from pasture, the women filled the *degs* with boiled spinach, salt and whey for them. Some sprinkled ground pea flour on top to add nourishment. A well-fed *dzongo* would reward them with more milk and butter. Surrounded by these unusual animals jostling the women shepherds, Tara was emboldened to feed several *dzos* with salt from her hand, as she balanced on a low rooftop to get level with them. Then one, more persistent than the others, climbed onto the roof after her. "Mum, help!" she cried and was saved by a woman who laughingly shooed it away with a stick. They are tame only in the sense that they know their owners.

I learned that Damsum is an "in-between" settlement where the women do not stay all day. They leave at dawn after milking and having sent the herds higher up to graze in the care of one or two girls, and then go down to the village to do their household and farming chores. They all have family—old parents, husbands, and older children to tend. As the sun begins to dip below the mountains, the *brangsa* comes alive again as the women return, carrying baskets of straw, blankets, *khurrba,* babies, and other supplies to begin the evening chores here.

"In five days we will go up to the higher pasture, where there is more grass," Sakina told me. "Come with us." Being higher up, the Hombruk

---

11　Another reason is that the religion of the Hushe valley is *Nurbakhsh*—a more liberal version of Shi'ite Islam prevalent in western Baltistan.

12　In the daytime when the sun is shining, the temperature may rise to 25 degrees centigrade, but when the sun goes down, it can plunge to 5 degrees, even in July.

pasture is ready later. We had been planning to follow Sakina, her family, and the other shepherds there, but now that they were our friends, it would be even more enjoyable. The shepherds make the move in two or three stages. First some take their goats, *dzos,* and *dzongos* which are not in milk to pastures at the foot of Mount Masherbrum, where they leave them in the care of a shepherd all summer. In the next stage a few take some of their belongings to the other higher *brangsa* and finally they all move there with the rest of their stuff.

Some choose to go to a higher pasture still called Alling, further to the west where they remain all summer. Those who go to Hombruk stay a month and then return to Damsum, when the grass has had time to regenerate. All these intricate arrangements appear to be routines that have been followed for decades according to an unwritten code. The women go where links have already been established by clansmen from their village, giving them rights to that pasture.

A few days later when we went to visit our friends as usual at sunset, we found everyone was hustling and bustling about and an air of excitement hung over the settlement. "Our men have come up from the village to help us move," I was told. Through the open doorways, we could see the men packing up bedding, filling bags with *khurrba* and other food supplies, rolling up rugs, tying them with *dzo*-hair rope, and filling sacks with pots and pans. Two men were minding babies, while the women called to *dzongos* to drink potfuls of *darba* before milking.

They left at 4:00 am. I heard the quiet rustle of feet, the lowing of cattle, and murmur of voices so I peeked out of the tent. The stars were still visible in a deep blue sky and people's dark shapes were outlined against it. I could make out a baby *dzo* slung across the neck of a man. The group left early so that they could milk the animals at their destination at sunrise.

The rains came the next day and delayed our departure. We sat disconsolately in our tent looking out at the green, sodden meadow, the dripping willow trees, and glistening wet rocks. Mashabrum was wrapped in heavy mist. Not even a bird could be seen. Our meals were served to us in our tent by a soggy porter, who would dash from the cooktent where the other porters sat huddled in blankets by the kerosene stove.

The cold came up through the groundsheet and our tent did not seem snug any more. We played gin rummy interminably, read the same books over again, and wrote in our diaries wearing woollen gloves. Rain in the high mountains in a tent is miserable. On the fifth day at daybreak the clouds began to lift. In a fine drizzle we gladly packed up to leave for Hombruk.

Setting off early, we headed south. The clouds blew away and the sun came out to warm us and dry our damp clothes as we walked at a steady pace, turning west just before the fields of Hushe village. At the base of the mountain we began the climb up a steep slope to the pastures on a narrow, rocky path made by countless feet. As we climbed, we could see down below us a number of rectangular terraced fields of peas and barley. Bundles of *kha-khating,* a flowering legume drying on rooftops and on large boulders for winter fodder, added a splash of purple to the greens and golds of the fields. Our winding path was edged with mullein plants in flower, buttercups, daisies, and small purple asters growing among the rocks. We passed by thorny bushes covered in pale pink, single-petalled roses, *gulab.* "We call them *marrgulab,* because of the smell," I was told. *Marr* means "dead" in Urdu and Farsi, referring to the bitter and surprisingly unpleasant smell of these Himalayan roses. Their Balti name is *sia.* (The Siachen glacier is known as the Rose Glacier).

We walked for three hours (a climb the women normally do in one hour) to reach the grassy ledge of the *brangsa.* Halfway up, at an altitude of about 3,500 metres, I began to feel dizzy and breathless, my lips dry and sweat falling from my eyebrows into my eyes. I was ready to turn back and would have, but for Fatima, a lively young girl who had befriended us in Damsum. She ran fleet-footedly down from the *brangsa* to escort us. Now she persuaded me to continue, pulling me along encouragingly.

When we reached the small plateau we were given a hearty (and female) welcome. Women came with gifts while we rested on the grassy verge. *Branjus,* a cake made of roasted barley flour that is kneaded with butter to form peaks in a flower pattern, was set before us. "This is special—we made it for you—you must eat it," we were told. A woman reached into her pocket for a small, sharp knife and cut thin slices of the rich, dense cake. Another woman brought a small pan of *dzongo* milk for Tara. Some brought posies of flowers, dahlias, wild roses, and marigolds, which they tucked into our hair or put in the pockets of our jackets.

They surrounded us, laughing, talking, and nudging each other in an effort to come closer to us. After this refreshing interlude we proceeded upwards, passing their settlement on our right. Our campsite was set up on the brow of a hill overlooking the *brangsa,* not close enough to infringe on their space, but close enough to be able to wave to each other.

This *brangsa* suffers from a shortage of wood. The landslide that came down a few years ago buried and destroyed much of the pasture and woodland. Now the girls have to take their animals across a log bridge to the other side of the narrow valley and climb higher still for wood, which they carry back in *chorrongs*. My immediate reaction was, "What a hard life," but I was wrong in my initial perception, as usual.

This is what I observed on my first morning. Sitting on a rock as I wrote in my diary, three women were visible walking bent down under heavy loads of wood that were tied with ropes to their backs. Another was driving some *dzos,* which had decided to return early, back to pasture. A couple of young men (the only men I had seen here apart from our porters) were rebuilding a roof. They had laid down branches across the cavity, then sod to cover it. Now several girls were tamping the sod down with their feet. As I watched, another girl set off up the valley with a *chorrong* on her back, presumably to search for firewood. This seems to be the main activity after the morning's rush of feeding, milking, and churning.

However, I soon discovered that it is not all work for the women. There is plenty of time for recreation, rest, and even play. In the evening, shrieks of laughter came from the direction of a big boulder on the edge of the settlement. A number of teen-aged girls, married and unmarried (including Tara), were enjoying a sliding game. The boulder was about twenty metres high and had a polished surface on one side that slanted down to the ground (worn smooth by many such games). After the game, Aminu and Fatima accompanied Tara back to the campsite, with flowers in their hair and their arms around each other. Tara had little braids in her hair in front, like the other girls. She was wearing a wool cap under her *dakhun,* a gift from one of the girls. In return, she had given them some of her bracelets.

Earlier in the afternoon, as I wandered around the laneways between the little huts, I came across old *apis* dozing in the sun while babies played happily around them in the mud; a young woman sat on a rock outside her door unravelling an old sweater. She was going to knit a new one out of the precious shop-bought wool. In a clearing, their *dakhuns* cast aside, a group of women were checking each other's heads for lice. It was not so much an inspection as a confirmation, a nit hunt in which nits were expertly crushed between two thumbnails. I obligingly sat down to have a woman go through my hair. My scalp had been uncommonly itchy lately! From where I sat I could see a group of girls washing clothes in the stream. There was time for fun too, as they splashed each other, standing ankle-deep in the icy water.

Our porters did not cause as much of a disruption in the lives of the women as we did. They belong to the same, or neighbouring villages and may even be kin. Fatima is engaged to be married to Rozy Ali, one of our porters. Indeed, it was at our guide's suggestion that we had come here. His family's livestock is being cared for by some of the shepherds and they address him respectfully as *kaka*, older brother. In return for caring for two *dzongos*, the shepherds will get between fifteen and twenty kilos of *mar* (*mar* sells for 150 rupees per kilo). The animals are sent up in June and will come back in September. Our guide's parents are old and he needs the help, because his young wife has to look after them, two small sons, and the fields! Many families from Haldi, his village, do the same. At mealtimes we were often sent a bowl of creamy yogourt from one of his *dzongos*, or a glass of fresh *dzongo onga*, straight from udder to table for Tara—a welcome change from powdered milk.

In the evenings, we made bonfires and sat watching the flames in the dark and silence. Storytelling is a popular pastime in the *brangsa* in the long evenings after chores are done and some evenings our guide would join us and tell us stories. Two tales were about bears, which live in the forests and mountains around here (as do foxes, wolves, and snow leopards, although hunting for skins has depleted their numbers in the last century. Killing snow leopards is legally banned).

First Story

"High above the village of Hushe, at over 4,000 metres, there was a cave where a bear—a *drenma*—was known to live. One day, a woman who had gone up to gather wood disappeared. Her family waited and waited for her to come home but she never appeared. A few years later, the family dog wandered into the cave. The woman was there. She took off her bead necklace and tied the *phallu* on him as a signal to her relatives that she was alive. So the village found out. She was living with the *drenma* and had children by him. The villagers banded together and came and got her by force. They drowned the children. The woman wanted to go back to the bear so they locked her up. The bear tried to get her back by clawing the roof and they killed him."

Second Story

"Two bears lived in a cave at Alling glacier. A man who was travelling in the mountains was overtaken by nightfall and took shelter in a cave where bears were sleeping. It was winter. In the night, an avalanche buried the opening of the cave, so the man was trapped inside. He thought the bears were dead and he ate one of them to stay alive. When spring came, the other bear woke up. He thought the sleeping man was a bear because he was dressed in a bearskin. The bear woke the man and clawed a way out through the snow. When the man got out and went back to his village, no one would believe that he had stayed alive all winter with a *drenma*. But the bearskin was proof."

•••

We had many invitations from the women to go into their huts, warm ourselves by the fire, or join them on walks across the bridge and up slopes as they foraged for wood. They told us the names of herbs and flowers and showed us how to make rings by plaiting the strands of long grasses. Or we were invited to watch them as they milked and fed the *dzos* in cramped, damp byres that smelled of hay, urine, and the sweet breath of cud-chewing animals.

As our friendship grew we were able to talk more freely and to share in the fun. We camped in that meadow edged by dark forests for a week. In the mornings when we awoke we would put our heads out of the tent and breathe in the clean air that smelled faintly of wood fires, dung, and baking bread. Sometimes in the night as we snuggled in our bags, we would hear the deep rumble of a yak and imagine that it had sensed a wolf.

Having spent some time in several men's pastures (in Nagir Province and the Basha valley in Baltistan), I feel that I can compare life in high pastures where mainly men go, and those worked by women. The difference lies in the variety and complexity of activities in the women's pastures. The women bring their small children with them, but also travel between village and *brangsa*, sometimes daily, to perform their household duties. They carry fuel wood and manure down to the village where they tend their fields, gather fruit and nuts, and do household-related chores before coming back up.

When they are in the pastures, the women grow vegetables like potatoes and turnips and rear chickens for eggs, which are a welcome addition to their diet and are also taken down to their families in the village. Having small children in the pastures, while adding to the work, also adds to the quality of life. Old grandmothers come up to help. Cooking and laundering are accompanied by childcare, knitting, and mending clothes. In order to carry out all these activities the women have set up complex arrangements to cope with time/space constraints.

In the men's pastures, on the other hand, the activities are less varied, since livestock herding, shearing, and processing the animal products are the main occupations, to which woodcarving may be added. Because men are not traditionally involved in child-rearing, raising chickens, growing vegetables, weeding crops, or nurturing and feeding the family in the village, the differences mainly reflect the multiplicity of tasks that are women's traditional responsibilities. However, while the work that women do is important, it is not necessarily more prestigious than men's work.

Women's pastures will suffer from neglect for the same reason that men's pastures are deteriorating. As men leave for downcountry jobs for cash, fewer women will be able to go up to the pastures. Men are needed for the heavier work of clearing land, terracing, digging channels, house building, and repairing houses. Not only in the high pastures, their presence is also important in the villages while the women are with the herds. This shows the interdependence and complementarity of men and women in traditional living, where each gender has its specific tasks.

Chapter 6   DISASTERS AND OTHER TRAGEDIES

Floods!

One day, when we were sitting in Loqpar having tea (something we did from time to time), I asked Rabia to tell me about the time of floods. She said, "I remember a flood. Four years ago, I came to Loqpar with Halima and Rafia, carrying baby Zahra on my back. We were working in the fields when we heard a distant roaring sound. As it got louder, I realized it was coming from the *nallah*. We ran closer to look and saw big water coming down the mountain, carrying boulders that bounced together and made a *khattarnak*, a fearful noise, *rdoom, rdoom*!

"I ran back with the girls to the path we had come on, but we were too late. The path was gone and the valley was filling up with water. Rafia was only three. You can imagine, all the children were crying. We had to climb the hill, and try to find a path over it. We were very frightened by the noise and the water. It took me a long time with the children because I had to carry both the girls over the mountain. When we reached the village, everyone was shouting *shwa*, flood! But *Allah shukur*, our house was safe (being higher)."

It is difficult to imagine that the little stream running peacefully in the deep gorge can swell to overflow its steep banks. The Basha River does not affect the village as much as this tributary called Phucchap does. It flows east to join the Basha between this and the neighbouring village. It is a glacier-fed stream and any snow melting on a sunny day, combined with heavy summer rains, swells it.

That is the scientific explanation, but in folklore there are others that explain disasters in terms of supernatural beings and impending evil. This story was told to me by a college student: "Once upon a time, a man happened to look up the (Phucchap) *nallah* and saw an ugly old woman with a bald head, digging a deep hole with her hands in the mud, beneath a huge boulder. He noticed that her feet were backwards, a sure sign that she was a *strinjao'n*—a witch. So he knew that something bad was going to happen. He looked past her and saw that water was roaring down the *nallah*. He ran and warned the villagers and told them what he had seen." "So the witch made the flood happen?" I asked. The boy shrugged. "I don't know, but that's what they say."

In normal times, the stream is used for irrigation and to supply drinking water to the two villages. Channels are led off into the fields north and south of it when the stream emerges from the gorge, so it brings both life and destruction—irrigation and drinking water *and* floods. In 1996 the *nallah* spread violently over its banks, carrying boulders as big as houses to smash into houses and spread detritus over the fields. The stream carried heavy rocks and boulders but not much soil, and deposited the rocks as it retreated, rather than debris.[1] The fear of that summer's flood brings back memories of floods. "Now when it rains a lot, we are always afraid. We can't sleep at night."

In the yearly cycle of activities, the possibility of floods varies with geographical location and aspect throughout the valleys. "After the *blo* has been cut (mid-October) if the weather is warm, there is the danger of *kakkar*, ice blocks, suddenly melting. If the weather is cooler, there will be no flood." It was Ahmad speaking, the *chowkidar*. We were sitting in his small, smoke-blackened kitchen, having a cup of very strong, very sweet tea. If I want to hear his stories, that is where I go.

I sit on the string bed and Ahmad squats on the floor by a small kerosene stove that gives off evil fumes and black smoke, but the door is open to the vegetable garden. He puts a plate of cream-filled biscuits on the tray. His youngest son, aged three, sits down at my feet and helps himself. Ahmad has access to store-bought commodities not only because he is a *chowkidar* with a monthly salary from the Pakistani government but also because he and his brother own two small shops.

"It was a summer night in '96, of heavy rains," he continued. "Someone shouted a warning *shwa*! The river started rising—there was a roar and then booming rocks as it spread into the village, between our house and Nurbano's. The water went 'round the *masjid*, stopping higher up. All my family was in our upper house (my brother's) but I stayed at home to keep

---

1   A debris flow is a moving mass of mud, rocks, and water. It may or may not be accompanied by a flood.

an eye on things. In the morning I couldn't open the door of my house because of water, but no damage was done. The water was standing a third of a metre deep around it. Our fields were ruined and ten to twelve threshing floors were spoiled—the threshing poles were washed away. Two or three houses were filled with mud."

He shifted his position to sit more comfortably and lit a cigarette. "The animals were still up in the high pastures except for the *dzos*. We opened the doors of the *phingkhan* to release them so they could run away and save themselves. The water carried huge rocks and frightened people took refuge in the *masjid* and around *Aghaping*.[2] Well, after the flood, many families rebuilt their houses elsewhere, leaving the animals in the old pens." In answer to my question he replied, "Yes, that means more work for those who have to feed and water the animals. But it has to be done."[3]

Later, when I got back home, I asked my hostess about Nurbano's experience. "Nurbano talked so much at the time of the flood, that she will not talk about it now. The memory upsets her. She gets angry if you mention it." At my request, we went to visit Nurbano in her new house. She received us graciously. We drank tea and ate sweet, greasy bread and I was introduced to her new daughter-in-law and grandchildren. But when I brought up the subject of the flood, she did not reply.[4] When we were leaving, she came out with us and gestured silently towards derelict fields that were clogged with rocks and mud. They were hers.

When we returned home, Rabia told me more. "I remember everything that happened that night. We were all sleeping *handok la*. We woke up to the sound of the big boulders in Phuchhap *nallah*. Maht Ali and his family [their immediate neighbours to the north, adjacent to the stream] ran to our house, to join us on our *handok*. The water did not reach them, but

2   This is rather like saying, "*chez* Agha."

3   Even though they rebuilt within the bounds of the village, it still meant a longer walk to the old animal pens and it is generally women and children who do this work. Since there is no land to spare in the village, they would have used one of their own fields for house building. While this means less land for food, rebuilding in the same village also means that their friends and neighbours remain the same, so feelings of disorientation are not as acute after the flood as would otherwise be the case.

4   Through reading disaster literature, I learned that the experience is traumatic and to speak of it brings back memories too painful to bear. People who have endured destructive and life-threatening disasters are near the edge of a breakdown even after the event. See Cuellar, "Unravelling Silence: Violence, Memory and the Limits of Anthropology's Craft," 160.

Phuchhap was too close, so they wanted to get away. It was a pitch-black night and raining hard.

"We could hear a lot of wailing and shouts in the dark, when people woke up and realized that the water was coming right into their houses, breaking down walls. We couldn't see them but we could hear them. People ran with children and belongings to the *masjid* for shelter. That is where Nurbano and her family also went with their belongings—whatever they could grab. Their bedding and clothing were carried away by the *shwa* and ruined. *Shwa khyonse, pshik say phanse*—the flood carried the things and flung them. They found them later, a box here, a rug there. Two rooms were completely destroyed, full of mud and rocks. Their boxes of grain were carried down into the *katza* through a hole in the floor. The flood lasted for an hour, but the families stayed in the *masjid* for a week."

Later, when the villagers helped the stricken families recover from their losses, the retrieval of muddy and sodden boxes, bedding, and other possessions which had been carried away by the flood waters was one of the main tasks. Drying, cleaning, assessing the damage, and rebuilding soon followed. One house had sunk below ground level, its *katza* completely removed and everything in it gone. The family had to carve steps down to the main floor which now sat where the cellar had been. There was no time immediately to grieve the tragedy that they had suffered.

The valleys in Baltistan lie mainly in the rain shadow of the summer monsoon, receiving some rain in late July and in August. That is also the time of late spring thaw, when the glaciers feeding the tributaries and streams high above the villages start to melt. This combination can be deadly, leading to intense flooding of settlements.

There were other floods along other rivers.[5] A month later when I visited friends in Ghursay on the Hushe River, further east, there were signs of flood damage. A neighbour, who had come to fix the kerosene stove where I was staying, said a lot of land had been cut off from the mainland by the floodwaters in the last flood, creating islands. These islands were now deserted.

Some of the people along the river, whose houses had been stranded by the water, were without fire because they had been caught unprepared and did not even have matches or enough food. Those on dry land then

---

5   An example is the flood in Gol, on the Indus in August 1993. The water came down a ravine, bringing mud flows that devastated fields, trees, and houses. Godwin Austin recorded a flood there in 1855. See Mason, "Indus Floods and Shyok Glaciers."

organized a rescue. They bound together logs to make a raft, using a strong rope made with *dzo* hair. This is the old-fashioned way of crossing rivers. In earlier times the rafts were traditionally floated on inflated goat skins, called *zaq*. But in the modern version the raft was floated on rubber tires. In this way, people and livestock were taken off the drowning islands. Later, instead of rebuilding in the village, some families chose to move to Khapalu further west. They were afraid because the water was still deep around Ghursay.

I went for a walk with my hostess's young son and daughter, accompanied as usual by a crowd of children—little girls piggybacking babies, boys pushing, laughing, and hitting each other in play and leaping up to knock down apricots. As we walked slowly, there was plenty of time to look around. When we reached the river, I saw the drowned land, dying trees, and abandoned *rinthaks* clogged with sand. The fields were covered with sand and stones too, through which spindly and stunted barley poked through. Here and there were the abandoned *bunds*—gabions or net-enclosed baskets of rocks—evidence of valiant but futile human efforts to restrain the river.

The Hushe, a mountain river over a kilometre wide in some places and fast-flowing, is mightier than any man-made bulwark can contain. Over the years it has been changing course, leaving the west shore at Saling to come closer to Ghursay, gouging into fields and widening its bed. The village is almost at the confluence with the Shyok River. The children pointed out a place on the other side. "Look, *baji*, my father says there used to be a wooden *zamba* between Ghursay and Saling when he was young. He could walk across it." It is hard to imagine a bridge there, almost a kilometre width across the river.

Later that night at supper, I asked my host about changes to the population. "People are leaving their houses to build higher up, closer to the road," he said. "I myself have left the house where I grew up, and have moved twice." First, his father's home was destroyed. Then he built one higher up which he has also abandoned, but he keeps the land for his kitchen garden and the rooms for his goats.

The house where he lives now is by the road and *masjid*. It is a whitewashed house of squared timber and stone. The doors are squared and the window panes have glass in them and even wire mesh to keep insects out in the summer. Some of the rooms in his new house have ceilings of wooden beams and painted plywood, but there is still turf on the roof for insulation.

His house is different from most other homes in the village and from his own earlier ones of logs and rounded stones set in mud, the turf roof packed between logs. Most people cook by kerosene stoves and occasionally use a fireplace. But the poorest are forced to use wood alone and they have a difficult time finding fuel.[6]

My host explained that, as far as he knows, the floods started in 1958. Since then three-quarters of the village have been lost to the river. Some people have migrated to other villages like Tallis and Haldi to the north. "In 1965, I would estimate there were four hundred homes here. Now there are not more than three hundred. When you think of the increase in population, that is really a lot fewer homes." While there has been no loss of life directly due to floods, a dangerous situation has arisen, with the proximity of a fast-flowing, turbulent river to the shore. In May 2000, opposite Saling two years after the last flood, three Ghursay schoolboys were drowned in the Hushe River.

On one of the first hot days in May after a long winter, the boys decided to play hookey from school to go swimming. The two older boys, aged ten and eleven, swam across to a sandbank in the seemingly calm river. The youngest boy of six had been told to stay on the river bank and wait by the shore but he jumped in to follow them. Finding the river too deep to wade in, and unable to swim, he started shouting for help, so the older boys dove in to rescue him. They were all pulled down by a strong, hidden current in the deep water. They had been playing on y-shaped concrete banions built to impede the flow of the river, which also had the effect of creating swirling undercurrents.

News of the accident reached their parents three hours later that afternoon. When the boys did not come home at the usual time, the families started enquiring. Some women working in their fields had noticed the children playing by the river, so they were able to point out the place where they had last been seen. By the time rescue efforts were made, it was too late to find the boys alive. Their bodies were hooked out of the river where they had been trapped in mud. This was a sobering event and tragically taught the villagers of the danger posed by the river. The roadside shrine draped with fluttering cloth flags and fresh marigolds as a memorial was still there when I visited it two years later.

In recent years, people have noticed that the water has become increasingly turgid. They understand the connection between this and

---

6   There is a lack of firewood in the village due to the loss of forests along the river from floods.

increasing deforestation in the *nallahs* which join the main river. For this reason, they have dug wells for their drinking water. Previously there was no need for wells because water came directly from channels led off the river, which intersect the village.

Now the water is stored and "rested" in the wells called *chhudong*, which have been dug at various intervals around the village. They are fed by groundwater and covered with heavy wooden lids. The pits have an inlet and an outlet that can be closed or opened to the underground channel. The water is usually exchanged in the morning when it is cleanest and is still during the day, *gnima phonget,* allowing the silt to drop down to the bottom.[7] I often accompanied my hostess's sister-in-law to the well nearest their house on her daily trips to fill their round clay pot. A tin canister anchored by rope to a boulder was dropped down into the well to bring up the water. This is heavy work for women, on top of all their other chores. My friend, even though she was a strong woman, balanced the heavy water pot on her shoulder with difficulty, her face red, her breathing laboured.

Late one night at the end of July, as we were having supper we had an unexpected visitor. The day had been long and busy for the two sisters-in-law, with the usual round of work. This was a home where the husbands, both schoolteachers in different villages, were absent during the school term. When the last chore had been done, the little black cow milked, cow and goat penned for the night, preparations for a meal were started: peeling, chopping, and washing herbs and vegetables—potatoes, mint, thyme, fenugreek, and green onions—freshly dug from the *drumba*. The little children were asleep, soothed by bowls of milk and stale bread.

Suddenly the door, which was locked at night, flew open and a man came in. Without pausing in what she was doing, our hostess welcomed him saying, "*Shukhs, shukhs,*" as she ladled a plateful of food just as if he had been an expected guest. The family knew him well because villagers from the same valley are not strangers to one another. A platter of *khurrba* was moved closer to him, a jug of drinking water, and a metal cup. He had come from the village further up the valley in order to catch a bus to Khapalu early the next morning. He told us he was going there for help from the police.

Khapalu, the main town of the region, has a hospital, several medical clinics, the police station, and the post office. Men go to Khapalu for medicines, to buy goods not found in the small village shops, for news,

---

7   Kreutzmann, Schmidt, and Benz, eds. *The Shigar Microcosm: Socio-economic Investigations in a Karakoram Oasis Northern Areas of Pakistan,* 67.

or to meet with officials in connection with work. The house where I was staying was beside the road where the bus to Khapalu stopped. It was not unusual for travellers to rest, have a bowl of tea, or even spend the night while they waited for the bus.

As he gratefully took a drink of water, Sodeh passed his hand over his face, murmuring *Bismillah*. His hands trembled and he was obviously overcome with emotion as he told us of a terrible flood that had come the night before north of his village. A glacial meltwater torrent had overrun its banks after a hot, sunny day. "It has completely destroyed Kandeh," he said, a village on the west bank of the Hushe River. "The *hotul* is gone, about sixty *chulas*, the school, trees, and fields, all drowned." One man had reportedly died. A rock as big as a house, in the Hushe River just past the bridge on the road that leads to the Siachen glacier, had moved slightly.

The villagers had some warning of the flood by the familiar booming sound of boulders earlier in the day. Realizing from past experience that a flood was imminent, they had already evacuated their homes. Men, women, and children rushed out of their houses as the rumbling sounds came closer. Rocks mixed with mud made the rushing river "look like *dalyia*, oatmeal porridge," a sight that made the people quake.

Sodeh had been with an expedition that was just packing up to leave in a tributary valley. When he heard the sound of the river, he had hurried down to his own village, fearful for his wife and children. Since women have to irrigate and work in far-flung fields, they are vulnerable to flash floods and mud flows. They are hampered further by small children who accompany them. His own fields were scattered over a considerable distance and away from his house.

When we heard his story, we remembered that our drinking water, which was always muddy, had turned a pasty yellow the day before with silt. "*Dirrin ishin thalba yut*, it is very muddy today," my friend had said. "We cannot use the water straightaway." This must have been due to the extra silt brought down by the flood. The next morning, a walk by the river revealed the huge boulder at the edge of the river north of Ghursay, as uprooted *chuli* trees floated by. The police were commandeering all jeeps and wagons on the road to carry relief supplies of food, drinking water, and blankets to the flooded village.

A few days later, as I took the road to Skardu by jeep, approaching Kiris on the Shyok River, we saw a sad reminder of the Kandeh flood. Men, women, and children were fishing in the shallow water at the edge for a strange kind of booty—timber and other items from flooded homes, which had floated down all the way from Kandeh. They were piling what they could salvage at the side of the road. As we drove slowly past we identified a threshing pole, bits of *shuck* walls, squared wooden beams from a house, and a hollowed-out log used as a flume for a watermill. Since the river at this point was slower and shallower, women were hitching up their *salwars* to wade in and retrieve smaller objects floating by, scooping them up in round, woven *kharriks*. Although their homes had been carried away, people had manged to salvage a few valued possesions.

Tragedies like this seem not to daunt the victims. Floods are not an uncommon occurrence here and people are used to the the government's neglect or inability to help them. They rely on themselves, using small-scale methods to cope, which involve their own labour and intensive land-use and management techniques based on past experience. These risk-aversion strategies work better for them than the cash-intensive, technological interventions so dear to government, aid, and military agencies, who cynically, according to some analysts, see each disaster as an opportunity.[8] The following year I heard that people were rebuilding their village painstakingly, house by house. There was a new and bigger school, cleared land, terraced fields, and newly dug irrigation channels. The new village is higher up on the slope, further from the tributary stream.

Ghorrocho—Grim Secrets

A gloomy place with a brooding air, Ghorrocho means Big Heap of Stones, (-cho being an honorific suffix which implies importance or respect). These rocks, marshy sandbanks, and stunted bushes are found where the Basha meets the Braldu River. Local legends abound to explain the place's origin and unusual features. They almost always carry a moral warning. One story goes that a holy man or *pir* hurled the stones that form Ghorrocho. He had come disguised as a hungry traveller to a prosperous settlement where the villagers refused to give him food when he asked, except for one old woman who gave him her last crust of bread. In return for this charitable act, he told her to get to safety before he destroyed the town because of its inhabitants' hardness of heart.[9] The scientific explanation

---

8   K. Hewitt, *Interpretations of Calamity from the Viewpoint of Human Ecology*"; Shaw, "Nature, Culture and Disasters: Floods and Gender in Bangladesh."
9   This story also illustrates the importance of hospitality towards travellers.

is that the place was formed by a huge landslide which came down the mountain slope from the western side in geological times.[10]

The place is steeped in stories. At the southern end of the island, in a stony, sandy, and rock-strewn plain, a smooth, rectangular boulder stands out above the others, famous locally for its size, colour, and shape. It is called *Tillanka* after Kesar's horse. Kesar was a legendary king who married the daughter of a *peri*[11] who had the power to turn humans into any shape and form. There is a saying that anyone who climbs that slippery brown stone will die (however, there were fairly recent stone cairns on the top).

This is also a place of grim mystery—a murder was committed here a few years ago. In this part of the world, such a crime is unusual—no one had a personal recollection of a murder. Some shepherds found the body of a middle-aged woman in the bushes as they were grazing their cattle one summer. The body turned out to be that of the female dispenser from the village of Seisco, further north. Clues led the police to her husband, who later confessed to the murder. He was younger than she and there was rumour that he had fallen in love with another woman. The story went that he had married his wife for her property, which she failed to inherit. It was of interest to me because eight years previously I had met the dispenser and heard her story.

That story begins with my visit to Ghorrocho in the summer of 1997. After leaving the village where I had been staying for some time in Rabia's home, I joined my husband on a trek. We drove south to Tissar and crossed the bridge. There we took our rucksacks and tents from the jeep and set off on a sandy track accompanied by two porters. Our feet sank into soft sand as we walked. After wading across small icy channels, we arrived at a place called Shukthang Brangsa at the northern edge of Ghorrocho. (The word *thang* means plain.)

Huge rocks and boulders covered the sandy ground, with stunted bushes and shrubs growing between them. In this men-only *brangsa* that belongs to Tissar, shepherds stay for two or three months in the summer with their livestock. It was here on this lonely moor that shepherds had made their sad discovery.

Caves, which appeared to be used by the shepherds, had been carved into some of the bigger rocks by weathering erosion. We put our heads

---

10   K. Hewitt, "Quartenary Moraines vs. Catastrophic Rock Avalanches in the Karakoram Himalaya, North Pakistan."

11   The English translation of the word as fairy does not do it justice, because *peris* are powerful and fearful beings, more like goblins or sorcerers.

into one and saw the remains of a fire, raised ground for a bed, and some cooking implements in a rough niche. Suddenly, a fat, hairy caterpillar, beige with two black dots, fell from a rock onto the bare neck of one of our porters. *"Balgosse!"* he cried in alarm, as he slapped at it. Within seconds, an angry red rash appeared on his neck. Baltis are wary of caterpillars, with good reason.

Inside one of the larger caves, sheltered from the wind, the porters lit a fire and made tea. We sat outside on a rock to drink the hot tea, dipping sweet *kultchas* as we watched little birds hopping around fearlessly for crumbs. After a short rest we resumed our walk and reached the south end of the island by late afternoon, where there was another *brangsa* called Kor Kor Sokh Bu.[12] This one was owned by Hyderabad, the village on the opposite side of the river. Shepherds from the two villages take turns using the pastures, although there was some legal dispute over them.

We walked past cows grazing in the lush, damp grass and chose a spot in a clearing on raised ground for our tent, avoiding anthills dotted about in the cropped grass. Our two helpers went off to the stone shelter where the shepherds lived to prepare our evening meal of *paillu chai* (courtesy of the shepherds) and *khurrba*. We could hear the rushing sound of the Braldu River behind us as we sat on the grass outside our tent with the shepherds, sipping the tea. The men smoked.[13] Birds flew among the reeds and bushes around us. A huge brown spider, as big as the palm of my hand, appeared out of the grass crawling towards us and a shepherd scooped it up in his hand and flung it back into the bushes. "It has a hard mouth," he said casually.[14] We spent three days in Ghorrocho, exploring the sandy, rocky landscape and identifying plants.[15] We did not see another soul beside the shepherds.

Now let me move back in time to 1989 to my meeting with the woman dispenser from Seisco. While I was living in Chutrun, I was fortunate to be able to go to Seisco with an AKRSP officer from Skardu, who had stopped on his way north to meet with farmers. He heard of my wish to

---

12 *Tsokh* is the name given to a low, thorny bush. A male calf or son is called *bu*.

13 Cigarette smoking is popular with shepherds, porters, and anyone who has cash. Deaths due to lung cancer have risen in the past twenty-five years and men are smoking less now, perhaps having worked out cause and effect.

14 That is, it is poisonous.

15 One of the common plants is ephedra, which yields ephedrine, a pharmaceutical ingredient used in decongestants. The sticky sap from its bright orange berries is used by shepherds as a remedy to staunch bleeding in cuts.

see as much of the valley as possible, and kindly invited me to accompany him. "You will be interested in meeting the dispenser—she is a woman," he said, adding, "She speaks Urdu."

The dispenser became my guide for the day. She was in her thirties then, a thin, quiet woman who had been trained as a midwife. With her I walked around the village, meeting women at home or in the fields, wherever they happened to be going about their work. Since she knew them well, I also received a friendly welcome. "*Salaam*, Sodehbe, who is this with you? *Angreze?*" they would ask. "No, she is Pakistani, she came with *kaka* Nasir. She speaks Urdu."

When we returned to her home she dragged a *charpai*—a string bed on a wooden frame—outside and made tea. From where we sat we had a view of the river while she told me about herself. "How did you come to be trained as a midwife? Where were you educated?" I asked. Her quiet demeanour and sad eyes spoke of a tragic past and indeed, Sodehbe's story was a sad one.

She had been the only child of elderly parents. Before her birth, her father vowed to educate his child, girl or boy, and send him or her to Iraq on pilgrimage. True to his promise, "My father taught me to read and write Arabic and read the Qur'an at home," she said. "But, when my mother died, he married me to a man fifteen years older than me." She was twelve.[16]

After marriage she went to live in Iraq with her husband. Her father died while she was away and in her absence her uncles (his brothers) occupied his land which was hers by right. Now that she was fatherless and landless, "My husband gave me *talak*—a divorce," she concluded simply. "How long had you been married?" I asked. "Ten years. I had four children. But he kept them all, even the girl."[17] Their three older sons were sent to an Islamic school in Karachi.

Here she was, barely twenty-five at the time of her divorce, alone and poor. But because of her education she was able to apply in Skardu and get a government job "like a man." She remarried a younger man who had no property of his own. But it was more respectable to be married than single

---

16 Young girls are considered at risk of losing their honour without a mother's care.

17 Usually, under Islamic law, in a divorce a girl child lives with the mother.

in her profession, because she was still a young woman.[18] "People talk," she said. All the while she fought a legal battle to regain the land that her father had left her.

Sodehbe pointed to her land. She knew that without her land, she was not her father's daughter. She did not belong to that valley, that place. She was nothing. I had the feeling that day and night it burned into her mind. It was visible from her one-room government dispensary home, across the Basha River, three *chulas*, which sent up smoke from her uncles' houses, solidly built of stone and wood. Ironically, she herself does not have a house of her own, or even a fireplace. The government house she and her husband occupy, she told me mournfully, is cold in winter and hot in summer, because it is made of concrete with a tin roof. "We have no *chula*. Only an iron stove."

While we talked, her husband lay on another *charpai* near us, watching us under lowered eyelids. Apparently he could not speak Urdu like his literate wife. He did not speak to me at all, not even in greeting. "Do you want more children?" I asked. She shook her head. "What is the use? I have no home." Some years after I met her, she was dead and her younger husband was accused of the murder.

Her second husband had met a younger woman, which may have spurred him to commit the crime. His expectations of possessing his wife's land had faded with time as she remained powerless against her uncles. Since he himself had no land or income, he had played the role of a kept man by his wage-earning (but landless) wife. But she did not have much either. Although she was a trained midwife, her work assisting in births gave her neither status nor significant income.

The husband and wife were pawns in a newly emerging cash economy, complicated by old, patriarchal values. Greed, lust, betrayal—these are sins that are common to humans everywhere and are not unknown among Baltis, of course. Yet to act on them to commit a crime of passion is rare in these parts.

---

18 Women are allowed to remarry after divorce or widowhood if they are prepared to forfeit the money settled on them by their husbands before marriage (called *haq mehr*). They are also able to instigate divorce. Although not common, it has been known to happen. Being a divorced woman, she was already atypical. With education and travel experience, she did what other women could not—worked for money.

Rape!

This is a sad story with an unsurprising outcome. Physical violence against women is fairly uncommon in Baltistan. In my travels in over two decades, there have been no reports to me of wives who were beaten or mistreated, although there was mention of bad-tempered husbands and more often, of "*ghunny*, bad, mothers-in-law. The word *ghunny* is always accompanied by a hooked forefinger, to signify crookedness or badness. I knew of at least one case where the wife left and remarried for that reason. However, an isolated instance of a rape was recounted to me.[19] In my view it happened because of modern values clashing with traditional ones. The rapist was an outsider who was employed in a salaried government job from another village; the victim was the illiterate young wife of an absent soldier.

A young woman who had recently given birth to a son went to the local dispensary to get medicine for a rash on her face. The dispenser was a government-appointed man from another and bigger village.[20] When the woman was inside the room, he locked the door and "had his way with her."[21] The woman's husband, who was in the army and had been away for several months, was from a prominent family. When he came home and saw his wife was pregnant, he soon found out who was responsible because nothing can remain hidden for long in a face-to-face society. There was a lot of hushed finger-pointing.

Yunus,[22] the husband, immediately did two things: he did what any "honourable" man would in the circumstances—turned his pregnant wife

---

19   There have been several accounts in Pakistani newspapers of rapes of foreign, white women who are tourists or trekkers. The assaults appear to have been committed by Balti men employed as porters, or by men who have met the women alone in remote, high altitudes. The assaults fall into a category by themselves. Such encounters would have been unheard of in the days of organized trekking expeditions (see Pratt, *Travel Writing and Transculturation*) when women travellers were formally accompanied. In modern times, not only are the women vulnerable because they are alone, but the men they meet may be stalking and preying deliberately on women they see as "loose" because they are alone and unaccompanied. In all cases the women appear to have talked to the men in a foreign language (English, Italian, German) indicating that the men had been exposed to Western culture themselves, perhaps through work, television, or movies in the bazaars of Skardu and Gilgit.

20   That is, he had no loyalties towards the people of this village.

21   This is a literal translation from Balti.

22   All names in this story have been changed, to protect the privacy of the people.

out of the home without their baby son Mahmud; and he approached the dispenser for an apology and compensation.[23] The accused man laughed and said, "Prove it." Since the dispenser was also from a prestigious family, the wronged husband was powerless either to remove him from the village or to get retribution.[24]

Yunus's son by his now-absent wife was given to the care of Yunus's extended family consisting of mother, sisters-in-law, and brothers. In time, Yunus remarried and started another family, still going away on long absences in the army. According to custom, his new wife moved in with the extended family. She clearly favoured her own three children, leaving Mahmud (who was very young when his mother was raped) to be brought up by the other relatives—so essentially he was motherless. When I first met Mahmud, he was a thin, nervous-looking boy of ten, clearly lacking the self-confidence of his cousins whose house he shared.

We came to know him quite well as he visited Tara and me often, giving us small, wizened apples and walnuts out of his grimy pockets, or offering to sell us curios like carved wooden boxes. I had a suspicion that his family was unaware of the treasures he carried about, which clearly came out of his house. In later visits, as he grew up, I learned that he had dropped out of school and was trying to get a job in Skardu as a server in a hotel. His male cousins meanwhile were still at school.

At times Mahmud worked for his uncle in his small business in the village. One summer, when he was about twenty, he went off to Skardu and got himself a job as a porter. While his father and uncles disapproved, they could not stop him now that he was grown up. After that, he came home less and less, drifting from one menial job to another.

Of his two older male cousins, one was preparing to go to college in Skardu, while the other finished high school and made a good marriage to the daughter of a wealthy landowner, which enabled him to start a business. When I first met Mahmud, I asked him about his mother. "Dead," he answered for that is what he had been told, although he must have come to learn the truth as he grew up.

Five years after my first visit, when Mahmud was fifteen, my hostess told me discreetly that a certain girl I had seen around the village was the daughter of the raped first wife. The woman had gone back to her father's

23 It is customary for the offender to pay a sum of money to the victim's family in retribution.

24 He would have to have been elite, in order to afford education, medical training, and have a government job.

house in her natal village to have the baby and live out the rest of her life, not quite as an outcast, but certainly without the prospect of remarriage. As soon as her daughter reached puberty, she had been married to an older man.[25]

When I saw the girl she was obviously pregnant. Dark-skinned (the dispenser was very dark), she was dressed in drab clothes and watched me with a sullen expression as I walked past her. She looked unhappy. It was whispered that she had come back to see her father (he did not hide his paternity now). "*Shargo*, poor thing," the women said pityingly, but no one approached her. They watched her from doorways and rooftops, *dakhuns* drawn disapprovingly across their faces, whispering behind their hands. Needless to say, faced with this lack of welcome, she soon left.

The dispenser meanwhile flourished in his job. He was a loud-spoken and well-dressed man, with oiled hair, shiny shoes, and all the other marks of wealth. Besides this he had the friendship of the local prestigious men.[26] Shortly after his daughter's visit, he moved away to another job. By an unspoken agreement, Mahmud's family stayed away from the dispensary until he left. Since they were wealthy in cash terms, they could afford to travel to Skardu Hospital for their medicines, even sending their womenfolk for treatment. For example, Yunus's old mother was taken there to see a doctor for high blood pressure.

Life had not been kind to the girl born out of wedlock. Poor, married, and with child when she was barely into her teens, both she and her mother were victims of a rigid, patriarchal system that punishes the weaker side and rewards the powerful. But, her half-brother appeared to be not much better off than she. Although his plight was less obvious because he remained in his father's house, he still bore the stigma with which his unfortunate mother had been branded by also living on the margins of his social world. Although they were aware of each other's existence, the

---

25 Probably done to save her from a fate similar to her mother's—she would have been vulnerable to rape, since she was the fatherless daughter of a homeless woman.
26 Men are not dishonoured for being sexual transgressors, but women bring shame on their blood kin if they even appear to have violated the code of honour. What happens is immaterial because blame is always attached to women and not men. Husbands, not being blood kin, can distance themselves from such wives and even gain honour in the process. There are many examples in Indian and Pakistani media which attest to this. So-called honour killings happen in extreme cases when the dishonoured girl's male relatives kill her to remove their shame, sometimes with the approval of the girl's mother.

two children grew up without officially acknowledging each other. Perhaps they subconsciously resented the other.

Death of a Baby

For some days, as I sat by the tent on our roof, women who stopped by for a chat began to talk of the sad case of the baby whose mother had to go to Skardu Hospital. "*Shargo tsuntse,* poor little one," they would murmur, shaking their heads sadly. As I passed women on the footpath they would stop and ask, "Have you heard about Sheikh Tariq's baby? His mother is in hospital." I thought it was simply because the baby missed his mother.

Then my hostess disappeared for hours at a time. I had grown used to her company on the *handok* while she cleaned grain or did some other chore. In answer to my question she replied, "I was at Sheikh Tariq's house. You know his son is very sick." "Why, what's the matter with him?" I finally asked, when it was clear that things were getting worse. "*Shess met,* I don't know" was the grim-faced reply. "He won't drink milk any more. *Sirrif julab, quai,* only diarrhea and vomiting." She went on to tell me that they had tried all their remedies. "His aunt gave him coriander and *mindoqskar* teas and burned *isman* flowers. They waved the smoke around his head, and the sheikh recited verses from the Qur'an." She shook her head hopelessly. Nothing worked. They had even sent for a religious cleric from the next village to dispel malignant spirits, in case the child had been given the Evil Eye.

"But who feeds him?" I asked. "The sheikh's sister has come from her village," she replied, adding admiringly, "The sheikh bought a *dabba,* a can (of milk), from Skardu and a bottle." This was contrary to the usual custom in such cases, when he would have been given to another nursing mother to feed. By her tone my friend implied that the baby was receiving the best (because modern) care. Yet I feared that it could spell trouble.

Bottle-feeding is alien to Balti culture. How could a bottle be kept clean, let alone sterile when it fell to the ground, or was handled with dirty hands? Did they feed the baby with milk that had been left in the bottle for hours, allowing bacteria to form? What kind of water was used to dilute the formula? For centuries, the sparkling meltwater from glaciers has fed the Balti people. Yet in recent decades as garbage and pollution have increased, the situation has changed—channels that come through the village are no longer clean.

How had the aunt measured the formula when she could not read Urdu or English? It is doubtful that the sheikh was by her side all the time—feeding babies is women's work, after all. Babies under one year old rarely drink anything other than mother's milk. Even when other foods such as *khurrba* soaked in *paillu chai* (called *pappa*) have been introduced, breastfeeding continues for a few more years. Meanwhile, breast milk is considered so pure that it is even squirted into babies' eyes to cleanse them. So putting two and two together I guessed what was ailing the baby and further enquiries confirmed it: he was dying of dehydration due to sickness, undoubtedly caused by contaminated milk.

By the third day, his condition grew steadily worse. At nightfall, as the women came from visiting him (he lived next door), they wiped tears from their eyes. "He is very sick. He doesn't even cry now." We sat without speaking, thinking of the beautiful, plump baby. I had met him on the paths in his mother's arms and although we did not speak, we had smiled and nodded to each other.

At that time I was fairly new to the village and had not been to see the sick baby, nor been invited. Now it appeared it was too late. "What is happening now?" I asked. The reply shocked me. "They are bleeding him," my hostess said simply. "They have made a cut in the forefinger to let *nakpo khrak*, black blood out." At my protests she just repeated, "The bad blood has to flow. That is our way. If it reaches the tip of his finger…." She shook her head. This was a last resort, when all other remedies had failed.

Early next morning, the wailing of women's voices gave us the news: the baby had died in the night. A stream of visitors came and went from the house next door, to pay their respects to the sheikh. His wife was brought home from hospital. It was a sad day; there were no happy noises of children playing as the village mourned with the family. People went up the steps to their house to mourn.

That afternoon, as I watched from my vantage point on the roof, a weeping procession of women came into view. The body of the dead baby was carried out of the house, wrapped in a small, white cloth covered with sacking. With it were father, mother, and other relatives. I watched as the group came to a stop outside a house and the man laid the baby down on the earth. The mourners crowded around—his face was shown for the last time and then covered. "Poor things, they are so poor they have nowhere else to put the baby," I thought.[27]

A woman, presumably the mother, fell to the ground on her knees, her head resting on the body as she sobbed. The other women helped her up and, supporting her with an arm on either side, the *janaza* (funeral procession) proceeded to the gravesite. I could see in the far corner of their field where a grave had been newly dug. After he was buried, stones were laid on the grave. The women dispersed to their homes to prepare *kho*, sweet black tea and *chapatis* to take to the sheikh's house where the mourners were gathered.

Later, from my readings I learned that traditional peoples respect the earth and regard it as sacred, which is why they had laid the baby on the ground before he was buried. It was an act of consecration.[28] What I had witnessed was a ceremony in touch with what is real. It was not ostentatious. It had nothing to do with wealth (the father was a wealthy sheikh). It did not mean they did not love the baby (he was their only child).

What makes this death tragic is that it was caused by inappropriate technology and could easily have been prevented. In most Pakistani urban areas, baby formula and milk bottles are advertised on huge billboards and are readily available, even to people who are not familiar with their use. This is not to imply that the local people cannot learn the dangers of bacteria and food poisoning and take the proper steps. They are more than capable of learning, but foreign corporations, by aggressive marketing and advertising techniques, have enticed people from poor countries into believing that simply using such products will magically give them

---

27 Poverty in pre-modern societies is measured in different terms. People are not poor as long as their culture is intact and they have sufficiency. I was thinking like an urbanite.

28 Eliade, *The Sacred and the Profane*.

healthier babies (or better crops, in the case of chemical pesticide use).[29] The sheikh had sent for what he believed would be the best possible food for his son: a plastic milk bottle and a can of baby formula showing the picture of a healthy, golden-haired baby being fed from a bottle. Of course, access to cash is another prerequisite, but in the sheikh's case this was not a problem. I will always regret not having offered a possible remedy. Oral Rehydration Salts (ORS) given when he first fell ill may have averted the death (that, plus stopping bottle-feeding).

Folk medicine and indigenous remedies have traditionally been used in the mountains for centuries, based on the rich flora. The tradition of culling wild flowers, herbs, and leaves with which to make infusions to drink or pastes to treat simple maladies—stomach problems, headaches, colds, rashes, fevers, cuts, and bruises—has continued even with the introduction of modern medicine (the availability of which is still unreliable). Many skills have gone underground, leaving old men and women as the main repositories of such knowledge, but it does continue. The story of the baby's death is not so much about local medicine as it is about its failure in a modern context—its failure when the cause of the problem is not based in the local culture.

---

29   In the early 1970s, Nestle engaged in aggressive advertising and marketing techniques in the poorer countries. By giving free baby formula samples to new mothers in maternity hospitals, the corporation encouraged mothers to feed its products to their babies instead of breastfeeding. By the time mothers realized they could not afford to keep buying formula and that their babies were not thriving, it was too late: their own milk had dried up. Studies found that there was a rise in deaths of bottle-fed infants compared to those who were breastfed, which led to a worldwide boycott of Nestle products in the ensuing decades. Nestle was prosecuted, and eventually agreed to stop this practice. In 1979 it became apparent that things had not changed, so the boycott is ongoing.

Chapter 7   LAST WORDS

Perils and Joys of Doing Research

Doing research involving people presents difficulties. It is definitely not the same as studying rocks and landslides. This is not to say that humans are absent from the latter research, or that physical geography is more predictable, but it does not involve close, everyday interaction with living beings.

While what I am about to relay is about situations where I felt uncomfortable or even threatened, let me affirm that was not the case everywhere. In Chutrun where I lived for lengthy periods (with or without my daughter), I felt perfectly safe to walk wherever I wanted. I knew the family names of most households, their relationship to each other (whose daughter was married to who, their family history, recent illnesses, births and deaths), and even recognized people at a distance by their gait and clothes. It was home.

One morning, in a village that was new to me, I went for a walk with two young guides, the son and daughter of my host. We walked along narrow pathways set among the fields. The barley was already waist-high, making it impossible to put a foot anywhere but on the path. Some fields were flooded for irrigation, the water spilling over the path, so I had to balance carefully on the slippery mud. For this reason, I failed to notice an old man until he came right up to me and shook his finger in my face. "Come on, come on, take it out of your pocket, let me see it," he demanded impatiently. He was bent over with age, so that his face was a little below mine. I stopped in surprise and said "*Salaam*," as is customary. He ignored this and kept haranguing me, turning his head to smile triumphantly at a group of women and children behind him. "Where is it? Where is it, take it out of your *jholi*." Their expressions were unsmiling. The hostility was unsettling.

I was taken aback. Then it dawned on me that "it" meant a Pakistani Identity Card, which I do not possess. The children with me explained to him that I am a Pakistani, but even they wondered why I did not produce it. I do have a Pakistani passport, but had no intention of "proving" anything. So I shrugged and went past him, squishing into the muddy field to do so. As we proceeded, with a crowd of children now following us, we met up with another group of people. A woman stepped forward and asked me where I came from. To be asked to identify oneself before greeting is considered rude by Balti notions of propriety and I began to feel uneasy. Women leaned out of the upstairs window of a house, calling out "*Jasoos*" and "*Memu*."[1]

During the period of fighting between India and Pakistan over Siachin (June 1999) the Government of Pakistan has offered a bounty of 50,000 rupees for the apprehension of spies.[2] There have been incidents of spies infiltrating both sides of the border, so with my rucksack and camera, as a woman travelling alone, I realized I was suspect. However, when I recounted this incident to my host, he merely said, "They're *jahil*, they know nothing of the world. Pay no attention."

But it was not an isolated incident. A few days later, I found myself wedged in the third row of a bus belonging to the Northern Areas Transport Company (NATCO) in one of the front rows reserved for women and children. We were a tightly packed crowd, pressing knees against women with babies, cloth bundles, and plastic shopping bags full of fruit.

One young woman carrying a baby had a bright green jug with a lid and a blue plastic cup tied to it. It was obviously new for the journey, and she was very proud of it. When we stopped to pick up a passenger by a freshwater spring near the road, she requested permission from the driver to alight saying, "Brother, just wait while I fill my jug." Thereafter, it was wedged between her feet, occasionally tilting when the bus went over uneven ground (often) and spilling onto my shoes.

Babies cried, were nursed, and slept; at times their heads lolled on another passenger's lap, who never complained. Behind the women's rows, men filled the seats in the rest of the bus. There were also men and boys travelling on the roof, among the luggage. Before we left the village, the

---

1   This is a derogatory term, applied derisively to foreign woman.

2   The village I was living in is in the Hushe valley, not far from the Line of Control between India and Pakistan. It is adjacent to the Siachin Glacier where a war is being fought sporadically. Foreigners are not allowed entry east beyond this valley without a permit.

driver stopped the bus, jumped out—leaving the engine running—and diverted water from the channel alongside the road, presumably into his field. Nobody minded.

I was taking my hostess and her nine-year-old daughter to visit the medical clinic in Khapalu. As a high-born Sayyid woman, my friend could not have taken this journey on her own without the protection of a man. Such a companion, called a *propha*, meaning escort, is usually male. But her husband was away, teaching in a school in the neighbouring village and her nephew, the only other male in the house, was too young. However, I, as a woman who had "knowledge" *ilm* — I could read and write, travel alone, and hold my own in the company of men—I could be trusted to guide them in the outside or public world.

Our journey to Khapalu went without mishap. By "chance" (since everybody knows everybody or is related to them) we met one of her female relatives who had been on the bus, sitting behind us. When we alighted from the bus, they greeted each other warmly, she taking little Samina by the hand and leading us by a shortcut through the fields to the clinic.

The clinic was a small concrete building and the doctor also "happened" to be related to her. When she had given her name at the door and her purpose for coming, the doctor's assistant beckoned to us to come in, giving us precedence over all the other women and children crowded into the little waiting room. We went gladly, although I spared them a guilty glance.

The office had a bare concrete floor and little furniture. We sat down on two small chairs in front of the doctor's desk, the child in her mother's lap. The desk was covered with closely written papers in Urdu, a fountain pen, an inkwell, a glass of water, and other paraphernalia. The doctor was a thin, tired-looking man with a stoop. An orderly or assistant squatted in the corner, awaiting instructions. My friend explained the symptoms in detail, but he was more interested in questioning me. Why had I come? What was I writing about? Was there any help that the government could give poor doctors like him? Like many others, he thought that I must have official authority if I was writing a book. Finally, after offering tea, he turned to the patient.

Her daughter was diagnosed with allergies and worms.[3] The orderly took us with the prescription to another room along the corridor where medicines were dispensed. This room was a little better furnished than the doctor's office, with shelves (almost bare), a rickety glass-fronted cupboard, a table, and several chairs. The young male dispenser poured some pills and a red powder from the cupboard into squares of paper torn from an old exercise book, which he then screwed up into packets. I paid the nominal fee and we went outside.[4]

We walked up the narrow, crowded dirt road back to the bus stop in the bazaar. Our bus had not yet come, so we wandered about among the stalls, the girl's eyes round with wonder as she clutched her mother's shawl. "*Ango*, I want *sharbat*, sweet drink. Oh, can we buy some *tarbuz*, watermelon?" There were rows of brightly coloured shawls hanging on a rack, handmade baskets, aluminum pots and pans, piles of fruits and vegetables in boxes, sliced watermelon on a cart, mounds of dried dates on a mat, candy in bins, and packets of biscuits stacked up in pyramids. Bottles of red, orange, and green pop were lined up behind a dusty window pane in a shop little bigger than a box.

My friend bought packets of biscuits for the children at home and a wedge of watermelon for her daughter. I bought us each glass bottles of the vividly coloured soda which we drank there by the stall (because of the deposit) and a plastic bottle of water for the journey. When the bus arrived we were at the head of the straggly queue and boarded first. Thankfully it was not crowded this time and we spread out comfortably on the first bench (a fact I would regret later).

It was not until we set off and had gone a short distance out of Khapalu that the trouble began. The bus stopped at the police checkpoint. Beyond it lay the Restricted Area where foreigners need a special permit to enter, but our bus was going to turn off before that.

When the door opened, a policeman looked into the crowded bus jammed with people, stopped when his eyes alighted on me in the front row and said with outstretched hand, "I.D. card." I handed him my Pakistani passport. He scrutinized it carefully, then carried it in to the

---

3   Roundworms are common in the Northern Areas. Their eggs are carried in the dust, so infection is easy. At some time or other, all children suffer from them. The treatment is simple: a pink liquid drunk daily for three days expels them (until rein-fection).

4   In return for living in a home as part of their family, I often did my hosts favours, particularly those that involved cash.

police station. "Please come in and sign the foreigners' book," he said on his return a few minutes later. I refused for two reasons. I was afraid that if I left the bus and was delayed inside the bus would go without me, leaving me stranded in an unfamiliar village until the next bus came along (tomorrow?). Second, if I signed the book I would be admitting I was a foreigner, which clearly I was not.

The other passengers moved restlessly around me but no one, not even the driver, told me that I was holding up the bus. The frustrated policeman went in to the office and came out a while later. "There is nothing wrong with your passport," he said. "Everything is in order. It's just that it is a problem you have a passport and not an I.D. card." "That's not my fault," I said, reaching for my passport, which he quickly pulled back, "I live in Canada. That's not a crime, is it? Millions of Pakistanis live abroad. Give it to me. You are holding everybody up."

He was almost persuaded. Murmurs of approval at my courage (or audacity?) came from the passengers around me. My hostess, behind her tightly held *dakhun*, smiled. But the policeman was not convinced. "I must phone my superiors in Khapalu," he said firmly. "Unless there is anyone on this bus who can vouch for you?" I pointed to my hostess, the wife of a well-known and respected man in the region. She shrank back into her seat, with the *dakhun* pulled even more tightly around her face, her eyes downcast. "She is a woman," he said with an apologetic smile.

Altogether, we waited forty-five minutes. Some discussion went on but I had a sense that the crowd was friendly towards me. An elderly man unwrapped a basket of cherries, and passed them to us. The young woman with the baby (she was also taking the same bus back) handed around her cup and plastic flask with water. A small child who had been sucking on a slice of watermelon threw up into her mother's strategically held *dakhun*. Everyone around her, including me, made helpful suggestions and sympathetic noises. The driver disappeared to say his prayers on the veranda of the police station.

Finally, the policeman came out, handed me my passport sheepishly, and waved the bus on. Obviously, he had got the right answer from a telephone call to his superiors. But why was I singled out in a bus holding at least sixty-five people, since I was dressed like all the women, in baggy pants, a long shirt, a *chaddar* covering my head and shoulders? The answer, I think is that several things gave me away.

My glasses, for one. Women do not wear spectacles in these villages, simply because they cannot read—education for girls has only just started here. Only a few elderly men wear them, and sometimes that is as a status symbol. There were other, minor give-aways. My grey hair made me look old, but my unweatherbeaten face belied it. Women, even if high status, get wrinkles early, due to the sun, wind, and dust they are exposed to, along with smoke from cooking fires, to say nothing of the fact that they will have borne several children before they reach the age of thirty.

More importantly, my full set of teeth set me apart as an outsider. Women in their twenties start losing their teeth to tooth decay. A gap-toothed smile is not uncommon even among young girls since the only cure for a toothache is extraction.[5] In other words, I do not have to speak in order to be identified as a stranger.

Since I have been a frequent visitor, possibly too there are stories going around about a woman, claiming to be Pakistani, doing untypical things like travelling alone or accompanied by a young daughter, with a rucksack and camera, carrying a passport and speaking English, Urdu, *and* Balti. It is very hard to remain anonymous here, so it is likely the policeman may have heard rumours about me and been on the alert. Perhaps he also thought he would catch me out as a spy.

My research involves more than fact-finding and analysis. In order to know, I have to get through the wall of suspicion and mistrust that surrounds a strange woman living in people's midst. The people who were more inclined to be suspicious of my intentions were "citified" male Baltis, who have worked or lived in the plains. The average villager—man, woman, or child—was pleased that I appreciated their food and way of life, whereas the so-called modernized Balti would wonder why I was living at their "primitive" level without my family, and doubted that I would do it for its own sake. There had to be some other motive.

Eyeing me mistrustfully as if to imply, "What are you doing here?" some men would say, "Why are you wearing those bangles (clothes, plastic sandals)? That is what *our* women wear!" One exclaimed almost disapprovingly. "Does your husband let you come here alone? You should be at home with your children." The hostility was thinly veiled. "*Kya azadi*!

---

5   This phenomenon is increasing as shop-bought sweets, biscuits, refined flour, and sugar replace traditional foods like dried fruit, nuts, and wholegrain bread.

What freedom!" some would say mockingly, as I lit a cigarette.[6] Men would watch me closely as I sat cross-legged on the floor, dipped my bread into a tin bowl of buttery tea, ate, supped the tea, and smugly returned my empty, wiped-clean bowl with the typical thanks, "*Barkat*!" I too had been watching closely. *Yerri shezdeh!* You're welcome! comes the reply.

In spite of some awkward moments, there were few threatening or physically dangerous ones. Indeed, they were so few that I can remember each one. In one instance, I was walking north along the Hushe River with my two young guides, aged ten and eleven, when we sat down to rest on a boulder by the side of the rough road. Presently, a boy came walking by, a little older than my companions. He stopped stock still in front of me. After a few minutes I said "*Salaam*." He did not reply, shifted on his feet, and continued to stare. I slowly took out a cigarette and lit it, an act that made him open his eyes wide in disbelief. Then a smirk appeared on his face.

My friends became uneasy. "Let's go," Muhammad whispered. But I stayed where I was and asked "What's the matter? Do you want something?" The boy laughed and started running in the direction we were headed, towards the next village. "He's a bad boy from that village. He means trouble," the children said nervously. "Come on, let's go back." We got up and started walking home in the opposite direction. Presently my young companions turned to look and said in alarm, "Hurry! He's coming back with his friends." The girl pressed herself to my side. I still could not believe that we were in danger, so I walked at the same pace.

A big, surly-looking youth came up beside me. He was dressed in traditional garments, but over his *kamiz* he wore an old mountaineering jacket, and on his head was one of the fake Pakistani army caps that were so popular with young men. With what can only be called a leer he asked in English, "Vhat is your name?" I answered curtly, now hurrying my footsteps. "Vhere do you come from?" he pressed on. "What business is it of yours?" I replied, answering in Urdu, looking at him sideways with a frown to show that I was not afraid and did not like his inappropriate manner.

---

6 I am not a smoker, but in the mountains I always carried cigarettes for several reasons. Even though I had companions, they were not from *my* world; smoking took away some of my loneliness. Also, due to language difficulties, the act of smoking sometimes filled an awkward void of silence. Another reason was that *women* were delighted to be offered a cigarette by me. It was a luxury they could not afford and were never given, even if their husbands were smokers.

We were still a long way from the first houses, on a lonely path in the fields. It was late afternoon, when there is a lull in the work and thoughts and feet are turned homeward, so the fields were empty. I noticed that he was holding up his right hand meaningfully. He wore a knuckle-duster! I knew instinctively that is what it was, though a second earlier I could not have described one. It glinted on his hand, a half glove of leather encrusted with pointy metal knobs on the knuckles, leaving his finger tips free.

Perhaps my grey hair peeking from under my *chaddar* disarmed him. At any rate, at the same instant that I began to feel uneasy, he slowed down. My young friends turned their heads and said, "They're all going back." That, I believe, is one of the times when I briefly feared for my physical safety in a village.

In villages that I did not know well, I always walked with someone from the house where I was staying, or with someone recommended to me, never alone. Because the narrow lanes and paths between the houses and fields are "private" rather than "public" spaces, they are an intimate part of village life and I did not want to be seen as an intruder.

At any time of the day, girls, women, and children can be seen sitting on the path beside a channel, washing clothes, dishes, or even themselves; old men and women rest in the sun (or shade); men engage in basket-making or spinning, get their hair cut, or enjoy being shaved by the *nai*; women clean grain, mind babies, or rinse spinach leaves. No outsider can pass unnoticed. At the very least, it is within the rights of any villager to ask you what your business is.

When the boy had stopped in front of me I was on a public road that was drivable by jeep where anyone can theoretically go uncontested. So why was I, a strange woman, walking instead of riding "respectably" in a jeep as my status indicated (rucksack, shoes, glasses, camera)? His suspicion was reasonable in that context.

•••

Problems with human relationships are not the only problems. At night, when I am snuggled into my sleeping bag, the bugs start crawling. I can feel them on my legs, then on my neck. I reach up and catch something. A flea. So I have to cope with many more kinds of life than I am used to—fleas, bedbugs, centipedes, spiders, lice, and mice sharing my personal living space. My host's daughter, as a sign of affection, brings her blanket and pillow into my room and lies down beside me. I appreciate the gesture, but in the early morning when I sit up, a louse jumps from my head onto my hand!

A trip to the village shop provides me with a canister of flea and tick powder. I sprinkle it all around the edges of the room. Munni, my young companion and guide, helps me to drag out my mattress and shake it. Then she sweeps the *dhurrie* under it with a twig broom. This raises more dust than it collects, but when that has settled the floor does look cleaner. We lay my bedding and bags down within the circle of insect powder. House-keeping here is reduced to a few elementary tasks. Tonight, I hope to have a carefree sleep.

But what is that scratching sound in the corner? Thump the floor to scare the rat away, I was told. It is a big white *bya*, I have seen its tail poking out of the hole in the ceiling. In the morning there is a tiny hole in the corner of my rucksack where there is a bag of toffees.

I have to surmount my own inhibitions of living in close proximity to people who are as alien to me as they would be to any middle-class urban dweller.[7] In another village, I am given a room to myself, but in the evening my host says, "We will arrange for someone to sleep with you." In spite of my protestations that I like sleeping alone, at bed-time Hamida, accompanied by Aftab her niece, and three smaller girls, crowd into the narrow space on the floor. They settle themselves comfortably on the carpet beside me, rolled up in their quilts. It is drizzling outside, and a pleasant breeze is blowing in through the window, which I have kept open. "Shut the window," one says, snuggling down under her covers. The room begins to smell stuffy.[8] As the smell of rancid butter becomes overpowering, I creep out of my sleeping bag and open the window when everyone is asleep.

But there are countless moments of delight to make up for these discomforts of living in constant close proximity. Munni makes a flask of tea, just the way I like it—weak, sugarless, and milky. First, she has to milk the goat and fetch water from the channel to fill the kettle. Then, she lights the fire with *burtsa* from a pile on the roof (she has to climb up a rickety ladder to do that) and puts the milk and water in a pot balanced on three

---

7   I long for privacy at night when I am in a village after being close to people all day. But what, to me, seems like an encroachment on my personal space as people crowd around me seems to my hosts a loving gesture, an act of friendship.

8   A common meal is *zan* with a scoop of fresh *dzongo* butter. After eating it, children lick their bowls and fingers clean so there is no need to wash hands or face before going to bed.

stones. When it comes to the boil, she throws in a handful of tea leaves, lets it simmer for a minute, and takes it off to steep, with a lid on the pot.

To bring it to me, she puts two handleless china cups on a tin tray, one for me and one for herself. She fills an old, much-used flask with the tea, which is smoky and stained on the outside but spotlessly clean and freshly rinsed inside. She also places a saucerful of sugar and spoon for herself. We settle ourselves on the patio outside my room. It is early evening, the time of day I like best.

Chhulung, the stream below our house gets louder. On a hot sunny afternoon it overflows its banks into countless irrigation channels that have been carved alongside. A large black bird with a long forked tail and yellow beak flies into the tallest poplar that grows at the side of the house.[9] It is joined shortly by its mate. Here the male sings a long, tuneful melody, as if playing on a flute. Other than the rushing sound of water and birdsong, there is silence. I sip my tea and gaze at the mountains above the treetops. Beside me, Munni lies on a mat, doing English handwriting under my guidance.[10] The whole world consists of our rooftop, the water, the mountains in the distance, and the tree.

Later, we all sit by the fireside, waiting for dinner. I enjoy these times of tranquility in the evening. There is only one lantern in the household, so the entire family congregates in one room at night, while Munni and her mother prepare our evening meal. Munni places turnip and beet leaves, spinach, green coriander, and mint in a basket. She sits on a mat, pushing down the greens with one hand and cutting with a sharp knife, until it is all chopped up. Hardly any spills out. Then she carries the basket down to the channel, and rinses them in the basket, which now becomes a sieve.

Syed Abid switches on the radio and we listen to the news. A little bit of the modern world (my world) comes into the mud-daubed room for half an hour. I feed sticks into the fire as Neesa expertly makes *chapatis* on the cast-iron pan. These flatbreads need consistent high heat to remain tender and puff up. The warm smell of fresh bread fills the kitchen, mingling with other delicious aromas of steamed rice and *sonma spachhus* simmering on the fire, reminding us that we have not eaten anything since the last meal at noon. The absence of snacks after a day's work has given everyone a good appetite.

---

9 Identified as a *drongo*, here and in Islamabad. Latin or English name unknown; apparently a Himalayan bird.

10 I paid her wages for being my companion, but I also tutored her since she was missing school.

No one talks for awhile after Neesa has passed heaping plates of stew and rice around, accompanied by a large platter of *chapatis*. The youngest child creeps into his father's lap and falls asleep, with a full stomach and a mouth ringed with traces of his meal. At nine o'clock when everyone has eaten and the last dish has been washed up in the large tin pan which doubles as a kneading tray, we go to our rooms, I, with the lantern.[11]

As the full moon climbs high in the sky, I extinguish the lamp and climb out of the window to sit on one of the two chairs on the patio, unable to leave it and go inside. When I first started coming to the villages, the sight of the full moon lighting up snow-capped mountains took my breath away. In the clear air, the light on the bare slopes turns purple and the snow shines with a strange brightness. It is almost light enough to read.

"What do you call that in Balti," I had asked my host, speaking in Urdu and pointing to the moon. "*Lzgot*," he said with a puzzled expression on his face. "Isn't there a moon in Canada?" At last, I climb back into my room with the moon and the snowy mountain peaks in the silvery purple light framed in the window. When I do lie down on my mat, a bright panel of light lies beside me. Now, there is only the sound of running water as I fall asleep.

Or, I walk into a neighbouring village with my host. A crowd of women, babies, and children appear in a previously empty clearing. We are urged to sit down. A goat hair rug is thrown down—to me its appearance verges on the miraculous—while everyone else perches on boulders, logs, or on the ground. A boy is sent to shake down a mulberry tree. Soon, a platter of sweet, juicy, purple mulberries is placed before me, along with a basket of cold, golden apricots. "*Zos, zos!*" I'm laughingly urged.

One of the women disappears into a nearby house. A quarter of an hour later, when we are preparing to leave, she appears with a flask and some china cups and pours the sweet, hot tea. The talk is good-natured ribbing and always involves questions. "Do you like our village?" "Do you have a lot of cows in Canada?" "Stay here tonight!" "How many sons? All daughters? *Allah!*" with thumping of breast in laughing unbelief. "Are they married?" "Grandsons?" They have all heard about me—some I may have met in "my" village.

Finally, there *is* one other problem for me: doing research on women with *women* as my guides. Spring and summer are the busiest seasons for the villagers in the high mountain valleys, which is also when I go to the

---

11 Instead of using soap to get out stubborn grease from the dishes, Munni scours them with hot ashes and a pad made of leaves and straw.

mountains. The women have to work incredibly hard and do not have time to be my guides unless I follow them as they work.

One of the reasons that women are so busy is that in more and more villages, men are away earning cash, either as porters and guides to mountaineering expeditions, downcountry in the service industry, or in the army.[12] Only women, children, and old men remain in the village, visible on rooftops, in fields, on the paths and lanes, and by the water channels. Occasionally, a husband or a son returns, is feasted and feted for one evening, and then mysteriously disappears again. There is an eerie absence of able-bodied men in the growing season.

Women are left to do not only their own traditional work, but also many tasks that they would have done jointly with men or that men alone would have done. I asked to accompany my young hostess one day to see for myself exactly what she did. Accordingly, after breakfast at 7:30 am I went *chuli sputz* (to knock down ripe apricots from the tree) with Khadija. Of course, her day had started earlier at 5:00 am when she went clambering the slopes to direct water into their fields, *chhu tama*, and I was still asleep.

Irrigating is hard work. It means walking to distant fields, digging out clods of earth with a hoe from the surrounding ridges, leading water from a nearby channel to the field, waiting while it is flooded, sealing up the ridge with the clod of earth, and then repeating the procedure in the next field.[13] Since land is not held in a parcel but scattered about the village, the different parts of people's property are visited and irrigated turn by turn in this manner.[14]

For apricot-picking, we set out with the baby tied to Khadija's back with her shawl, basket in hand. Sometimes she can leave the baby with her *ghunmo*, deaf mute sister-in-law, but today Nargis was also busy, harvesting with her elderly father. When we reached a grove of their trees, Khadija put

---

12   Cash is in demand for modern items like school fees and supplies, electricity, antibiotics, and luxuries like pressure cookers, radios, watches, and toaster ovens (now that electricity is available in the evenings).

13   Where is Khadija?" I had asked, as her mother-in-law poured my tea. And she had explained," *Chhu tama la gwerra,*" at times using her hands to show me how she did it.

14   Having fields in different parts of the village is one of the people's strategies to minimize risk. If there is frost lower down, the crops on a ridge are safe. If one field is ruined by strong winds, another in a more sheltered location will be safe. It also means that everyone gets a chance to have a mixture of soil—alluvial, sandy, or stony.

the baby down on the ground, who then began to pick up mud and stones by the handful. Khadija climbed up the tree and knocked the apricots down with a stick. She was not alone. Everywhere there was the sound of apricots being knocked down by women engaged in similar work. While she was up there, Khadija pruned the tree, breaking off brittle branches and dropping them on the ground. They would be useful for kindling. When she climbed down, we both squatted on the ground and rapidly picked up the apricots by the handful, both whole and rotting, and put them in the *kharrik* she had brought from which, when full, they were tipped into a *chorrong* she had left for that purpose on the previous day.

The apricots were sticky and squishy to pick up, and by the end of it my hands were encrusted with juice and mud. Many a time as I passed women engaged in *chuli tama, chuli phet*, working with apricots, extracting apricot pits, they would wipe their grimy hands on their *dakhuns* and hold them out, *"salaam, liachmo yut?"* Etiquette demands that we shake hands, but I was sorely tempted to hide mine behind my back!

Khadija, the baby, and I moved on to another spot, where she continued to work on another tree, while I alternately sat on a boulder, stopped the baby from eating mud, chatted with other women nearby, or ate some apricots. I crushed the pits with a stone on a flat rock worn smooth by use and shared a few with a little boy who suddenly appeared.

An hour later when *chuli sputz* was finished, Khadija went across to the field where a lot of her apricots had fallen from an overhanging branch. Her relative, a young girl of about sixteen, was cutting barley there. Khadija deftly picked up the fallen apricots, then, sitting down beside her, picked up a curved knife that was lying nearby to help with *sniget nas*. They talked rapidly as they worked. In their busy day, women seldom have time to go visiting, so they socialize whenever and wherever they are. No doubt, her friend will return the favour another day.

We returned home, Khadija carrying the basket, heavy with wet apricots and kindling, on her back and the baby in her arms. She nursed the baby for awhile, then put him down in the dirt yard, where he promptly started crying. He'd had enough for one day. But Khadija still had to climb the wooden ladder with her basket to tip the apricots on to their roof to dry.

Her mother-in-law picked the baby up. *"Ayo, ayo"*, her three-year-old son suddenly appeared, tugging at his mother's *salwar*. He'd also had enough and wanted his mother's attention. But Khadija left again for *chhu bourba*, finding water, which involves going up and down hill looking for a channel that is not already being used by someone else. The strenuous climbing must be hard on nursing mothers, yet, in the absence of men, it is the young and strong women (married, with small children) who have to do it.

I ate *bara zan* in the smoke-blackened kitchen with Khadija's old mother-in-law and the children.[15] This meal typically consists of *paillu chai* accompanied by a loaf of unleavened bread. "If you like our tea, you will like us," a woman had said to me when I first tasted it. As we ate, *api* sat by the *thap* with her grandsons, ready to refill my cup, ladle poised. In between tending to me, she popped morsels of *pappa, khurba* dipped in *chai,* into her grandsons' mouths.

She told me that Khadija still had to pick up a load of cut barley from a distant field before returning for her *zan*. I went to my room for a rest. Later I heard that Khadija had also had to wash a bundle of clothes (hers, her children's, and her parents-in-laws') before she ate. When I emerged from my room after a couple of hours, she was on the rooftop, splitting the apricots we had picked for their pits, placing them in two piles of sweet and bitter kernels. The dried flesh of the apricots would be fed to the animals in winter and the kernels would be shelled for their oil.[16] And so the work went, on and on. Despite my best intentions, I couldn't actually keep up with her in the one day I had set out to follow her.

So unless I am prepared to work with the women through the day, I have no one to accompany me on my walks through the village, or to show me their work, or answer my questions. If I attempt to go alone, I am seen as an intruder rather than a welcome guest and am followed by children, usually boys (girls are too busy) heckling, pushing, and jostling.[17]

One of the consequences of being there in the busy season is that young children, usually girls, but sometimes an especially quiet and reliable boy will become my chaperone, guide, and translator. When they are as young as eleven years old, it can cause problems.

On one occasion, I was in my room alone with two young children—my host's son and a neighbour's daughter. It was a religious holiday for the villagers, which meant that women and children were at home cooking and

---

15 Literally, twelve o'clock food, but it may be eaten later than that.
16 Sweet apricot oil (*ngarmo chuli mar*) is used for cooking and eating with *zan* or *khurrba*. Bitter (*kho chuli mar*) is used medicinally as hair oil, for earaches, on cuts as an antiseptic, for bruises, or as a liniment for sore muscles. Its healing powers are valued.
17 Except in the village I call home.

preparing for a festive dinner after the prayers, while the men were in the *masjid*. But keeping me company could be tedious for the young if more interesting things were going on elsewhere. No food was being prepared in our home because we had been invited to dinner in my girl companion's home that afternoon.

"I'm just going to see if *ango* wants any help," the girl said and disappeared. "You must stay here," I told the boy. "Remember your father said I was not to be left alone." But he grew more and more restless. "I'll see why she hasn't come back," he said and also ran off. I locked the door of my room and went to sit by the low window which opened on to the patio. I tried not to feel panicky. This was a fairly new village to me. Although I had been here briefly two years ago, it was a big village and I did not know my way around its twisting alleys, or even know many people. Also, language skills seemed to forsake me when I was nervous. But surely I'm safe here, I told myself. Who would bother me?

There was a thump on the sod roof. Although the outer door to our house had been securely locked at my request, due to the proximity of the houses it was quite easy to climb onto our roof from a neighbouring one. I peered out of the window and looked up. Three big girls, about fourteen or fifteen years old, were standing above me, eating mulberries off the tall tree that shaded the house. They bent down and waved. Soon they dropped down and squatted outside my window, blocking the light.

I began to feel apprehensive, but smiled and tried to answer their questions. "What is your name?" "Why do you come here?" "Show me the camera," "What is that?" pointing to the sleeping bag. "Can I touch it," "Do you have a lot of *penne*? Are you rich?" "Do you know where Hala is?" I asked finally. Hala was my girl companion. They stared back. One made a sign of not knowing. They whispered to each other and started running about on the patio, giggling and shoving, pelting each other with leaves. The biggest girl tried to come in through the window, pushing past me. They shouted "*memu, memu*" and mimicked the way I spoke. "Please go to her home and tell her to come back," I pleaded.

My anxiety increased as things got out of control. The girls disappeared out of sight and a lump of dried mud sailed past my face through the open window and landed on the sleeping bag behind me. One of them suddenly reappeared at the window without smiling. Her expression was unfriendly. "Go away!" I cried and tried to shut the window while she pushed against it. Her laughter taunted me.

Just then my host arrived! He had gone to the friend's house where we were to have lunch, noticed that both my young companions were there without me, and hurried over. At his appearance, the girls leaped over the wicker fence and jumped down into the alley, their bare feet thudding as they ran, followed by his angry shouts. My relief was so great that I burst into tears, something I had never done before.

It may seem strange that I was intimidated by teenaged girls, but their language and mannerisms were strange to me and I felt confused when confronted by their hostility. Hala's mother was indignant when she heard of my mishap. She had of course, scolded her own daughter for leaving me alone. She knew the girls who had teased me by my description. A few days later she was with me when we ran into one of them and she let loose a stream of invectives against them, their families, and their descendants, which made the girl turn and hide. I had no more problems from them after that.

I had already realized that not everyone in the villages I visited was friendly towards me. In the evening in this same village, while sitting with my back to a small, open window in the kitchen at dinnertime, I felt water splash me. It happened on several occasions until I stopped sitting in that spot. My host went to the window and peered out but there was no one to be seen in the gathering dusk.

There are several possible reasons for hostility: I am a woman travelling alone; some think me foreign; even if they accept that I am Pakistani, my behaviour is not typical. The Pakistan government has a patronizing attitude towards Baltistan and the Pakistani tourists who do come tend to stay in hotels in Skardu and not in villages.

This means that they seldom meet a Pakistani woman in the village. The Pakistani men they may see are on treks with porters and tents so they are also distanced. Another reason for their distrust may be that I am rich (that is, in cash terms) yet choose to live with them which leads them to suspect that I am a spy. This makes it all the more remarkable that mostly I feel safe and welcome wherever I go.

All in all, the problem of not having an adult woman as my guide can be frustrating. While I am prepared to work with the women, I cannot keep up with all that they do in a day. They on the other hand, are always concerned about me, urging me to "*duk aram se*, sit and be comfortable" due to their extreme sense of hospitality. There is also the undeniable fact that as a newcomer, I am ignorant and untutored in their ways, so I hinder them in their work—although they are too polite to say so.

Once the growing season starts, everything ripens and is ready for harvesting at the same time. Women and children work hard and quickly to process it, so that nothing spoils or is wasted. The commodities pile up in bags, sacks, baskets, and bunches—a satisfying reward for their labour. Women cannot sacrifice that to my need for their company, or waste time teaching me to do what has taken them generations to learn.

Here is a plaintive excerpt from my diary that speaks of my complicated position: "I am back at the Indus Hotel (in Skardu) feeling a bit of a failure. They are very kind, but the women have no time for me in the busy season. Since I cannot keep up with them, there is no other place for me, but to stay in my room. Human research is *very* difficult. I'm tired—physically and emotionally." I had returned from my intended six-week tour four days earlier than planned. But I *had* finally mastered the Balti language!

Rumours and Resistance

By now it should be obvious that I had developed a great respect and admiration for many of the village women. The intention has not been to romanticize them or their lives, which in certain respects can be best described as tough. Likewise, while I convey their extraordinary kindness towards me, this does not mean that all went smoothly, or that we were not sometimes torn in different directions. I have also wanted to portray the sense of mutual respect and sensitivity about our different faiths and observances. Nevertheless, in some families, the way in which religious fundamentalism reinforces patriarchy sometimes caused difficulties for us.

In some religiously conservative villages, elite men have advanced into positions of authority and power, ostensibly because of their lineage (Sayyids, descended directly from the Prophet Muhammad) but in reality because of landed wealth and status as aghas, sheikhs, or non-elected heads of villages. All of this opens new opportunities for them because as the wealthiest individuals in the village they are at the forefront of any innovative venture or opportunity presented by governmental or international development.

As religious leaders they are often associated with a stronger or more persistent sense of patriarchy which is reflected in the treatment of women. Unexpectedly, perhaps, women from wealthy religious families are more controlled and confined to their homes than are the women from poorer or peasant households who need to be free to work. Elite women are also likely to have more children.

This story illustrates these dichotomies, including how "modernization" can bring about what seems its opposite—a reinforcing of more traditional values and relations, especially for women. It shows how so-called religious fundamentalism is more about economics and social control than it is about religion. Arising from these considerations, I became more aware of how the perils of women's situation may have to take precedence over what an outsider, however well-meaning, might want to see happen—especially if the outsider's well-intended changes put the women at risk. And finally, all of this is set in the context of complex interpersonal relationships.

In a village, after an initial and enthusiastic welcome into a home, I came up against a sudden turnabout in my hosts' attitude towards me. Mysteriously, there seemed to be attempts to block my access to the women of the family; attempts in the form of empty rooms or closed doors in a house where I had previously been free to enter.

More alarming were the rumours. The rumours were not of a sexual nature (because I was careful to keep to the company of women and to behave according to the moral codes of the society) but rather they portrayed me as a spy and alternatively, as questionable and dangerous because of my religious beliefs. I began to realize that I was meeting with strategies of resistance[18] and that these rumours were spread among the very people I had thought of as my friends.[19]

First let me repeat that whenever I went into a new village, it was in the company of someone from that village, or with an introduction to my new hosts, to be assured of a welcome and so I would not appear to be trespassing. I was introduced to an elite family of three brothers, their wives, and children of varying ages, some married with babies of their

18 Halvorson, "Geographies of Children's Vulnerability: Households and Water-Related Disease Hazard in the Karakoram Mountains, Northern Pakistan," (125). In her research in a Balti village, on children and women's health, the author mentions that often when she was invited for a meeting, she would arrive, only to find the front door locked. Or, she would be the only one there and none of the other women who had promised to come would turn up.

19 Nyborg, "Yours Today, Mine Tomorrow? A Study of Women and Men's Negotiations over Resources in Baltistan," 134. Resistance is often taken as a liberating struggle, for example, of women demanding their rights from men, as in this study on men's and women's access to resources. In my case however, it was in the form of an opposition aimed at me by some women and men. Perhaps a better phrase for it is *reaction to my presence*.

own. The family welcomed my daughter and me into their large, rambling home where each married couple had a separate room and all shared the communal kitchen and *balti*.

Before long, I was going in and out of the house without invitation. Indeed, if I missed going for several days, a child would be sent to ask me why. It became my custom during my daily walks around the village to climb up the bamboo *kaska*, walk through the airy balcony, and step into the kitchen unannounced. One or another of the wives would be cooking dinner—a stack of *khurrbas*, a big pot of *spacchus*, or a bubbling cauldron of *namkin chai* would be balanced in the *thap*. She would turn around with a smile to wave me in, "*Onn'n duk*," inviting me to come in and sit down, a cushion placed for me, crumbs hastily cleared away, babies removed from that space.

It was nice to sit in a home, be given a cup of tea, and have people to talk to. One of the things I missed most on my trips to the mountains was my home. After some weeks, Twahira, a young childless woman who was married to one of the brothers, shyly asked me to read from an Urdu book which was lying around.[20] "Can you read?" I asked her. "*Chhun chhan se*, a little bit," she confessed. She had gone to school in her own village before marriage, but only up to primary level.

In no time I was giving her regular reading lessons. It was good for both of us, because in this way I learned Balti and she, Urdu. She would bring her nephew's Urdu *qaida*[21] and we would sit down comfortably and start. Without children to care for, she welcomed my company as we sat reading and talking, a crowd of children always around us. "You should open a school for all these girls," I said half jokingly, for there was as yet no girls' school in this village. She blushed and smiled, happy to dream, but we both knew it could never happen. "Respectable" women do not work outside the home and never for money.[22]

Soon, a teenaged girl, the bride of one of her nephews, began to join our gatherings. She had not met me on my previous visits. Rashida was

---

20　When I had first arrived in the village, she came to see me about her wish to have a baby. Even though I explained I was not a doctor, we became friends. One day, she pulled up the shirt on her back and showed me a dark stain, like a birthmark on the left side. "Perhaps it is the pain in my heart because I have no children," she said sadly.

21　A school textbook or reader.

22　"Our women do not work," an elite woman informed me proudly, while women were busy working in field, yard, and kitchen.

literate, having been brought up in Skardu where there are girls' schools and she had even studied beyond primary level. She would peer over Twahira's shoulder and read the word aloud quickly while Twahira was trying to sound it out. This began to happen every time we read. I reprimanded her in mock severity and everyone thought it funny. I thought she did too. Later, I began to wonder whether she, being a newcomer, had resented my taking too many liberties in her family. It may have been one of the reasons our lessons began to sour.

There were other warning signs which I ignored. One day, as we were having our lesson, the wife whose turn it was to cook came up to us and put her baby down in front of Twahira. "Here," she said brusquely, inferring that Twahira was doing nothing. Normally, Twahira, the favourite aunt of the family, loved being handed a baby. This time though, she laughingly brushed her sister-in-law aside and continued reading. That wife was the wife of the oldest brother. Certainly, she had not been pleased to have to cook and hold her baby, or be turned down by someone lower in the familial social order! I also remembered later that one of the young nephews would often make fun of his aunt's lessons and hide the *qaida*. "Why do you do this? She is too old to go to school!" Perhaps he had been trying to tell me something.

However, we continued with our weekly or biweekly lessons for a couple of months. One afternoon, while we were reading, Syed Hassan, the oldest brother and head of the household, walked through the kitchen. By now we were a larger group of women and children as more friends joined us every time we met. Sometimes, to their great amusement, I would sing the Pakistani national anthem, or an old film song, spurred on by an appreciative and uncritical audience. On this particular occasion, a tray of tea lay beside us, babies were being dandled by their sisters, and I was telling them a funny story about life in Canada. Meanwhile, Twahira continued to read. We may have been especially noisy that afternoon.

A hush fell over the women, as it does when an elder male enters the room.[23] *Dakhuns* were rearranged, expressions made serious, and eyes were downcast. As he left, he muttered something to the wife by the fireplace whose *bari* it was to *zan bya*, turn to cook. One of the older nephews beside us translated quietly for me, "Uncle says no one is working." Quickly, we

---

23   Tual, "Speech and Silence: Women in Iran," 54, in Dube, Leacock, and Ardener, *Visibility and Power: Essays on Women in Society and Development*. When a man enters any space occupied by women, the space automatically becomes male space, since he is the dominant person due to the balance of power in a patriarchal society.

dispersed, Twahira hastily going to help with the cooking and I took my leave.

A few days later, Tara, who had been out with her friends (among them some girls from the Hassan family) gave me a disturbing piece of news. She said, "I just heard that before we came Syed Hassan had asked Rizwana (our hostess) not to keep Farida and Tara." We spoke in a mixture of English and Urdu and our hostess, who was listening from her seat by the fireplace, picked up the meaning from the names.

She nodded saying, "Yes, he did. But I would be very sad if you left. I want you to stay five or six months. That family has always envied us because we have more land and fruit trees than they do. You know you can always stay with us. This is your home." Their land adjoined the Hassan land and they were neighbours, two of the largest households in the village. But while one was a well-to-do farmer's house (Rizwana's) the other was the house of a Sayyid, so more prestigious.

I thought back on the last few days and realized that I had sensed that things were not the same. Lately, whenever I went to visit Twahira and her sisters-in-law, the kitchen would be empty, although clearly there were signs of cooking, even a pot on the fire. I would call the women by name, but there was no answer. As I walked through the dark passage, all the doors would be shut. Suddenly a young girl or boy would appear. When I asked the child where so-and-so was, I would be told "She's sleeping," "Out for a walk," "Working in the *drumba*," or "She's gone to visit someone who's sick." Now I saw them only in the distance, on paths across the fields, or leaning out of their windows, waving and smiling at me, but no more than that.

A few days later, Twahira did a strange thing. She came over in the morning at breakfast time ostensibly for eggs (Rizawana kept chickens). She had never come before on such an errand, which was normally child's work. She said something to Rizwana so fast that I couldn't catch what she said. Then she went out, came back, and emptied a heap of shelled walnuts in my lap from her bundled-up *dakhun*. Speaking rapidly to Rizwana, she said "I would like to invite Farida for dinner but all my brothers-in-law and sisters-in-law would have to agree, so I can't do it. I'm sorry." Then she left abruptly. Slowly, Rizwana translated what she had said. We shook our heads.

We had an interesting talk about why I am suddenly not welcome in that house. "Perhaps I give the women new ideas and their husbands don't like that," I suggested. "They don't want the women to be educated, maybe they will want more freedom then." She nodded happily, *"Aqal barabar yut, we think alike."*[24] Even with language difficulties, she and I could converse about abstract matters. This was partly due to her knowledge of spoken *farsi*, from her instruction in religious writings (Urdu and *farsi* share some of their main nouns), and partly to my ability to speak more Balti. We smiled at each other. We were friends, which felt especially good now that others, suddenly and bewilderingly, were not.

Then more rumours started circulating, still without any change in the situation. Rizwana heard talk at the village shop that I was a spy and that I had been questioned by the police in Skardu when I'd left the village the last time. There was even talk that I'd spent some time there in jail! Another, and more unsettling rumour was that I had been Muslim when I was younger and converted to Christianity when I went to Canada.[25]

Was I being paranoid, or was there a difference in the way people behaved towards me? When I went for a walk, a group of men and women were sitting under a tree. Normally, they would have called out a greeting. Now they suddenly stopped talking and watched me in silence as I walked by. Later, I went to the home of one of the women whose husband owns a shop. "Can I buy some kerosene for my lamp?" I asked. She clicked her tongue. *"Met.* No oil," she said shortly. Previously, she would have urged me to stay and have a cup of tea. However, it must be said that Tara's young friends from the family in question maintained their friendship. They still called for her; when she lay in her room with a fever, one of them, a young married girl of fifteen, even brought her new baby with her.

All this time Syed Javaid, one of the young nephews (the one married to Rashida) continued to come to our room every afternoon to have English conversation lessons. It gave me a certain satisfaction that at least one member of that family was loyal to us! He was eager to learn English and get himself a job in Skardu away from his paternal home. His own father was dead and he had been raised by his uncles. He confessed to me that he felt he would not progress to a worthwhile career while living at home and teaching in the local school. "Uncle makes me give him my salary," he complained. "I get to keep just a little bit of it for myself. This is no way for a man to live. I want to become someone." Of course, it could be argued that since his board and lodging and that of his wife's and infant

---

24 Literally this means, "Our intelligence matches."

25 The truth is that my mother was a Christian and my father was a Muslim. I was raised as a Christian.

son's were looked after by his uncle, what need did he have for money? But I took his point.

Shortly, Rizwana's mother-in-law arrived from running an errand to give us another disturbing piece of news. *Api* had met Rashida on the path, who told her that she did not like her husband coming to our house for lessons and that she would stop him because he (her husband) was afraid of her. Aware that propriety must be preserved, whenever the young man came I made sure that the door of our room remained open and that there were always a few women and girls in my room, including Tara. At that time she was thirteen years old, just a couple of years younger than Rashida. Rizwana said, "*Baji, fiqr met. Rashida la hassad yut*—don't worry, Rashida is jealous (of Tara). That is why she doesn't want her husband to come here." She added scornfully, "She is just the daughter of a shopkeeper. *Tamiz met, sirrif penne*, she has no manners, only money."[26]

Several days passed after I heard this news. Syed Javaid continued to come for his lessons every day. Sometimes he seemed so depressed that it was hard work to get any conversation out of him. One day, when we were persevering with our English lesson, Rashida burst into the room carrying their infant son. She sat down without greeting anyone, then abruptly got up, plunked the baby rudely into her husband's lap, and left the room, shouting something at him. The chatter in the adjoining room stopped. Only a fly buzzed.

Into the silence Syed Javaid said sadly, "She is angry with me." We said nothing, looking down at our hands in our laps. I waited for him to continue. He said, "Uncle wants me to stay in the village and not study any more at Skardu College. He just wants me to be a schoolteacher here, but I want to prove that I can be more. That is why I want to learn English. Maybe," he added bravely, "I'll come to Canada to visit you." But the heart had gone out of him and soon after that he left, carrying his baby. Later, Rizwana, who had also been in the room, translated what Rashida had shouted as she stormed out of the room. "*Haramzada! Nalbu!* bastard (in Urdu and Balti). Why do you come here? Here! Take *your* child *yourself!*[27] I have work to do at home!" Our lessons stopped.

---

26 Rizwana spoke as the daughter of a respected, albeit poor, landed farmer who was now deceased.

27 *Khirri; khyang.* She used the rude forms of the pronouns *yerri* and *yan*, which are only spoken to an inferior, or a dog. For a wife to speak in such abusive and derogatory terms to her husband is unthinkable.

On the advice of a schoolmaster who was a friend of Rizwana's family, Tara also curtailed her activities around the village. "She is a young girl, *jawaan*. People talk. Don't let her wander too far from home," he said kindly. "But you are both always welcome in this village because you respect our ways." This is not all he said.

As we sat around the fireplace, he smiled and gestured towards the pot of *namkin chai* and plate of *khurrbas* in the ashes beside the fireplace, small children climbing over their mothers, the mess of food crumbs on the *chhara*, the bundle of dirty clothes in a corner, and added proudly, "Our women have not changed the way they live and work since olden times, and we like it that way. It is our Balti way—*yehhi hamara watan hai—this* is our land."[28]

On reflection, I traced the beginning of "the resistance" to a combination of factors. They were: my Urdu reading lessons to a married woman, the jealous feelings of a young wife who was a newcomer to the family, and, perhaps the most important, through our conversations in the kitchen on all manner of topics, introducing the married women to new ideas. These may have seemed to the senior, conservative male members of the family daring and foreign—by extension, non-Islamic or even Christian—which they equate with North America; ideas that might stir feelings of unrest or discontent in the women.

There may have been other disturbing factors. My presence in the intimate spaces of the women's quarters in this large and wealthy household could have been cause for unease among the senior men. What secrets was I, an outsider, privy to? What was I writing in my notebook as I sat there drinking tea? In a simple farmer's house there is a direct relation between material goods and work. It was well-known that the Sayyid had a bank account, land, and houses in other villages and was engaged in projects brought by important government and development officials, but the *details* were not known, which I might be learning about.

---

28 Men often dressed and looked different or more modern than women. This teacher was smartly dressed in a white *salwar kamiz* and checkered waistcoat with a silver watch-chain across his breast. His hair was oiled and combed, his hands smooth, his nails short and clean, his shoes (which he kept on as he was sitting on the edge of the rug) were polished. He would not have looked out of place on a street in Islamabad. His young wife, on the other hand, wore traditional baggy *salwar* and a stained, voluminous shirt, which looked slept in. Her hair under her *dakhun* was messy. Her bare feet were rough and chapped, as were her hands (from working in the fields).

My unmarried daughter may have been the reason the young wife had reported our reading sessions to Syed Hassan.[29] For his part, he may have wondered why I, a newcomer to the village, was teaching a married female member of his family to read? He had deliberately walked through the kitchen on that fateful day to see for himself. Otherwise, he rarely came into the women's quarters except at mealtimes when the space's function changed to family room.

Five years later when I returned to the village, many changes had been made to their house. There was a high wooden stockade going all the way around the back. Surrounding the house and garden in front there was a high stone wall with broken glass embedded in concrete at the top (something seen only in cities).[30] Inside the enclosure where once there had been fields, a small house had been built for one of the married nephews. There was a new addition at the back as well where guests were now received: a squat, square building with two separate rooms presumably for men and women, a kitchen at the back. No longer did visitors drop in to the family house unannounced, by climbing up a ladder.

But such changes came later.[31] To go back to the time of the rumours about me, after a while, I began to get inquiries and invitations from some of the women in Hassan's family, mainly from the younger ones. "Mariam has had a baby," one of Tara's friends came to say. "She wants you to come and see her." "Why do you never come over now?" a nephew asked. So gradually, our relationship assumed a new pattern. I started to drop in, but only when invited. I was served tea in the outer balcony (not the *balti*) and made polite conversation. Our friendship became formal.

---

29   This suspicion was confirmed five years later. When I was on a trip to the village, I went to their house to pay my respects after the death of a family member. I was led to the *mehmankhanna,* the guesthouse. As usual, women and children of the family crowded around. Tea and special breads were offered, befitting a guest. Rashida came into the room and greeted me with a handshake, her eyes darting around to see if I had come alone. After a few minutes she left the room and came back with a worn-out *qaida* in her hand. "Here *baji*," she said, sitting down beside me, "teach us how to read."

30   I asked one of the villagers the reason for the wall with broken glass. "Because they want to protect their fruit trees," he answered. Then, with a smile: "Because they have a lot of money."

31   I do not mean to imply that the changes happened solely because of me. But I believe I was part of the reason for the new privacy. As the family's wealth and acquisitions increased, relations within the household and with the village became more complex.

The old camaraderie was gone. And I never tried to teach literacy skills to married women again.[32]

If You Could Have a Wish

One day when we had been in the village for three months, I posed a question to a group of people. By now almost everyone in the village, if not in the entire Shigar-Basha valley, knew me or at least about me. This made it easy for me to talk to them.[33] The height of the growing season was in full swing, young men were either in the high pastures, in college in Skardu, or working somewhere downcountry. Mostly, only women, elderly men, and small children were visible on pathways and rooftops.

As I wandered around, nodding at passersby, greeting one or two, photographing a house or fields or sitting down on a rock, I came upon two women and a baby in a shady lane. They were busy with a large pestle and mortar which here is somewhat like a public utility—every village has several, dotted about in various locations. It is simply a large boulder with a worn-out hollow in the centre and a round, smooth stone for crushing. The women were pounding sheep and goat manure in the mortar while the baby crawled around bare-bottomed.

When it has been reduced to powder, the finely pounded manure is roasted in a large skillet reserved only for this purpose, over an open outdoor fire. The *beel* as it is called, is then placed in a heavy cloth bag into which the baby is inserted, feet first, and then the bag is tied under the baby's arms. The powdered manure absorbs waste as a diaper would. It is changed every two or three days by being emptied into a field, when the bag is thoroughly washed (but not in the *chhu*)! While this practice is being discarded by some as old-fashioned, *gopi zamana la,* I would still come across women pounding manure on my walks through the village.

Seeing me, a number of women and men who were walking by stopped. No one worried about the time (although many men wear wrist watches). It

32 This incident was a wake-up call to me not to presume too much in a culture with which I was not familiar.

33 Pratt, *Travel Writing and Transculturation*. Referring to Mungo Park's travel narrative set in Africa in the late eighteenth century, Pratt writes, "Reciprocity ... is the dynamic that above all organizes Park's human-centred, interactive narrative" (80). That is similar to the way I interacted with the villagers. The women gave me their stories, taking what they needed from me—medicines, a voice to speak for them in public space, or status in their community because of their perceived closeness to an educated woman.

was a warm summer afternoon, but pleasantly cool and shady in the lane. As they seated themselves on the ground or a rock nearby, they seemed to be in the mood to talk. So I asked them turn by turn, "What do you want most out of your life?"

The first one to answer was Fatima, a bright-eyed, pretty young woman, the wife of a schoolteacher with three small children. Her husband is not only a salaried worker, but also owns land with his brothers, so they are *phyukpo*, rich, in both modern and traditional terms. "Everything!" she replied with a laugh. "Cream for my face—my cheeks are dry!" On a more serious note, she added, "*Talim*, education, for my daughters. Look at me—I can't read or write like you. It makes me feel useless. I am *icchat*, bored in winter." Then with a laugh, "*Quaid*! I feel I am a prisoner in the *katza*!"

As I wrote, she leaned over my shoulder to look admiringly at the words. She was curious about life in Canada and asked many questions, "How long does it take to get there? How much is the *karaya*, fare? What do you eat? How do you make bread? Do you make *khurrbas* like us?" She was surprised that my family owns neither land, trees, nor livestock. "*Ali*! How can you live? You even have to buy bread!" Even when Baltis have jobs, their cash income is not their basic source of wealth, but is in addition to their ownership of land.

Another woman, poorer, with five sons and less land, said seriously, "*Penne*." "Why money? Why not land, or food?" I asked. "Money will get health and food for the children," she replied. "Now we have nothing. No food, no clothes, no education, no health. Nothing." She looked at her husband for confirmation. He worked at odd jobs, in construction, as a *nai*, a barber (he would set up shop outside his house beside the *rshka* where he could dip his razor and comb), as a cook (making large pots of *halva*, *pullao*, or goat curry for weddings and feast days), as well as a government job as *dakpo*, postmaster.[34] He said slowly, "We want enough for our needs,

---

34 As postmaster of Chutrun, he had a rickety red metal mailbox attached to the wall by his front door, where you could leave your letters. To get there you had to walk through the muddy *harral*, the yard where his cow was tethered, and climb up a bamboo ladder. But it was better to give him the letter in person because, being a busy farmer, he seldom had time to look in the mailbox. Inside the house he had a wooden box with a lock where he kept stamps, pens, scraps of paper, and a bottle of glue. He could sell you a stamp and, being literate, even write your letter for you. The mail was given daily to runners who carried it in turn down to Skardu. Bad weather, floods, or broken roads could stop the mail for days. The wonder is that mail did arrive for us, even from Canada.

that's all. Now we work hard but what do we have in return? We don't even have enough flour to last us the whole year, let alone a surplus."

"This is a narrow valley," he continued. "There is no more land left to reclaim. The boys will have to accept what *Allah* has in store for them. Who knows what they will do for a living? My father came here from Khapalu before I was born and managed to get land and build a house. But how much land can five sons inherit? I was lucky because my father left me the house, but I do not have much land—my brothers got most of it. Some of my land is in Hamesil a kilometre away. By the end of the growing season we have made about thirty trips a day carrying manure to the fields. It's the same in early March. We work ourselves to the bone. And at the end we have nothing to show for it." He looked down sadly and there was silence when he had finished. To some degree, everyone shared in his experience.

Then Amina spoke. She was another young, lively woman, the mother of three children, two girls and a boy. She and her husband were both newcomers to this village (i.e., not born here). Her husband had a shop, and was a noted hunter for *markhor*. They were well off, with a big, new house and no other dependants. "Don't know," she answered pertly. "I want lots of children, five boys and two girls. Then when the boys grow up, they will study and become doctors and teachers and bring me their salaries. I will be rich!" "Lots of children means lots of sickness and worry," I suggested. "No, not really. A few children are no good—there are not enough to work when we are old," she replied.[35]

I turned to Ali, who had land, brothers, three sons, and a comfortable government job, so materially he was well off. "*Talim* for the children," he replied. "After that, a partner with whom one is happy, who matches one in intellect and everything else. Husband and wife spend so much time together—if a man's wife is no good, life is not worth living." It was rumoured that he and his wife did not get along because she was not his equal.

Rabia answered next. She was a capable, intelligent young woman with four daughters and one son at the time. She is my friend who has appeared in many stories. Her husband, a talented craftsman, gardener, and singer of religious songs, had inherited considerable land and a big house built by

---

35　In later years she had two more girls but the family continued to prosper and built another house in the neighbouring village, her natal home. Her eldest daughter was married to a cousin at the age of fourteen. This strategy decreases the expense of rearing many daughters and also brings a son and his labour into the home.

his father, but had no way of earning cash for their increasing needs. Being the only son also placed him at a disadvantage because he had no one with whom to share the burden of work except his wife. But as a woman, there were many tasks that Rabia could not do. "Education for daughters and sons. Then they could make a better life for themselves than we have," she said. "But here we have no hope of doing that unless we send our children away to school in Skardu. We need *penne* for that."

Her husband nodded, "I want the same, I suppose. What she says is true. I have plenty of land, but I can't produce more from it than I am already doing. The children are small and there is no one to help me. Here it is not like Pakistan (i.e., the lowlands) where you can get four crops a year off the land. We can only get two, with difficulty. I suppose I would like to be able to produce to have a surplus to sell. Since I have no salary, that is the only way I can earn cash."[36]

Finally I asked Nurbano and her elderly and ailing husband. Nurbano was a strong woman, known for her hard work, quick temper, and independent spirit. She and her husband were wealthy in terms of land, had two capable sons, and one a deaf-mute. She replied in her forthright typical fashion. "Not to be *muhtaj*, dependent, is important. Then to be able to provide food, clothes, and a house for oneself and one's children." Her husband, many years her senior and now unable to work, added slowly, "To have good health. Then to be able to provide food, clothes, and shelter for one's children."[37]

Overall, the answers were practical and sensible—about better education, health, and the fulfillment of basic needs. My companions were mainly positive and optimistic that their endeavours would lead to *tarraqi,* progress. I also discovered gradually that most people thought that my living with them and writing about them would make a lasting difference in their lives; sadly, I explained, it would not.

---

36 The solution, which he took ten years later, was to hire himself out as a porter to foreign expeditions in the summer. This, while providing him with cash (and I say *him* deliberately because cash remains in men's possession) took him away from his fields and pastures, burdening his already overworked wife. Recently, in 2005, he has started working for the electricity company in a neighbouring village.

37 His wish was not granted, at least not for himself, because he passed away the following year. Seven years later, Nurbano's house was destroyed in a flood. She and her son, with the help of friends and relatives, built a new, bigger house on her land, where her extended family continues to live in comfort. If her wish came true, it is mainly due to their hard work and initiative.

Once a man said wistfully, "What will your book do for us? Will it help us? Will people read it and come and see what we need?" We were sitting in his dark, smoke-filled kitchen with his wife and four (out of five) poorly clad sons. The dirt floor was partially covered with a threadbare and stained *chhara*. As we talked, his wife was making *khurrbas*, piling them into a broken basket while her youngest child cried listlessly beside her on the bare floor. Occasionally she stopped to wipe his runny nose with her grimy *dakhun*. This family appeared to be among the poorest I had seen in the village, poor even by standards where wealth is not counted in cash terms. Instead of hope, there was despair in the home.

The man looked around the dark, shabby room and continued, "Have you ever in your travels seen poverty such as this? I have seen how people live in Islamabad. We can never reach their level, no matter how hard we try." Then he added bitterly, "The government did nothing for us when the flood destroyed our fields. An officer came to assess the damage and he never returned." He had lost several fields under wheat and beans to the flood of 1988, which severely strained his ability to feed his family and to give them land for their inheritance. For this reason, he was planning to send his oldest son into the army when he was sixteen, and hoping that another son would become a teacher or find work as a porter.[38]

At one time, Baltis flourished in spite of the rugged terrain and extreme climate of their homeland. But a hundred years of Dogra rule demoralized the people and decimated arts and crafts, so that today, much traditional knowledge and skill has been forgotten.[39] Few practise skilled woodcarving, weaving, or other crafts for which their neighbours to the south and west are famous (Hunzakuts and Kashmiris). Balti woollen cloth is said to be inferior to that made in Hunza and Nagir, because their looms are "simple," that is, without the mechanism that provides a third layer of stitches.

But in *gopi zamana,* olden times, it was different. In old houses in Shigar, Askoli, and elsewhere, beautiful designs have been carved in house doors and arches and many homes have ornately carved pillars ending in

---

38 As usual, it was through their own efforts that their prospects improved. Ten years later, the family was better off. The grown-up sons brought in an income, while their marriages to two sturdy girls added labour and grandsons to the family. A third son who had a crippled leg opened a shop in the village and so was able to earn for the household. With the extra money they built an extension on their house to accommodate their growing family.

39 See appendix for more on Dogra rule.

ram's horns which support the ceiling. The Shigar *masjid* with its delicately carved pagoda is another example of early Balti architecture.[40] If asked, the houseowner will often produce intricately carved salt boxes, spoons, ladles, cylinderical containers for spun wool, and little storage chests with puzzle locks, which are no longer in use. These and many more items have been replaced by shop-bought aluminum, plastic, and metal wares.

Old grandmothers unlock deep, wooden chests and dig out rich and ornate silver jewellery, rings set with big stones, dangling earrings that loop over the ear for extra support, necklaces set with large turquoises, garnets, and rubies. The heavy *phallu* placed on a velvet band is tied around the throat with finely braided threads. In Arindu and Askoli women wear *nattings* with elaborate silver chains laced over the black woollen cap, a *tomar*, which is a tradition that stretches eastwards to ancient Tibet and Ladakh.

Sturdy footwear made of the hides of yak, *dzo*, goat, or sheep used to be worn by both men and women. The boots were of four kinds: one called *polla* had a leather sole and strap; *mosho* was all leather with the tougher leather on the sole; *fusho,* a soft indoor shoe, was made of lighter leather; and *tawootse polla* was the strongest boot, usually made for royals. It was fashioned of strong leather with a fur border on the cuff, and was often embroidered with coloured wool and leather. Women's boots had *yung-drunpa* design for good luck. Interestingly, this is a swastika-shape in reverse, dating from Bongchus times (a pre-Buddhist period, pre-seventh century). Now plastic shoes have replaced the leather footwear. They are cheaply bought in the local shops and bazaars, waterproof, and easily replaced. Of course, cash is needed, which is why the poorest go barefoot, or with mismatching, ill-fitting shoes. Some of the garbage lying around in fields and channels consists of broken plastic slippers, shoes, and sandals.

In spite of hardship, almost everyone I talked to has strong, positive feelings for Baltistan, for their land, and their home village in particular. I also loved the children, who were so appealing with their golden skin and delicate, slightly Mongol features. And there are lots of children! I once asked a friend jokingly if he would give us his two-year-old son to take back to Canada. "We'll send him to school and he can become a doctor,"

---

40 Afridi, *Baltistan in History*, dates *khanqahs* (prayer houses) and mosques which were constructed after conversion from Buddhism, reflecting the influence of Buddhist architecture. The exact date of the Shigar *masjid* is difficult to ascertain, but it is believed to have been constructed by Raja Hussain Khan (1718-1815). The one in Skardu is believed to be earlier.

I said, knowing that they value doctors. His answer was immediate and unequivical as I had known it would be: "No." But I was still curious. "What will he do here?" I asked. "*Aram se baithey ga,* live comfortably (literally sit)," was the reply.

A young man who was going to Skardu to college for two years spoke about his feeling of sadness at leaving his home as he went around saying goodbye to all his friends. "You'll soon forget the village when you're in town," I said. "No," he replied, "I am in love with every rock and stone in Chutrun. I will never get tired of it." "Are you happy to be here?" I was often asked, with the expectation that the answer would be *yes.* Then people would nod their heads saying, "There is *sakun* here." *Sakun* means tranquility.

The women seldom or never leave their village.[41] If they do, it is to go to neighbouring villages or to return to their natal homes for a visit. Only one or two prestigious women in any village had travelled to the plains of Pakistan or abroad, generally to go to Iran or Iraq on pilgrimage.

My daughter and I would often tell our hostess Rabia how we would love to take her back to Canada with us—what we would show her, how she would travel on the airplane, sit on a chair, and have electricity all the time. And a flush toilet! Taps in the house! She had seen airplanes in the sky, high above the mountains. "I have never even been to Skardu," she would reply. "That will be enough for me."[42]

•••

I hope I have conveyed the hopes and desires of ordinary people for a better life, for many of the benefits of modernization. Change is coming fast to these once-remote and relatively isolated villages. But what kind of change is another matter. Has it improved the quality of life for the poorest of the poor? Has it been in accordance with the wishes of the majority? Or is it creating a bigger division betwen the haves and have-nots? My own experience over a period of two decades, living in close contact, suggests that the answer to the last question does not involve good news.

---

41 This was the case in the late 1980s. Fifteen years later, with more jeeps and wagons on the road as more Balti men started a business as drivers, women began to go to Skardu, Rawalpindi, Lahore, and Karachi. Many go for extended visits to their sons who work as cooks in Chinese-Pakistani restaurants. Rabia has been to Skardu several times, always accompanied by her husband and one child.

42 Now she has even been to Rawalpindi and, in 2006, to Karachi.

The rich are getting richer as well as more secretive and less generous towards their neighbours. This of course affects the quality of social relations and the well-being of individuals at the bottom of the ladder, who traditionally have depended on goodwill and patronage from those in power.[43] Also, women are not keeping pace with men, which is not to say that they do not share in the benefits of material wealth (more varied foods, bought clothes, bigger houses). They do, but they lose out on intangibles like education, freedom, and decision-making in their own lives and in public matters—they are still not on an equal footing with men. Therefore, with regards to poorer people in general and women in particular, it seems that not only are their modest hopes too rarely met, but new developments have often driven them back a step.

Thresholds of Acceptance

I was showing a group of friends in Canada some slides of my last trip to the mountains when I was asked this question: "What was your threshold of acceptance in the village? Where was the line drawn, beyond which you could not go?"

My admittance into village society was not sudden but a gradual process. Physically, Balti villages are complex collections of narrow, winding lanes, close-set mud houses with attached courtyards, kitchen gardens, and animal pens, enmeshed between water channels, ponds, and groves of trees, all of which belong to someone. These spaces cannot be entered by outsiders and strangers unobserved.

Entering Balti villages requires active consent and participation from at least one villager. Someone from inside has to be willing to invite or welcome a person from outside. Even when a person has allowed someone to live in their village (i.e., to set up a tent) Baltis do not easily let strangers into their homes and more importantly, into their hearts. I explained at the beginning of the book that I was able to gain people's trust and friendship primarily in three ways: by learning their language, by being accompanied by a child, and by giving them medicines.

There were a variety of responses to my presence among the people. Responses differed between men and women and again between young and old. "She is a spy." This was the initial reaction. Older women were inclined to be suspicious, based on the fact that I am not Muslim. Their

---

43   In *Veiled Sentiments*, Abu-Lughod writes that such relationships were not of domination and subordination, but of protection and dependency, 85.

questions showed genuine puzzlement. "How could you be a Christian when your father was a Muslim?" "Aren't you afraid of dying?" One asked simply, "Do you feel angry when we say the *nimaz*, prayer"? Since the women see themselves completely within a faith-based world, they could not imagine the day's round of activities outside of their religious beliefs. They could not comprehend how I could be different.

Younger women were more tolerant and also more curious. Young men were inclined to be rude if citified and curious if not. Older men were like old women, but more distant and reserved. Children were generally eager to be friends. Some boys were jeering and a nuisance until they got to know us. Girls were friendly and helpful, perhaps because of Tara.

I also have to admit that initially it was not the Balti villagers who drew the line, but I, both figuratively and literally. By this I mean that when I first began to live with my daughter in a tent on the roof, on the second morning I bent down outside the tent and drew a line in the mud before a crowd of people who had gathered and I said "Do not step over this line, this is *my* side!"[44]

As people gradually began to accept my presence in the village, I learned to recognize them, remember their names and relationships to each other, and which house they came from. One day on my walk, I saw an animal being slaughtered. A new house was being constructed and the sacrifice was to ensure a blessing upon the project.

Later, when blood had been sprinkled from the young *dzo*/cow hybrid on the site, a meal was prepared on an open fire by the men. "Come and join us," the men invited. A huge cauldron of stew was bubbling on the fire, while children gathered hopefully around. My invitation had been given out of courtesy to me, but since none of their wives was present on this occasion, I realized I should not be either. "*Metpi*," I replied, "*Bustryn la liachmo men.* Certainly not. It's not right for women." They laughed approvingly.

One of the men suggested that I should buy a plot of land and have a room built for myself. "Then you can come back whenever you like. You are so much at home here. You are like a Balti now." This was said half-jokingly, but sincerely meant. We had been there seven months.

By then, my daughter appeared indistinguishable from the other little girls with whom she spent the day. She too had dry, sunburnt cheeks, uncombed hair covered with a little *chaddar,* rough, chapped hands, and dusty clothes. She'd had boils and lice and worms. Arms around each

44 See note 26 in chapter 1.

others' shoulders, the little girls roamed the village when they were free from their chores.

Of course, Tara had no household or farm duties, no siblings to mind, no hens to shoo in at dusk, and no kindling or water to fetch, but she enthusiastically joined in with her friends' tasks. She taught them songs in English and they taught her games to play with stones, how to build a fire out of sticks in the field, and how to roast scavenged potatoes. Where I held myself back, she was well and truly integrated.

That changed a little for me when we began living in one of the homes in the village and became a part of the family. The children called me *amma,* an affectionate term for mother, borrowed from Urdu. I helped them find things, brush the girls' hair, or mind a little one when her mother had to go to the kitchen garden or cellar. At night, before the evening meal the youngest would lean against me sleepily while her mother was busy at the fire. On more than one occasion, the oldest girl would come and lie down in my room in order to escape her grandmother's never-ending demands. I realized just how much I was accepted by one incident.

My husband and I decided to stay in a little "hotul" built by one of our friends in the village on a later visit. It was a concrete two-room building, with a somewhat modern toilet that flushed with a bucket of water. At our friend's request, we stayed there two nights on our return from a trek. Since we were accompanied by porters and a guide, we felt it would be easier to stay here rather than in the house where my friend would have to cook and care for our group. In order to thank all our friends and show how much we appreciated them, we decided to throw a *dawat,* a party, which our porters prepared.

Among the guests was the family I usually lived with, who came with their younger children (but not the older marriageable daughters, because it was mixed company).[45] The youngest child, aged about two, looked at me wonderingly when they arrived. Spreading her palms upwards and turning to her mother she said, "*Gnutti amma gnutti nanu met!* Our mother is not in our house!" Her mother explained to me that on the way to the party, the little girl had kept asking where I was, because it was not

---

45 Although all the guests were local men and women, "mixed" gatherings are not the norm. Men and women are segregated at gatherings, for example, weddings. It was a tribute to how comfortable they felt with us that they came at all. As it was, the younger men stayed outside the door, squatting with the porters as they drank their tea and ate the delicacies. The women and children sat in a circle in the room with us, along with a few of the older men.

usual for a grandmother to disappear and appear living elsewhere than her own home.

I have written about doors shut against me, which was a very definite line indeed. I have also mentioned other times when certain villagers appeared hostile to my presence, because of suspicion I was a spy or an intruder bringing unwelcome foreign ideas to women. But generally people were welcoming and hospitable, which says more about their generosity of spirit and kindness to strangers, than anything I did to deserve it.[46] All in all, while lines were sometimes drawn, mostly their hearts and doors were open for us.

Because she was a child when she first went and therefore was adaptable, Tara was even more loved and accepted than I was. I would apologize for her walking into a house at mealtimes and sitting down to eat as if it was her right. I'd be told "Let her be, she is a child," "She's always welcome," or "She's like one of our children." When she was sick there was a steady stream of visitors who came to ask about her. Her young friends naturally came, but so did their mothers and aunts, with gifts of nuts and apples and herbal remedies.

By and large, Baltis are friendly. When women meet for work or play, they like to hold hands, sit close together, touch clothes or hair, or lean against each other to show their affection. They also have a lively curiousity about the outside world and an appreciation of anyone who cares enough about theirs to learn the language and live with them. The girls loved Tara because she brought them new ideas yet seemed to enjoy doing what they did. A photograph of Tara shows her with a group of young girls in a high pasture settlement. She is in the centre and every girl's hand is reaching out to touch her.

---

46   Compare my experience with that of Rory Stewart *The Places In Between*. He writes about his travels across Afghanistan from Herat to Kabul. Along the way he meets both nice and nasty people. Mostly, he receives a welcome, food, shelter and water.

Appendix

The Balti World: Background to the Stories

There is no written record of the early history of Baltistan, a world physically unique, culturally complex, and politically unstable. This is partly due to its geographical location and physical features. To the west and south are the better-known regions of Hunza-Nagir and Chitral which offered routes to travellers from Europe to and from Russia and China in the days of colonial exploration and conquest in the sixteenth century. To the east lie Ladakh and Tibet, which again were better known and provided passage to China. To the south and east lies the beautiful valley of Kashmir. The mountainous landscape of Baltistan with its large glaciers, craggy mountains, and few easily negotiable valleys were avoided by most explorers and officials of the Raj, which kept it relatively free of Western influence.

The first historical reference to this region occurs in Ptolemy in the second century BCE who refers to it as Byaltae. The Baltis themselves refer to their homeland as Balti-yul (Land of Baltis).[1] Since the region is geographically part of the high plateau of Tibet and was for centuries ruled by Tibet, it is often referred to as Little Tibet, or Apricot Tibet (a reference to the main crop). Ethnically and linguistically it was also influenced by Tibet. The earliest written account of travels in the Karakoram mountains are by Chinese scholars who travelled to Buddhist shrines in northern India in the fifth century CE. They kept meticulous records of their journeys, which are among the important sources of knowledge for this region.[2] Further historical clues have been provided by carvings and Tibetan inscriptions on stone, which have been deciphered by archaeologists.[3] Later

---

1   Abbas Kazmi, "The Balti Language."
2   Francke, *History of Western Tibet,* 33.
3   Jettmar, *Rock Carvings and Inscriptions in the Northern Areas of Pakistan.*

sources include the writings of British and European scientists and military officials, Indian scholars, and Jesuit missionaries.

All the northern mountain regions of Pakistan and India have witnessed waves of infiltration, migration, and invasion over the centuries.[4] The present inhabitants of Baltistan are refugees from ancient exploitation and conquest by peoples of the surrounding mountains and plateaus of Afghanistan, China, India, and Tibet. Their mixed ancestry is apparent today in their facial characteristics, apparel, dialects, food, customs, and architecture.

The Baltis were ruled by Dogras, princely Sikhs from Kashmir, for a hundred years. Their rule is remembered as cruel and oppressive—a period in which Baltistan was robbed of its wealth.[5] Arts, crafts, and culture decayed. There are many anecdotes about Dogra rule. Stories give an insight into what really happened, in addition to historical facts. This is what one man told me:

"During Dogra rule, Agha Shah Abbas, the grandfather of the present agha, lived in this village. His influence was felt right up to Kashmir. In fact, he was regarded as the uncrowned king of Baltistan. A Dogra who became a Muslim ran away from Skardu to this valley, seeking protection from Shah Abbas. The Dogra Governor of Baltistan, known as the *Wazir-e-Wizzarat*, came after him with troops. When he reached Chutrun he stopped with his men across the Basha River, not daring to come into the Agha's territory and he demanded the Dogra to be returned. The agha came to the edge of the river and said, 'This is not the Kaffiristan of Skardu.[6] This is the Islamic State of Shigar. And now, since you have insulted me by coming close to my land, I do not take responsibility for your safety.' So the great Dogra hastily retreated downriver. This happened over a hundred and fifty years ago."[7]

A folktale concerning Balti dance in Dogra times is called *Chogo Prasal*, The Big Feast: "A Dogra raja took Balti prisoners to Ladakh, where he made them dance for his entertainment at a feast. The prisoners said they needed something to dance with, so they asked for and were given

---

4   Cunningham, *Ladak*; Keay, *When Men and Mountains Meet*; *The Gilgit Game*; Hopkirk, *Trespassers on the Roof of the World*; *The Great Game: On Secret Service in High Asia*; Allen, *A Mountain in Tibet: The Search for Mount Kailas and the Sources of the Great Rivers of India*.

5   Afridi, *Baltistan in History*.

6   That is, land of unbelievers.

7   Personal communication, Afzal, PIA Transport Supervisor, Skardu, 1989.

swords. The Dogras were so confident of their control over the Baltis they had no fear of a revolt. There was much drinking and eating late into the night. The Dogras, known for their excesses, drank heavily of the local brew called *arak* and fell asleep after the meal.[8] The prisoners, waiting for just this opportunity, cut off their heads and escaped to freedom. The dance celebrates this every year."

When Dogra rule ended in 1948, Baltistan joined the newly formed government of Pakistan.[9] It was ruled by local petty chiefs and rajas who were removed by Zulfikar Ali Bhutto in 1973.[10] While the government of Pakistan has been responsible for building schools, hospitals, and dispensaries since then, these institutions are at best poorly equipped and sometimes the services are present on paper only which reflects the marginalization of the Northern Areas by central government.[11] While aware that politically they are a part of Pakistan, Baltis always refer to themselves as Baltis, as though Pakistan is a foreign nation.

The region has seen many changes in the last four decades. Perhaps the most significant one has been the building of "jeepable" roads to replace dirt tracks, following the construction of the Chinese-funded Karakoram Highway in the mid-1960s. The introduction of electricity, the building of schools for boys (and later, girls), and the promotion of trekking and tourism, are all part of an effort to "develop" the region economially.[12] However, in the provision of amenities, the government has favoured urban locations at the expense of rural areas and the fulfilling of male,

---

8   *Arak* is a potent spirit distilled from mulberries and was once popular in the Northern Areas. After prohibition during General Zia's government, its distillation has gone underground but it is still available.

9   This is disputed territory with India, similar to Indian-held Kashmir.

10   He was the head of the Pakistan People's Party. After a coup, Bhutto was replaced by General Zia-ul-Haq and hanged in 1977.

11   In 2009 the name Northern Areas changed to Gilgit-Baltistan and a governor was elected. If it were to become a full-fledged province, then India could legitimately keep disputed Jammu-Kashmir and the Line of Control would become an international boundary.

12   Many villages are still not wired for electricity, or else supply is sporadic or unreliable. Heavy rains and high winds can disrupt the flow of water supplying power. Most villages receive power for only three to five hours in the evening, and again at dawn for one hour at prayer time.

elitist demands rather than the needs of peasants and women. This appears to be in keeping with mainstream development policy in general.[13]

Islam was brought to Baltistan in the late fourteenth century by proselytizing missionaries from Iran, who travelled through Kashmir. Syed Ali Hamdani, a Persian-born Sufi, is credited with converting the people from Buddhism to Shi'ite Islam. A simple stone mosque in Ghyari is said to have been built by the saint. Although pockets of Buddhism (and even animism which existed earlier) remain among hill people,[14] most Baltis belong to the Shia order, but there are also Nurbakshis and Sunnis and those who are known as Ahle-Hadis, followers of the words of the Prophet.[15] Shi'ism is an Orthodox branch of Islam that upholds Ali, the son-in-law of Prophet Muhammad, as his spiritual successor.

There is no difference between Shias and Sunnis, the two main branches of Islam, at its basic level. *Allah*, Muhammad, and discussions of death are central themes in both.[16] Both Shias annd Sunnis believe in *sharia*, the Quranic law, to varying degrees. Both belong to the *ummah* or family of believers which celebrates the glories of Islam. The differences lie in history rather than theology and began in the seventh century CE when Ali, the husband of Muhammad's daughter, failed to succeed his father-in-law as Caliph and was later assassinated. His two sons, Hasan and Husain, were also killed, believed martyred. The Holy Prophet, his daughter Hazrat Fatima, his son-in-law Hazrat Ali, and his grandsons, Hasan and Husain, are the *panj tan pak*, the Pure Five, for Shias.

Shi'ites believe Husain, who was killed at the battle of Karbala, should have succeeded Ali, the fourth caliph.[17] His story is reenacted every year during the ten days of *Muharram*, which marks the beginning of the

---

13   Mies, *Patriarchy and Accumulation on a World Scale: Women in the International Division of Labour*; Banderage, *Women, Population and Global Crisis*. Waring, *Counting for Nothing: What Men Value and Women Are Worth.*

14   They are called *brokpa* (dwellers of high pastures) who come down occasionally from their mountain homes to trade and barter. They have Mongolian features and wear colourful woollen robes encrusted with buttons, beads, safety pins, and bottle caps. Their hair is long and finely braided under woollen caps. Their language is more closely related to Tibetan. People who resemble them physically but are sedentary and Muslim can be found in the higher villages like Askoli, Arindu, and Hushe.

15   Afridi, *Baltistan in History*, 27.

16   Ahmad, *Pakistan Society: Islam, Ethnicity and Leadership in South Asia.*

17   According to Abdollah, *My Father's Notebook* (56-57), Shi'ites await the coming of the twelfth imam, the Mahdi, who is descended from Husain's brother Hassan. Hassan was imprisoned until his death.

Islamic calendar, when Shias flagellate themselves in mourning. Shias do not recognize the elected caliphs who succeeded Ali. Nurbakshis are a liberal and more recent offshoot of Shi'ism, found mainly in eastern Baltistan in the Hushe valley. They were converted from Buddhism to Islam by Syed Muhammad Nur Baksh, a nephew and disciple of Syed Ali Hamdani.

Fasting (in the ninth lunar month of the calendar—the Islamic calendar is about ten days shorter than the Gregorian calendar, which is why *Ramadan* begins on a different date every year) is one of the five pillars of Islam. The others are *Shahada* (profession of faith in the recitation of the *Qalma* or creed), *Nimaz* (prayer performed five times a day), *Zakat* (charity or almsgiving), and *Haj* (pilgrimage to Mecca and Medina), which all Muslims are expected to make at least once in their lifetime.

The missionaries from Iran were Sayyids, who are believed to be direct descendants of Muhammad. They carried the title of agha, as do their elite converts. Out of this class have come the petty chiefs or leaders of mountainous villages of west and central Asia, stretching from Kurdistan in the west, through Iran and Afghanistan to North Pakistan. They are dominant figures in the villages of Baltistan, prestigious because of their descent and because they belong to a wealthy, land-owning class. Village society depends on aghas to provide local justice, laws, and the allocation of precious resources. Access to agricultural land, grazing rights, and water use are traditionally granted by aghas.[18]

Part of the reason that aghas are powerful and their authority is accepted is that 50 percent of the villagers may be related to them through marriage. In the past, aghas were polygamous while the rest of the villagers were monogamous. This meant that the agha's family increased while the village population remained static, or even decreased. Marriages outside the family are still controlled by the agha. Judicious marriages to the daughters of neighbouring chiefs (themselves aghas) consolidate and expand their wealth.[19]

The respect given to aghas is shared and maintained by their women, who are usually, but not always, of Sayyid stock. A shortage of agha women has led to the necessity of finding wives outside the Sayyid lineage. The children of such marriages are then given Sayyid status. To be a Sayyid woman in day-to-day life involves strict segregation from non-family males, the practice of minimal contact with outsiders, and the covering of heads

---

18   MacDowell, *The Khurds: The Minority Rights Group, Report*, 23.
19   This is an example of how women are "commodified" to gain power.

and the lower half of their faces in the presence of senior male clansmen. In Baltistan, Sayyid women are addressed by the title *ascho,* honorific for elder sister.[20]

The agha controls interaction with important outsiders since it is only in the agha's house that there is a well-provisioned larder, which is stocked by the villagers; at religious festivals when people come to the agha's house to pay their respects, they give tributes in the form of walnuts, apricot kernels, grain, and *ghee.* These gifts maintain the agha's power, which in bygone days would have been threatened if a rebel chief had broken this social link. Now, in the last thirty years or so, new socio-economic factors have arisen which have affected and eroded their power. These factors include: mechanization of agriculture with different requirements from traditional labour; increasing control of land by wealthy individuals other than Sayyids who contest the power of the aghas (they may have gained wealth initially by engaging in small business locally, then expanded their activities into Skardu and even the Punjab and abroad to the Middle East); and the increasing seasonal migration of young Sayyid men to cities in the plains for employment, causing a breakdown in the extended family system as well as a loss of their own and their wives' labour. These men, dissatisfied with their secondary position as younger sons who lack control over their personal lives, break away from the larger family by obtaining employment in the cities and take their immediate family with them. Finally, the introduction of education for women and the opening up of opportunities for them is beginning to affect the established order and bring structural changes within the family.

Some aghas have been quick to jump on the development bandwagon by taking advantage of new cash coming into the region in order to increase their own wealth in modern terms. They have done this by acquiring vehicles that they can rent out, opening bank accounts, setting up residences for sons and nephews in the major cities of the plains, forming political links with foreign NGOs, or representing central government in official positions by giving and receiving favours.

Even their daughters, in a region where women do not generally have an education, are being sent to school in Skardu, to be trained as "lady teachers" and "lady health visitors" (considered respectable professions for women because they do not challenge the *status quo*) as new opportunities

---

20 Kazmi, in "The Balti Language," this shows the linguistic connection with Ladakh and Tibet, *-cho* being a suffix which denotes respect. A hired farmhand called me *ascho* to honour me but also as a joke, shared between us.

open up for women in the village. In other words, they have adapted to changing times by controlling or taking advantage of any innovation or wealth that enters their valley by reason of their elite position.

In general, change is coming rapidly to this mountain world. In over two decades of going there, I have experienced and seen some of these changes. To mention only a few that affect daily life in the villages, I start with the toaster oven. It has replaced the raked-up coals and ashes of hay, straw, and goat manure, which were used to bake *kultchas* in improvised ovens. Some say there has been a loss of flavour and their crisp texture, but it certainly frees the woman of the house from that arduous task. Now, a young daughter pops a tray of *kultchas* into the toaster, plugs it in, and sleeps beside it until the cakes are baked. Of course, she can do this only between the hours of 6:00 and 11:00 pm when electricity is available.

The diesel-fueled thresher has replaced *dzos*. It clatters noisily and dustily along verges, threshing grain laid down in bunches (no need of *herris* and worrying about rains), but also destroying the carefully banked edges of fields. Valuable topsoil flies in the air, to say nothing of diesel fumes and noise. The harsh call of large black and white *ghashap*, magpies, is lost, as they hover overhead, waiting for their share of grain. The main impact of course will be on the *dzos, dzongos*, and on the dual economy of cereal cultivation and livestock rearing.

School text books, exercise books, and ballpoint pens, pencils, and erasers have replaced the wooden tablet, quill pen, and bottle of ink. The latter items were relatively cheap and reusable. Now cash is needed for school supplies in an economy where not everyone has access to cash.

A welcome change has been the construction of metal pipes and taps to lead clean water from springs high up, which run continuously into *bearzings,* throughout the village. The only disadvantage is that sometimes the pipe is severed, and no one seems to be responsible for its repair.

I have recorded for the reader some of the time-consuming, age-old ways of doing things to feed, clothe, and house the people that still continue alongside the innovations. Combined with songs and stories, such actions add to the rich texture of social and cultural life that make Baltis unique as a people.

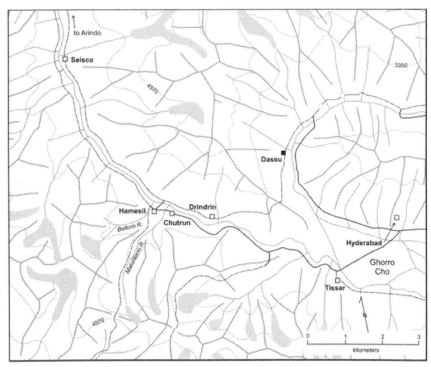

Detailed Map of Chutrun and Region

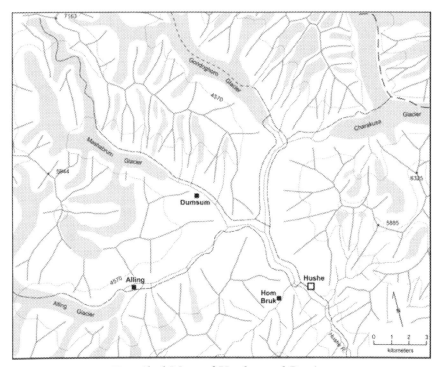

Detailed Map of Hushe and Region

Glossary

Urdu words, including Farsi, are indicated by (U). All other words are in Balti.

Aa jao. (U) Come on
Allo. Hollyhocks
Ango. Mother
Angun. Common living room and kitchen
Api. Grandmother, old woman
Apo. Grandfather, old man
Ascho. Honorific title for Sayyid woman; *ashe* + *cho*
Ashe. Older sister
Ashipa. Husband
Astana. Burial monument for aghas
Atta. Father
Ayo. Short for *ango*, mother
Azab. Difficult
Badal. (U) Change
baji. (U) Elder sister (title)
Bakhstrun. Wedding
Baksheesh. Thanks
Bal. Sheep's wool
Ballay. Dumplings in gravy
Balti. Family room, with iron stove. Also called *meh balti*
Baltilog. Baltis
Ban. Cow
Baraat. (U) Wedding procession
Bari. (U) Turn
Bari zan bya. Turn to cook
Barkat. May you be blessed (giving thanks)

Bearzing. Pond

Beel. Ground sheep and goat manure for baby's diaper bag

Bles. Rice

Blok Bosset. Thunder

Blukmi. Shepherd

Bluy kattal. Uproot buckwheat plants

Bokhari. Cast iron stove for heating and cooking in *balti*

Bongo. Daughter

Brangsa. high pasture settlement

Bro. Buckwheat

Burtse. Roots of dried artemesia plant

Bustryn. Women

Byabjon. Egg

Byafo. Hen

Byango. Rooster

Canada la ango chuchu minnet? In Canada do mothers breastfeed?

Chaddar. (U) Veil for women

Chadung. Wooden vessel for churning salt tea

Chai. (U) Tea

Chai thuns, chai thu'nwerra? Will you drink tea?

Chakor. (U) Partridge

Chalaki. (U) Cunning

Changchang. Naughty

Chapati. (U) Flat bread

Chaphe. Roasted flour sprinkled on tea or eaten with *ghee*

Charpai. (U) String bed on wood frame

Chara. (U) Fodder

Chham. Stop

Chhara. Woven *dzo-* or yak-hair rug

Chharfa. Rain

Chhargul. Nose ornament

Chhu. Baths at hot spring

Chhu chhu dacchal. Plant that yields soapy suds

Chhun chhan se. A little bit

Chi'bya? What's the matter?

Chi'in? What is…?

Chicpa. Alone

Chorrong. Conical basket slung on back with leather straps

Chowkidar. (U) Keeper

Chula. (U) Fireplace

Chuli. Apricots

Chuli sputz. Harvesting apricots

Chuskoo. Curdled cream like yoghurt

Dakhun. women's veil

Dal. (U) Lentils

Dana. Boils (swelling and inflammation resulting from an infection in a skin gland)

Dastarkhwan. (U) Cloth laid on floor for meals

Dawat. (U) Invitation

Dena. Then

Dhurry. (U) Cotton floor mat

Dirrin ishin thalba yut. Today there is a lot of mud

Drulba khurba. Walking

Drumba. Kitchen garden

Duk. Sit down

Dzo. Yak-cow hybrid (male)

Dzongo. Female yak-cow hybrid

Dzua. Wooden vessel for milking

Fotoo chik. Take a photo

Fusho. Indoor boot of soft leather

Gar gwe? Where are you going?

Ghee. (U) Butter

Ghiopa. Trusted male escort in wedding party

Ghobus. Wooden pillar supporting roof that ends in carved ram's horns

Ghot. Deaf-mute, male

Ghunmo. Deaf-mute, female

Ghunny. Bad

Girri. Apricot kernels

Glu. Song

Gna la ishin fiqr yut. I am very worried.

Gna la jahil yut. I am illiterate.

Gniarma. Green chilies

Gnima duet. Sun sets

Gnima phonget. Sun is shining

Gniopa. Bride's daytime companion for two days

Gnis. Two

Gno. Take

Gnutti amma gnutti nanu met. Our mother is not in our house.

Gopi zamana la. In olden times

Guinsett. Headache

Gul chin. Marigold

Gunchas. Clothes

Gunmo. Women's shirt

Haboo. Centipede

Hacchu. Piggy-back ride

Halva. (U) Semolina pudding

Handok la. On the rooftop

Haramzada, nalbu. Bastard, in Urdu and Balti

Harral. Fenced yard for animals around house

Hassad. Jealousy

Herris. Stacks of grain

Hrstwa. Weeds for fodder

Hummal. Pregnant

Hyuk. Yak

Icchat. Bored

Ishin. Very

Isman. White wild flower

Janaza. Funeral procession (U)

Jasoos. (U) Spy

Jholi. Rucksack

Ji. (U) Word denoting respect, like Sir, Madam

Kaccha. Underwear

Kacchu. Wooden bowl with handle, for ladling and measuring flour. 1 *kacchu* = 3 cups (imperial measure)

Kajal. (U) Black eyeliner

Kaka. Older brother

Kamina. (U) Mean

Kamiz. (U) Shirt

Karol. Small, handleless china cup

Kaska. Wooden ladder

Katza. Cellar

Kharrik. Small round basket with handle

Khattarnak. (U) Dangerous

Khirri. You (rude)

Khirtee. Loops of spun wool

Khlarrat. Tired

Khlia. Wooden churn for butter

Khling. Paddle for churning butter

Khrak. Blood

Khrok barrik. Lightning

Khurrba. Round loaf of unleavened bread

Khuyyun. Threshing grain

Khyang. Your (rude)

Khyonse. To bring

Kisik. Fleas

Kohl. Black eyeliner

Kultcha. Sweet cake

Lamgan. Poppy

Lapke skya. Carry a bundle on the back

Lappko. hand

Las. work

Le—khers. Here—bring it

Lemma. Bride's female companion for two weeks

Liachmo. Good, okay

Limik chhu. Hot springs bath with key

Lu. Sheep

Ma'gnuss. Don't cry

Mahir. (U) Expert

Mar phyungma. To extract butter by churning

Markhor. Wild mountain goat

Marrgulab. (U) Rose without perfume, dead rose; Himalayan rose

Marsia. Mournful religious song about persecution

Masjid. (U) Mosque

Meethi chai. (U) Sweet tea

Meh. Fire

Mehman. (U) Guest, visitor

Memu. Foreign woman (derogatory)

Met, men. No, not

Mez. (U) Table

Mintakpo. Name

Mohstung seremosing, Balti seremosing. May you have long life and health.

Mosho. All-leather boot with strong sole

Mubarik. (U) Congratulations

Muhtaj. (U) Dependent, slave

Mungurr. Tin bowl for tea or food

Nakpo. Black
Nallah. (U) Valleys, settlements in interior
Nana. Grandfather (honorific)
Nas. Barley
Natting. Woollen cap worn under *dakhun*
Nnongo. Younger sister
Odong. Face
On'n duk. Come, sit
Onga. Milk
Onga tsirrba. To milk
Onn'wa. Yes, that's right.
Oosoo. Green coriander
Osey. Mulberries
Paillu chai. Salt tea
Pappa. Bread soaked in tea for child
Parandah. (U) Coloured tassels plaited into hair
Parantha. (U) Flat fried bread
Peet. Spring
Penne. Money
Pharring. Dried apricots
Phingkhan. Animal byre
Phingma. Felted mat
Phoongma. Wheat and barley straw or chaff, for fodder
Phurrgan. Partridge
Phurrpa. Weeding tool
Phyakma. Twig broom
Phyukpo. Rich
Plu. Son
Plupla. Children
Polla. Boot with leather sole and strap
Propha. Male companion for women on journey
Purdah. Veiling or seclusion from men
Pyjamas. (U) Narrow tapered pants for men
Qaida. (U) Text book
Qar. Woven woollen blanket
Qasida. Joyful religious song of praise
Quaid. Prisoner
Rafsal. Formal family room
Ragasha. Beautiful

Ral. Goat hair

Rawak. Goat

Rbyarr. Summer

Rdungma. Pound in mortar with pestle

Rdwa. Rocks

Rgunn. Winter

Rinthak. Water mill

Rohmi. Male and female labourers paid in kind

Roti. (U) General name for bread, food

Rshka. Water channel

Rukhsati. (U) Departure of bride to groom's home

Sakun. (U) Peace

Salaam. (U) greetings

Salleh. Rooftop room

Salwar. (U) Baggy trousers for men and women

Samik. Mixture of yogurt, ground green chilies, green coriander, and salt

Sang gwit. Go together

Sehrla. For a walk

Sembu. Sleeping bag or bag for *beel*

Seremosing. Farewell

Sehrla gwerra? Shall we go for a walk?

Shakhang. Storeroom for grass and straw for animals in cellar

Shahri mi. Citified man

Shargo. Poor

Shess met. Don't know

Shhu. Vegetable or cereal garden bed

Shikari. (U) Hunter

Shokhmo. Quickly

Shukhs. Welcome

Shwa. Flood

Shwa khyonse, pshik se phanse. The flood picks it up and throws it down.

Sia. Himalayan rose

Sirrif julab, quai. (U) Only diarrhea and vomiting

Sman. Medicine

Sniget nas. To cut barley

Sningpo. Heart

Sonma. Spinach

Sonma spacchus. Stewed spinach

Spacchus. Curry or stew

Standal. Large sieve for grain

Starga. Walnuts

Strinjao'n. Witch

Stu. Milky residue of crushed apricot kernels

Stu rdungma. Pounding kernels to extract *stu*

Stunn. Autumn

Sung. Go away

Talak. (U) Divorce

Talim. (U) Education

Tamiz met, sirrif penne. No manners, only money

Tanse. Pour

Tarraqi. (U) Progress

Tawootse polla. Strong boot with fur cuff and embroidery; for royals

Tawwara. Mournful religious songs about martyrdom

Tayyar. (U) Ready

Thalba. Dirt, mud

Thalo. Wooden tray for kneading flour

Thap. Fireplace

Thar thar yut, aram yut? Are you well, are you comfortable?

Tharrat. To love

Thhanchu. Resin on apricot tree

Thimboo. To pick up stray grain with hands

To. Cast-iron griddle

Tokhs. Hunger

Tomar. Silver beaded crown for bridal *natting*

Tro. Wheat

Troktrok. Dirty

Truss. Wash

Tsenmo. Embroidered border on woman's *gunmo*

Tshalba. Thorny rake weighted with stones

Tshelba onget. I feel shame.

Tsillsirr. Wood ashes used as fertilizer

Tsungma and chadung. Wooden paddle and churn for salt tea

Ungeethi. (U) Metal kerosene stove

Yan. You (polite)

Yerri. Your (polite)

Yerri shezdeh. You're welcome

Yurma. Weeding
Zamba. Wooden or rope bridge
Zan min. Give me food.
Zanphapsbikba. To clean grain

Acknowledgments

I am grateful to my brother Aslam and his family in Islamabad, who patiently put up with my journeys to and from the mountains, sometimes carrying unwelcome guests like lice and fleas; to AKRSP officers and jeep drivers in the initial year, who helped me get to the villages from Skardu; to the women who were my teachers and friends in the villages; and to my daughter Tara who enthusiastically joined in my research.

Thanks to my friends in Elora, where I began writing this book, for their interest, comments and many cups of tea.

I am grateful to my husband Ken, for his advice, support and encouragement, both in the field and here, without which I would have given up long ago.

I am grateful to Pam Schaus of the Geography Department at Wilfrid Laurier University, Waterloo, for her help in making the maps and diagrams. Finally, my thanks go to my editor, Jacqueline Larson, for her questions that made me explain more clearly what I took for granted, and her help in efficiently pulling everything together.

Bibliography

Abdollah, Kader. *My Father's Notebook. Trans. Susan Massoty.* New York: Harper Collins, 2006.

Ahmad, Akbar S. *Pakistan Society: Islam, Ethnicity and Leadership in South Asia.* Karachi: Oxford University Press, 1986.

Abu-Lughod, Lila. "A Community of Secrets: The Separate World of Bedouin Women." *Signs: Journal of Women in Culture and Society* 10.4 (1985): 637-57.

———. *Veiled Sentiments: Honor and Poetry in a Bedouin Society.* Berkeley: University of Calfornia Press, 1986.

Afridi, Banat Gul. *Baltistan in History.* Peshawar, Pakistan: Emjay Books International, 1988.

Ask, Karin, and Marit Tjomsland, eds. *Women and Islamization: Contemporary Dimensions of Discourse on Gender Relations.* New York: Berg, 1998.

Allen, Charles. *A Mountain in Tibet: The Search for Mount Kailas and the Sources of the Great Rivers of India.* London: Futura, Macdonald and Co., 1982.

Banderage, Asoka. *Women, Population and Global Crisis*: A Political-Economic Analysis.* London: Zed Books, 1997.

Bertaux, Daniel, ed. *Biography and Society: The Life History Approach in the Social Sciences.* London: Sage, 1981.

Birth in South Asia: Midwives and Female Healers. American Anthropological Society. Session 112. Available at: <http://www.aasianst.org/absts/1995abst/southasi/sases112.htm>

Bowen, Elenore Smith. *Return to Laughter: An Athropological Novel.* New York: Anchor, 1964.

Brohman, John. *Popular Development: Rethinking the Theory and Practice of Development.* Oxford, UK: Blackwell, 1996.

Courtenay, Bryce. *The Power of One.* New York: Ballantyne / Random House, 1989.

Cuéllar, Alejandro. "Unravelling Silence: Violence, Memory and the Limits of Anthropology's Craft." *Dialectical Anthropology* 29.2 (2005): 159-80.

Cunningham, Sir Alexander. *Ladak.* London: 1854.

Dainelli, Giotto. *La Esplorazione Della Regione Fra L'Himalaja Occidentale e il Caracoram.* Bologna: Publicato Sotto la Direzione di Giotto Dainelli, 1934.

Dove, Michael R., and Abdul Latif Rao. "Common Resource Management in Pakistan: Garret Hardin in the Junglat." Paper presented at conference on common property regimes, sponsored by Aga Khan Rural Support Program. Gilgit, 1986.

Dube, Leela, Eleanor Leacock, and Shirley Ardener, eds. *Visibility and Power: Essays on Women in Society and Development.* New Delhi: Oxford University Press, 1986.

Eliade, Mircea. *The Sacred and the Profane.* New York: Pantheon, 1957.

Eliot, George. *Middlemarch.* 1874. London: Penguin Classics, 2003.

Francke, August Hermann. *Baltistan and Ladakh—A History.* 2nd ed. Islamabad: Lok Virsa, 1986.

———. *History of Western Tibet: One of the Unknown Empires.* 1907. New Delhi: J. Jetley, 1995.

Giles, D. "Medical Aspects of the IKP." In *The International Karakoram Project.* Vol. 2, ed. K. Miller, 351-59. Cambridge, UK: Cambridge University Press, 1984.

Hartmann, Betsy. *Reproductive Rights and Wrongs.* Boston: South End Press, 1995.

Hartmann, Betsy, and James Boyce. *A Quiet Violence: View from a Bangladeshi Village.* London, UK: Zed Books, 1988.

Halvorson, Sarah J. *"Geographies of Children's Vulnerability: Households and Water-Related Disease Hazard in the Karakoram Mountains, Northern Pakistan." PhD Thesis, University of Colorado, 2000.*

Hewitt, Farida. "Women in the Landscape: A Karakoram Village Before 'Development.'" PhD Thesis. Waterloo University, Waterloo, ON. 1991.

———. "Women's Vulnerability and the Case of the Missing Men." Paper presented at the Canadian Association of Geographers, 31 May 2002, University of Toronto, Canada.

———. *"Women's Work, Women's Place: A Gendered Ecology of a High Mountain Community." MA Thesis. Waterloo University, Waterloo, ON. 1987.*

Hewitt-Azhar, Farida. "All Paths Lead to the Hot Spring: Conviviality, the Code of Honor and Capitalism in a Karakorum Village, Pakistan." *Mountain Research and Development* 18.3 (1998): 265-72.

———. "Floods!" In *Disaster-Development Linkages in South Asia*, New Delhi: Duryog Nivaron Press, 2007.

———. "Women of the High Pastures." (Karakoram-Himalaya box) In *Mountains of the World: A Global Priority*, ed. R. Messerli and J.D. Ives, 65-71, Box 4.1. New York: Parthenon, 1997.

———. "Women of the High Pastures and the Global Economy: Reflections of the Impacts of Modernization in the Hushe Valley of the Karakorum, North Pakistan." *Mountain Research and Development* 19.2 (1999): 141-51.

———. "Women's Work, Women's Place: A Gendered Ecology of a High Mountain Community in Northern Pakistan." *Mountain Research and Development* 9.4 (1989): 335-52.

Hewitt, Ken. *Interpretations of Calamity from the Viewpoint of Human Ecology.* Boston: Allen and Unwin, 1983.

———. "Quartenary Moraines vs. Catastrophic Rock Avalanches in the Karakoram Himalaya, North Pakistan." *Quaternary Research* 51.3 (1999): 220-37.

Hopkirk, Peter. *The Great Game: On Secret Service in High Asia.* London: John Murray, 1990.

———. *Trespassers on the Roof of the World: The Race for Lhasa.* Oxford UK: Oxford University Press, 1982.

Horseman, Jennifer. *Something in My Mind Beside the Everyday: Women and Literacy.* Toronto: Women's Press, 1990.

Illich, Ivan. *Gender.* New York: Pantheon, 1982.

Jettmar, Karl. *Rock Carvings and Inscriptions in the Northern Areas of Pakistan.* Lahore: Allied Press, for National Institute of Folk Heritage, 1982.

Johnson, B. "Childbirth with a Traditional Birth Attendant in a Khatmandu Valley Newar Village." Paper presented at South Asia Session 112, Birth in South Asia: Midwives and Female Healers conference, 1995. Washington, DC.

Kazmi, Syed Abbas. "The Balti Language." In *Jammu, Kashmir and Ladakh: The Linguistic Predicament,* ed. P.N. Pushp and N.Warikoo, 135-53. Himalayan Research and Cultural Foundation. New Delhi: Har-Anand Publications, 1996.

Keay, John. *The Gilgit Game.* London: John Murray. 1979.

———. *When Men and Moutains Meet: The Explorers of the Western Himalayas, 1820-75.* London: Century Publishing. 1977.

Kohli, Martin. "Biography: Account, Text, Method." In *Biography and Society: The Life-History Approach in the Social Sciences,* ed. Daniel Bertaux, 2-75. London: Sage, 1981.

Kreutzmann, Hermann, Mattias Schmidt, and Andreas Benz, eds. *The Shigar Microcosm: Socio-economic Investigations in a Karakoram Oasis, Northern Areas of Pakistan.* Berlin: Centre for Development Studies, Freie Universitaet, 2008.

Ladurie, Le Roy. *Montaillou—The Promised Land of Error.* New York: Vintage, 1979.

Lefebvre, Henri. *Everyday Life in the Modern World.* New York: Harper and Rowe, 1958.

Lama, Abraham. *Peru: Traditional Knowledge Enhances Modern Medicine.* Third World Network. 2000. Accessed 1 October 2010 at <http://www.twnside.org.sg/title/enhance.htm>

Maguire, Patricia. *Doing Participatory Research: A Feminist Approach.* Amherst, MA: The Centre for International Education, School of Education, University of Massachusetts, 1987.

Marhoffer-Wolff, M., and G. Stober. "Medical and Cultural Innovation in the Yasin Valley." In *Occasional Papers 2, Pak-German Workshop:*

Problems of Comparative High Mountain Research with Regard to the Karakoram. University of Tubingen, Germany, 1992.

Mason, Kenneth. "Indus Floods and Shyok Glaciers." *Himalayan Journal of the Himalayan Club* 1 (1929): 19.

McDowell, David. *The Kurds.* The Minority Rights Group International, Report 23, London, 1985.

Mies, Maria. *Patriarchy and Accumulation on a World Scale: Women in the International Division of Labour.* London, UK: Zed Books, 1986.

Murphy, Dervla. *Where the Indus Is Young.* London: Arrow Books, 1977.

Nyborg, Ingrid. "Yours Today, Mine Tomorrow? A Study of Women and Men's Negotiations over Resources in Baltistan." PhD Dissertation. NORagric, Agricultural University of Norway. 2002.

Pratt, Mary Louise. *Travel Writing and Transculturation.* New York: Routledge, 1992.

Read, Arthur F.C. *A Balti Grammar and Vocabulary.* London: Royal Asiatic Society, 1934.

Rogers, Barbara. *The Domestication of Women: Discrimination in Developing Societies.* London, UK: Tavistock, 1980.

Seierstad, Asne. *The Bookseller of Kabul.* London, U.K.: Little Brown, 2003.

Schutz, Alfred. "The Stranger: An Essay in Social Psychology." *The American Journal of Sociology* 49.6 (1944): 449-507.

Seneviratne, Kalinga. *Traditional Medicine Often Lauded But Neglected.* 8 December 2000. Third World Network <http://www.twnside.org.sg/title/lauded.htm>

Shaw, R. "Nature, Culture and Disasters: Floods and Gender in Bangladesh. In *Bush Base Forest Farm.* Ed. E. Croll and D. Parkin. New York: Routledge, 1992.

Shah, S. "Community Perception of Some Major Diseases and their Curative Practices." *Culture Area Karakoram Project, Newsletter 2.* Ed I. Stellrecht. University of Tubingen, Germany, 1992.

Shiva, Vandana. *Monocultures of the Mind.* London, UK: Zed Books and Third World Network, 1993.

Stewart, Rory. *The Places In Between*: Picador, 2004

Vigne, George. T. 1844. *Travels in Kashmir, Ladakh, Iskardo.* 2nd ed. Karachi, Pakistan: Indus, 1987.

Waring, Marilyn. *Counting for Nothing: What Men Value and Women Are Worth.* Toronto: University of Toronto Press, 1999.

Whiteman Peter T.S. *Mountain Oases: A Technical Report of Agricultural Studies (1982-1984) in Gilgit District, Northern Areas, Pakistan.* Gilgit: FAO/UNDP, 1985.